G. P. A. HEALY

American Artist

G. P. A. HEALY

AMERICAN ARTIST

An Intimate Chronicle of the Nineteenth Century

by

MARIE DE MARE

Introduction by

ELEANOR ROOSEVELT

DAVID McKAY COMPANY, INC. • New York

759.13
D39g
35574
November, 1957

Library of Congress Catalog Card Number: 53-11377

MANUFACTURED IN THE UNITED STATES OF AMERICA

VAN REES PRESS • NEW YORK

TO THE MEMORY

OF

GEORGE P. A. HEALY AND

LOUISA HEALY

AND TO

THEIR DESCENDANTS

THIS BOOK

IS LOVINGLY DEDICATED

ACKNOWLEDGMENTS

WHOM should I thank first? My grandfather himself, for being a man whose memory remains so vivid? His children, whose active interest, whose help, moral and financial, enabled me years ago to gather inestimable data, the many friends who brought me throughout the long years accounts of his work, of his personality, anecdotes where Healy's life touched theirs? How can I name them all? A list too long for these pages...

Yet among those innumerable contributors one figure stands out, the friend of a lifetime—young, to me always young, Edward Sheldon, the noted playwright, who, snatched suddenly from the activities of life and from the enjoyment of his brilliant success, spent years in darkness and physical immobility, shedding light and cheer for the privileged ones who could visit him. He proved a constant inspiration for this book, which he liked from its beginning. To him also I owe the invaluable advice and commendation of Mr. Van Wyck Brooks, who, after hearing his friend Ned Sheldon speak of the Healy biography, asked to see it and gave me the needed courage to continue a work which my invalidism made at times very arduous.

That the great American, Mrs. Roosevelt, should have written the Introduction is an honor for which words fail me, and it is one of my most cherished memories that even in the terser first version of my book she found bits of sufficient interest to read to our beloved late President.

With deep gratitude I mention the loan for several summers of the E. R. Mathews' New Hampshire home where I worked at the Healy biography. It has been my good fortune that a lecturer's life took me to many cities on both sides of the Atlantic where Healy's work can be seen.

Illness arrested my travels and personal research, but the kindness of correspondents has vastly enriched my store of information while the care, generosity, and help of family and friends—particularly of vivid and lovable Lila Tyng—enabled me to continue writing in spite of inevitable interruptions. I feel greatly obligated to my faithful secretaries—Miss Copeland, Miss Cosgrove, and Mrs. Queena Hazleton.

From every direction answers came with a wealth of details I could no longer gather personally. In Cambridge, Mr. Henry Longfellow Dana opened his Appleton-Longfellow files.

Boston, where I lectured in 1928-29 yielded data through the Museum of Fine Arts, the Athenaeum, the Boston Library, the Massachusetts Historical Society, where Mr. Tuttle found several Healy letters to Webster; Faneuil Hall's custodian told me that the historian Claude M. Fuess, then working on his masterly Webster, had found the Healys' address of 1813.... Though the fire of 1872 destroyed many Boston homes, the city no doubt still holds a mass of untouched Healy data.

Here, in New York, the Frick Art Reference Library with its abundant collection of Healy reproductions is the Mecca of my research. For nearly thirty years its charming and able librarians, Miss Ethelwyn Manning and Mrs. Harry Howell, have answered every request I made. I am deeply grateful to Dr. Allan Nevins for his invaluable help and encouragement. At the New York Historical Society, Mr. Shelley gave me excellent photographs of their Healy pictures, among which is the only miniature I ever saw by my grandfather. The Metropolitan Museum of Art, the New York Genealogical and Biographical Society, the rich New York Public Library and its Cathedral Branch were also most helpful. At Mrs. Lamar's gallery, years ago, when she arranged a Healy exhibit, I met a number of Healy owners. Mr. Davidson, of Knoedler's, has most kindly kept me informed of his Healy "finds," among which was the "Peacemakers," brought over from Europe and now at the White House.

In Washington, D. C., the Corcoran Gallery, the Capitol, the White House, and private homes—Mrs. Field's, Mrs. Grant's, Mrs. Robert Lincoln's—showed me long ago that the country's capital held some of Healy's finest work. From Mrs. Edward Pinney I received revealing Healy letters written at the time of the Civil War to Mrs. Goddard-Dahlgren of Washington, D. C.

In 1913, the Chicago Art Institute celebrated with a large exhibit the artist's centenary, and in 1943 the Chicago Historical Society showed its own important collection, which, with several loans, made an imposing exhibit. The Healys' residence in Illinois from 1855 to 1866 accounts for a great many of these paintings.

In 1930, the J. B. Speed Memorial Museum of Louisville, Kentucky, had a well-attended Healy exhibit, and in 1950 an outstanding Healy exhibition was held at the Virginia Museum of Fine Arts. The interest shown by its director, Mr. Leslie Cheek, Jr., has never flagged.

The list of persons to whom I wish to extend thanks is too long, but I must name also my cousin George W. Healy, Jr., of the *Times-Picayune,* grandson of Thomas Healy, G. P. A.'s younger brother; Miss Herma Clark, of the *Chicago Tribune;* the artist Julien Binford and his lovely wife; the Most Reverend Archbishop of Baltimore; Mr. Menefee, of Louisville, Kentucky; Dr. J. Hall Pleasants, of Baltimore; Miss Anna Wells Rutledge, of the Maryland Historical Society; Mr. Larkin, of Smith College; Miss Alice Kendall, of the Newark, New Jersey, Museum; Miss Fitch, of Nekoosa, Wisconsin; Mr. F. W. Coburn, of Lowell, Massachusetts; Mr. McCorison, of Cambridge, Massachusetts; Mrs. Elizabeth Washburne Wright, of Washington, D. C.; the Cleveland Museum, the Virginia Museum of Art, the Charleston Museum; the Sacred Heart Convents of Albany, St. Louis, and Chicago; Mount de Chantal in Wheeling, West Virginia; the

Albany Historical Society; the Newberry Library in Chicago and the Illinois State Hospital in Kankakee. The Versailles Palace and the Blerancourt Art Collection had before this last war a number of Healy paintings.

Special thanks are due to Prince and Princess Alexis Droutskoy, and to Mrs. John Alden Carpenter for their help and encouragement; and to the innumerable friends here and abroad, who have enriched by letters and documents the growing mass of information about G. P. A. Healy.

I am also very grateful to Mr. Thomas Robson Hay, historian, who kindly verified much of the data I had accumulated throughout the years, thus satisfying the publishers that facts presented in the manuscript are actual episodes of the artist's full and varied life.

To all, named and unnamed, I here renew my thanks with the assurance that without their help this book would indeed be poorer, and with the hope that their continued interest will make truer and richer the knowledge of George P. A. Healy, American artist.

This is not "fictional biography." Every incident, date and place has been carefully verified. The conversations, if not always in the exact words are nevertheless true, based on authentic direct reports such as the artist's own letters and other contemporary diaries and letters combined with my personal recollections of him and of the many stories he told as we sat—often unwillingly—for the portraits now so precious to us. Events recalled at various times by my grandmother and her daughters, especially by my mother blessed with a memory, startlingly exact, that brought back vividly that much maligned and amazing XIXth century.

After so many years of extensive research it is impossible to compile a full list of written sources, but, as well as I could, I have indicated where I found them.

MARIE DE MARE

CONTENTS

LIST OF ILLUSTRATIONS

FOREWORD

THIS life of George Peter Alexander Healy, written by his granddaughter, seems to me to have come to us at a very opportune time. We are going through, in this country at present, a period in which men and women need what courage they can muster to meet new conditions. It is, therefore, worth while for us to read of some of the men who made our reputation when we were still a very young country.

To many of us today it would seem that the difficulties in George Healy's path were almost unsurmountable. How could a lad succeed in a country where painters were hardly considered necessary in the absorbing struggle of conquering a new world, educate himself, build up a reputation, support a family, and educate his own countrymen to the point of looking upon art as something for which one might well spend a little money? Yet he never lost heart, and he succeeded in a most extraordinary manner.

There was plenty of incident in his long life; there were tragedies and comedies, but his joy in his work never waned, and energy such as his can only be drawn from the life of a new country.

Much of his life was spent away from this continent, but his loyalty never faltered, and the democracy that was an ideal of so many of our people in those days made it possible for him to meet people the world over, be interested in human beings primarily whether they were kings or beggars, and treat them all alike with that kindliness and geniality that characterizes his human relationships.

He was fortunate, indeed, in his wife and family and their understanding and appreciation of his work. They made it easy for him and gave him a sense of background without curtailing his freedom, which would probably have injured his work.

We have so few early American painters that it seems a great loss that we are not more familiar with those who made their mark in the nineteenth century, and this book is worth while, not only as a historical contribution, but also as a story of an interesting, vivid personality.

As this book develops, it tells, of course, the story of the period. It brings in a much wider picture than one would expect the life of an American painter of that period could possibly cover. In its pages one can find the record of many people in many countries so that it should have an appeal not only at home but abroad.

In these days when the United States is finding that we live in a very small world and that from every angle our country is tied to the countries and the peoples of the rest of the world, it is well to find roots beginning to intertwine so many years ago, and a name that should be well known in our own country will have meaning in many other countries.

ELEANOR ROOSEVELT

G. P. A. HEALY

American Artist

"You say a portrait painter has only to copy? His model is there: all he has to do is to reproduce it? But within the features that outline a physiognomy, the artist must find the soul."

—EUGÈNE DELACROIX

Chapter I

ART CLAIMS NO CITIZENSHIP

ONE hundred years after the French Revolution, in April, 1889, the Paris boulevards gay with horse chestnuts in bloom and noisy with a babel of tongues, visitors arrived in shoals for the opening of the great Universal Exposition.

On the Montmartre hill, in the vast high-ceilinged studio of G. P. A. Healy, 64 rue de la Rochefoucauld, the clear spring light vividly flooded a colorful array of pictures. Called upon to help form a committee for the American art section at the exposition, George Healy stood as a symbol of achievement in the world of American art. Interrupted in his work, he had reluctantly set down his palette to listen to an excited and irate compatriot whose words tumbled excitedly.

"Why, Mr. Healy, tell me why your committee chose my two pictures and now informs me they are rejected?"

"Mr. Parker, you know that only about three hundred of the thousand or more paintings offered can be placed; the jury decided—"

"I've a good mind to go and tell each member of the jury what I think of him!" And Parker stamped angrily toward the door. Healy followed him.

"Don't do that...." The kindly voice caused the visitor to pause and turn as Healy continued: "You know how much I would like

3

to see your work accepted, but there is nothing I can do," and placing his hand on the other's sleeve, he counseled smilingly, "If I were you, I'd just call for my pictures and say nothing."

With a sigh Parker reluctantly agreed.

"I suppose you're right...." Dejection succeeded anger as he walked out of the studio.

Healy listened to the lagging steps going down the stairs. It always pained him to see artists suffer; he would like to let them all in, give them a chance; but the jury found him much too lenient. Those younger men stormed against what they called mediocrity, apt sometimes to label mediocre any painting that did not conform with their own impressionistic ideas.

George Healy liked the new generation of artists; their happy effects of light delighted him who so often regretted that portraits did not give a painter sufficient scope for color. He watched the young men, listened to their arguments; if sometimes he overheard their disrespectful "old G. P. A." or familiar "Pop Healy," he detected an affectionate tone in the terms used—he had helped so many of them!

There was young John Sargent—one of the best, whom Healy advised to make art his career. Many others, John Alexander, Blashfield, Kenyon Cox, the ardent young Childe Hassam, showed talent. Most of them already had an appreciative public. It was not in vain that Healy's generation had worked to bring about the recognition of art in America.

George Healy glanced around his studio; that tulip picture he had bought from Hitchcock made a bright splash of vivid yellow; John L. Brown's horses were spirited, full of life; three canvases by Inness held his eye. Yes, his country had reason for elation; the space given to the United States at the exposition marked an apex for his century of American art.

Taking up his brushes and palette again, he stepped back from the easel, head tilted, ready to resume work on his canvas, when the sound of a voice arrested him.

"Monsieur has not forgotten that this is Thursday?"

"Oh! I didn't hear you come in.... Is it time, Isidore?" As he spoke, Healy raised his eyes to the handsome Louis XIV clock that always ticked the hours too fast to suit him. It was Thursday, and visitors would soon come trooping in. He submitted to Isidore's ministrations and slipped on a fresh black velvet coat in place of the rumpled one he had worn since morning.

Isidore felt a sort of protective devotion toward this American master, quite sure that without his prompting Monsieur would forget all the important things such as meals or visits and the names of prominent people. How young Monsieur Healy still looked with his brown curly hair barely peppered with gray; no one would believe this active, energetic man to be nearly seventy-six!

Healy walked around his studio, changing a canvas here or there, while Isidore quickly dusted and straightened chairs and table.

Voices filled the hall; Healy's daughter, Mary Bigot, came in accompanied by two Frenchmen as dissimilar as could be. One typified the *bohème* so often depicted in Montmartre with beard, open collar, and arrogant step; it was Desboutin, painter, engraver, and the inventor of a new process of lithography. Healy greeted him warmly, but soon Desboutin became absorbed in the pictures, shunning the social atmosphere. The other Frenchman was small, natty, and attractive with a humorous mouth and piercing eyes. Jules Lemaître's literary criticisms were the sensation of the day; his caustic wit could make or blast a book. He went straight to an unfinished portrait of Jules Simon, the noted educator and statesman, and across the studio, while talking to other newcomers, from the corner of his eye Healy watched Lemaître stop abruptly before the full-length portrait of Lincoln, exclaiming under his breath, *"Magnifique! Magnifique!"* Mary also saw him and smiled at her father.

Isidore was letting in more people. General Winslow, U. S.

Commissioner for the exposition, and his wife arrived. Conversation buzzed. Everyone discussed the new features of this exposition, particularly the fantastic tower of steel erected by Monsieur Eiffel. "A marvel of engineering," said one. "Hideous," protested another, while many praised its slender boldness.

Two sculptors came in, amused by the discussion and the penetrating American voices; Bartholdi immediately joined their group; for over two years his Statue of Liberty had stood on Bedloe Island, the symbol of a new brave world. Barbedienne, a bronze artist, contemporary and friend of George Healy, had some twenty years before cast for him in Rome the nervous magic hands of Liszt and the exquisitely feminine hands of Elisabeth of Rumania. Healy was showing them to his guests, while one of the McCormicks told Bartholdi about their exhibits and those of Bell and Edison.

During a lull, the painter mentioned La Farge's opaline glass; the beautiful Memorial Window, he felt sure, would win French honors.

"But stained glass is not new," a visitor remarked.

"His is," replied Healy.

Desboutin, ready to leave, interrupted.

"La Farge? La Farge? He's French!"

"His father was," answered his friend, "but John La Farge was born in New York and belongs to us in spirit and citizenship."

Desboutin laughed, shrugged, and as he walked to the door, threw out a last challenge:

"Art claims no citizenship!"

Around Healy the visitors now wanted details about many portraits; there was lovely Carmen Sylva, Queen Elisabeth and her handsome Hohenzollern husband Carol I of Rumania, whom Healy had twice visited at Bucharest and Sinaia; Gambetta of the leonine head and magnetic eyes; Thiers, first president of the Third Republic, small and round-faced with twinkling eyes and a mouth difficult to paint, said the artist, for it never kept still. On the other wall their archenemy faced them—Bismarck, very Prussian and military, who had told Healy that he was really kindhearted and should have been Pope! Lord Lyons and Lord Lytton, the former in impeccable dress and the latter very.handsome in full ambassadorial regalia, looked out from their canvases with diplomatic impassivity. There were many American generals—Grant, Sherman, Sheridan, McClellan, and also Beauregard, painted in New Orleans just before the outbreak of war.

A portrait of the aristocratic-looking Count de Paris recalled Healy's early paintings of and for King Louis Philippe; Cardinal Gibbons' ascetic quality and Archbishop Kenrick's superb portrait stood out amid the feminine beauties surrounding them; Mrs. Caton, who later would hold salon at Washington as Mrs. Marshall Field; Miss Horsford, charming in pink satin; Mrs. Potter Palmer wearing the latest fashion; the noted singer Emma Thursby, draped and bustled and regal in blue silk and lace. Fingers raised in a blessing, Pope Pius IX seemed to bestow his benign approbation over the heterogeneous gathering.

As the light grew dim, Edith shepherded the remaining guests across the courtyard and garden that led to the Healy home next door at 66 rue de La Rochefoucauld. In passing a portrait of Mattie Mitchell who was soon to marry the Duc de La Rochefoucauld one of the ladies remarked: "How charming! And what a beautifully simple gown!" "Yes," answered her mother, the outspoken Senator's wife: "That damn simplicity that costs!" Edith was glad her mother could not hear this remark.... At her silver laden tea table, in the white and gold drawing room, Mrs. Healy, short and stout like Queen Victoria, but still pretty and gracious, greeted the guests with pleasure as her eyes sought her husband and seemed to send a comforting message; "They'll soon be gone and you can rest" ... During their fifty years of marriage she had thus responded to his every mood.

After tea, when the last guest had departed, George Healy, as was his custom, stretched out on his favorite sofa, let his body relax, and closed his eyes. But sleep eluded him; the committee's wranglings, the artist's anger at having his paintings rejected, and some absurd remarks about Chicago still rankled. It all seemed so alien, so ignorant of the growing nation.... Healy let his thoughts span the Atlantic. During his last visit home, in Washington, in Chicago, in Boston, many had urged his return to America; the idea was taking root. His mind turned back to Boston and childhood days. His thoughts ceased churning; peace descended; his eyelids grew heavy in complete surrender. A loud snore informed his listening wife that George Healy was asleep.

Chapter II

A BOY AND HIS HERO

THE Healys of Dublin were descended from Cormac Cas, son of Olliol Olum, King of Munster, and Sabia, daughter of Con, King of Ireland. When the uprising of 1798 broke out in violence, the three sons of the Dublin estate were sent by their father to London—the two older ones to reach the colonies, the youngest, William, only fourteen years old, to find some work in the great city. Each boy had been given forty pounds, the best their father could do in the emergency.

At the East India Company docks, William, a quick, active youth, soon found work, and he must have proved a good sailor, for we find him shortly thereafter in the port of Boston and owner of his own ship.

Corsairs were active in the Mediterranean, and the young captain found himself pursued off the coast of Portugal. He managed to land his crew, blow up his ship, and somehow escape, for we find him next back in Boston, an accepted American citizen and quite a hero, whose portrait the great Gilbert Stuart painted. Boston shipowners liked him, and success seemed to come easily, but the War of 1812 changed all this. His ship seized by the British and himself their prisoner on the island of Antigua, his prospects were slim, and when an exchange of prisoners brought him back to Boston, the first thing he did was to tell beautiful young Mary Hicks that their marriage must be postponed, since he had nothing to offer. However, the girl would not listen, and even won over her widowed mother. So Captain William Healy

9

and Mary Hicks were married in the Catholic church of Boston by Reverend Father Matignon on June 22, 1812. The first child, George Peter Alexander Healy, was born July 15, 1813.

While details of the first year of this romantic family life are lacking, an old family Bible indicates the birth of other children in Albany, New York.

Why Albany? Intense research of maritime records have yielded little. But the Albany Historical Society, delving into old directories, found that a William Healy was in the Intelligence Service—a likely occupation for a fighting captain in the American Merchant Marine.

The Healy children after Boston-born George were: a brother John born in 1816; a sister Ann Elizabeth, who for some reason was called Agnes by her brothers born in 1818; another boy, Thomas Cantwell, 1820; and William in 1822; then baby Samuel, born in 1823, lived only a year, by which time the family was back in Boston. In 1825 occurred an incident that remained ever deeply etched into George Peter Alexander Healy's memory. There had been illness. The children recuperated, save George, who limped so that the parents felt the need of doctors' consultation. Called in, the doctors advised amputation, and the mother almost fainted. After they had gone, she came to George's bed and told him to stretch his leg over the sheet. Then, all at once, with all her weight, she sat on it. George screamed and must have fainted. But having recovered consciousness, he heard his gentle little mother tell him quietly that it was as if God had told her to do this; and George got well and never limped again. "Inspired bloodless surgery," said doctors of a later age.

And in June we see George, twelve now or almost, scampering with comrades through the streets of Boston, to watch the never-to-be-forgotten pageant of Lafayette's arrival.

It was the day of the big parade. Church bells pealed, columns of marching men formed, bands blared forth their martial music. From all the houses, from every street, men, women, and children emerged, mingled and finally blended into an irresistible human stream.

George pushed his way in and out among the crowd; his legs hurt, his body trembled with heat and fatigue, but he was determined to reach the outer edge and come as close to the procession as was humanly possible. They had come out early, his mother, his sister Agnes, and two brothers, John and little Thomas; the crush of people hurt them; for a while they watched the troops, the riders and carriages, and acclaimed the music; then, tired, they begged to go home, but George stayed on.

This was Boston's great day. Here, at Bunker Hill fifty years before, men had fought and died and laid the cornerstone of independence. Fifty thousand Bostonians and three times as many visitors from all over the United States were assembled to lay the cornerstone of Bunker Hill Monument.

Wheels and legs passed before small George's eyes till he felt dizzy, but the shadowy figures of history took shape and became human beings, real persons to remember and revere. Suddenly he was hemmed in, lifted, carried along by a new surge of the crowd as a deafening clamor rose.

"There he is! Huzzah! Huzzah!"

The voices reached a monstrous crescendo.

"Lafayette! Lafayette!"

In an imposing buff and blue low-slung open barouche, drawn by six white horses, stood a large-faced, big-nosed, tall, dignified man in becoming peruke, blue coat, and white cashmere trousers. His prominent eyes lingered over the stirring scene as he bowed repeatedly to the cheering throng.

George, too, yelled at the top of his lungs, for on this seventeenth day of June, 1825, twelve-year-old George Peter Alexander Healy experienced his first lasting hero worship, and he felt a tremendous exhilaration that wiped out all fatigue.

Catching sight of some comrades, George skipped along with them, climbed trees, leaped to porch roofs to escape the crush,

stopped here and there by a strong arm or a manly voice calling
out: "Hey, lads! Careful!"

At the base of Bunker Hill the procession, which had started
at ten, halted. Wooden benches had been erected to accommodate
some fifteen thousand spectators. There was a long wait. Devouring his hero with hungry eyes, the boy tried to picture
Lafayette as a young marquis fifty years ago; his imagination
could not quite evoke from this elderly gentleman the picture
of a dashing officer of eighteen. Like every schoolboy George
was familiar with prints representing Lafayette, tall, slim, and
elegant, standing beside the still taller General Washington.

Listening to comments around him, George heard someone
quote the toast of the French General in answer to the gift granted
him of perpetual American citizenship.

"To the perpetual union of the United States. It has already
saved us in times of storm; one day it will save the world."

A hush fell upon the crowd as Lafayette, holding a silver
trowel, made the symbolic gesture of laying the cornerstone and
in the stone's cavity deposited a casket containing coins and other
mementos.

Reverend Joseph Thaxter, the venerable chaplain of Prescott's
Regiment, stood where he had ministered to dying soldiers fifty
years before, and delivered the opening prayer. Daniel Webster
then came forward to speak and his thunderous voice held the
crowd enthralled.

During the applause George got up and stretched, ready to
scamper down the hill again. However, there were more speeches,
a hymn in which all joined, a dirge in memory of Washington,
then renewed yells of "Huzzah! Huzzah!" and the procession
wended its way back to the city.

With the music of bands still ringing in his ears and the joy
of these past hours pounding in his blood, George turned home-
ward.

Agnes, John, and Thomas rushed to meet him, clamoring for

an account of the ceremonies on the hill. Their brother picked
his words carefully, seeing in his mind the vast canvas of color
and life. For his mother and grandmother, the boy grabbed a
pencil, and on paper he scratched little drawings of the things
he had seen, the flags that had so impressed him. Shyly he turned
to his grandmother, Mrs. Hicks, whose paintings always fascinated him:

"Grandmother, do you think—" He controlled the eagerness
of his voice with difficulty—"do you think I could paint this?"

"Maybe, my boy...."

He watched her bright old eyes and caught the quick exchange
of looks between the two women. He knew then that he had
won his point and that his birthday, July 15, might bring the
painting material he so desired!

"Someday I'll go to France!" he exclaimed. "I want to see
the General in his own home."

His mother understood her son's enthusiasm; like him she
felt the romantic appeal of individuals who represented great
ideals. She had wept over Byron's death at Missolonghi in Greece
—another fight for liberty, a fight repeated all over the world.
South America was seething with it; in Venezuela, in Colombia,
and now in Peru, Bolivar caused men to cheer and women to
grow emotional. Republics replaced dependent colonies, and
President Monroe's declaration expressed the will of the United
States when he warned the nations of other continents not to
interfere with those of this hemisphere....

In the Healy home, as in most Boston homes, such matters were
discussed in the presence of the children and explained to them as
an important part of their education, for they must become aware
of things greater than play and ease. So George Healy thrilled at
heroism, and his mother sympathized with his new eagerness to
visit other countries where men had fought for freedom.

Chapter III

A STUDIO ON FEDERAL STREET

ON Federal Street one crisp October day of the year 1830, a young man of medium height, slender body, and quick movement stood admiring a new sign that bore the legend "G.P.A. Healy, Artist." Above it, swaying gently in the breeze, hung the portrait of a student wearing a jaunty cap, Rembrandt fashion. Any passer-by might have recognized George Healy's likeness as he contemplated this symbol of a hope achieved.

The young man took out his key, his first personal key; he walked up the stoop to the front door, entered, and mounted the straight stairway, at the head of which a door carried his name on a plaque. The room, not very large, was well lighted with its tall wide window; his easel faced a model's table on which stood an inviting armchair; on a stand by the easel were the paints, brushes, turpentine, and palette.

With a trace of swagger George seized his palette and brushes, spreading in a very professional manner the red, blue, yellow, sienna, white, and black paints, experiencing the same delight he had known at sight of his first rainbow—the magic of color. Here at last he could give himself wholly to its perpetual joy; he was his own master, could direct his own life.

A timid knock at the door interrupted this mood of exultation. He stopped his work and went to the door.

"Oh, it's you?" Agnes smiled at him from the threshold as he let her in.

"I just wanted to see how it looks now and watch you work,"

she murmured wistfully. "I thought it might be lonesome without any sitters...."

"Not for long," bragged her brother. "You'll see them trooping in...."

They both laughed, and Agnes wandered around the room, touching various objects, unconsciously trying to give a lived-in atmosphere to the new place. Then realizing that her brother had stopped working and that perhaps he preferred painting without an audience, she left.

Immediately George returned to his canvas, set two mirrors at the proper angle, and after a few bold strokes of his charcoal pencil took up his palette. He was soon absorbed enough in the work to forget the newness of his quarters or the need of other sitters; there was an almost religious devotion in his handling of his material, in the way he softened or thinned the paints, wiped the brush, or scraped with palette knife held in surgeonlike fingers a wrong color on the canvas; he had entered the sacred world of creative art.

It was not vanity that led George to make his portrait again and again; of necessity he became his own best model; untiring, he practiced tone effects, tried to make the flesh alive, the eyes expressive. Faithfully he gave what the mirror showed him—a rather heavy nose against ruddy cheeks, a round firm chin, strong despite the slight cleft (his mother called it stubborn Irish), blue eyes so deep-set under the dark brows that they seemed at times almost black; a somewhat sensuous mouth, optimistic with its upturned corners. His wavy brown hair parted on the side framed the face in a flattering bob that girls would adopt a century later.

In the late spring of 1830, Thomas Sully came to Boston to paint a portrait of Colonel Perkins. After the death of Gilbert Stuart, Sully, who had been his pupil, stood at the head of American artists, and therefore Boston lionized him. His sharp but refined face, his courteous manner pleased the fastidious Bostonians who crowded his painting room. There one afternoon

Miss Jane Stuart captured the artist's attention long enough to tell him of "little Healy," the son of friends, a remarkably gifted boy for whom color was a vibrant, living force. Sully expressed himself eager to see the young fellow.

"Let him bring me some copies of your father's work and several original sketches," he told Miss Stuart.

So it happened that shortly after this, George found himself at the door of Mr. Sully's painting room, facing a knocker that suddenly appeared formidable. . . . He shifted his portfolio, and with a burst of his fast-waning courage he grabbed the knocker so vigorously that its loudness brought the artist in person to answer his impatient caller. On the threshold Thomas Sully saw a breathless youth who stammered a fervid, "Mr. Sully . . . sir . . ."

"Come in, young man, come in," said the amused painter in a reassuring tone as he ushered the trembling lad into a room filled with pictures. "You must be Mr. Healy," he remarked, pointing to the portfolio, and at once George felt more at ease as he carefully placed his burden on the table indicated by his host.

However, instead of opening the folder at once, he went as if drawn by a magnet to a portrait placed in a good light on an easel. It seemed to him the loveliest woman's portrait he had ever seen—a sweet face delicately painted with its soft white scarf around the head; George wished he could paint his mother that way. Then remembering his manners he turned apologetically to Mr. Sully, who, far from resenting this involuntary compliment to his latest portrait of Mrs. Sully, watched with pleasure the boy's animated countenance.

"You like it?" he asked.

"Oh! Yes, sir!" There was no doubting the sincerity of his admiration.

The artist smiled and suggested that he bring out his work. George's feverish hands fumbled a little in untying the tapes of his portfolio. Used to the familiar tone of family and friends, he felt proud and slightly awed at being treated as a man. The artist examined first George's copies of Copley and Stuart and laid them aside when George handed him an original sketch. As his eyes fell on it, Sully gave a start, then looked attentively at other sketches.

"My young friend," the artist's voice had a warmth that immediately quieted the boy's jangled nerves, "I advise you to make painting your profession!"

With a deep sigh of relief George listened enraptured while Sully pointed out mistakes and explained how to remedy them. For over two hours they spoke of art, line, and color and of the help derived from studying old masters.

"Someday you will go abroad," the forty-seven-year-old artist told his young admirer, "and you will learn more from copying masterpieces in those European galleries than you can imagine; but remember that the only way for an artist to achieve even a small part of his ambition is to work constantly, to paint and paint and paint."

So now on Federal Street, George painted and painted while the days ran without money returns but in definite progress. His walls were covered with sketches—some bits of sea- or landscape showing his sense of color in sunny pastures, golden sunsets, or stormy waves and lowering skies; but a stronger feeling of life and likeness caught the eye in his numerous studies of faces, hands, figures. He could not afford a model, difficult to obtain in Boston, where any occupation out of the ordinary aroused a suspicion of sin; so his mother and sister and brothers posed for him as often as he could induce them to do so, while he waited hopefully for outside sitters. It was a long wait. Day after day, when he returned home at sundown, he would answer their questions with forced cheerfulness.

"No—not today...people don't seem to need portraits just now. But I saw the butcher, Mamma, and he said he would take his portrait in payment of the bill...."

That was good news, yet poor comfort to the aspiring painter.

George's stubborn optimism suffered a severe strain during those
long months of waiting. Once, Captain Healy, home from some
expedition, spoke harshly.

"You'll have to give up this wild plan of yours, George, and
get to work—I mean a real job!"

Stung to the quick, George looked at his father angrily, his
eyes burning with a growing challenge. What right had this
parent to reproach him when for years his own efforts had failed
to provide enough for the family? Did not Grandmother tire
her old eyes painting water colors to sell in order to help them
out? Hadn't he, himself, taken willingly any small chore that
offered and painted various tradespeople to pay some of the most
pressing bills? All this the Captain could read in the youth's
telltale face, and sadly he walked away, but a new tension developed between father and son, painful to the sweet woman
they both loved and wanted to protect.

Friends as well as family criticized young Healy; the romantic
seaport where men grew rich and ships brought new treasures
or thrilling tales of adventure gave scant recognition to native
art. True, Copley and Stuart had achieved fame, but not until
Europe acclaimed them; Benjamin West had lived in England;
Peale remained a little apart because he had taken an active part
in the battles he depicted and also because, like Dr. Franklin, he
used his active mind for many inventions. No sensible person
would encourage a young man to choose art as a profession; it
was impractical, morally dangerous, and financially unprofitable.

The most sympathetic stranger turned out to be George's landlord, Richard Tucker, one of Boston's great merchants, who
knocked one day at his tenant's door and viewed with interest
the paintings and sketches. He was amused at the ingenious
arrangement of double mirrors for his self-portrait.

Pleasantly talkative, Mr. Tucker eased the young man out of
his painful shyness and little by little drew from him the story of
his life at home. In the lively account of ordinary circumstances,

the older man sensed a curious mixture of easygoing, devil-may-care Irish outlook and serious puritanical sense of duty. The name Healy suddenly struck a familiar chord.

"Was your mother Miss Hicks?" he asked. George looked up in surprise.

"Yes, sir. Do you know my mother?"

"No, but I have heard the Higginsons speak of Mrs. Hicks and her daughter...."

Listening with one ear, Richard Tucker now prodded his memory; it must have been some eighteen years ago, during the War of 1812, that he had heard of pretty little fourteen-year-old Mary Hicks marrying a sea captain twice her age—a Dublin sailor who had joined the East India Company when the Irish rebellion of 1798 ruined the Healys, and who later arrived in Boston with his own ship and became an American citizen. A brave man apparently who caught the fancy of a romantic girl; there was a story about the corsairs; attacked, William Healy managed to land his crew on the coast of Portugal and blew up his ship rather than let it fall into the hands of those pirates.

George was speaking of the time his father had lost his ship to the British and been taken prisoner in 1812, then exchanged with other prisoners from the Island of Antigua. Captain Healy, a Catholic, had married fourteen-year-old Mary Hicks, a Protestant, that same year, in the face of much disapproval by the descendants of witch hunters who still perceived an odor of brimstone at mention of Rome.

Yes, thought the visitor, criticism of Mrs. Hicks was rife then, women shaking their heads over mixed marriages and repeating the old saw:

> Change the name and not the letter,
> Change for worse and not for better....

When the second term of rent came, George was caught flat of purse and greatly distressed. What could he do but confess to his landlord his inability to pay? Unexpectedly the generous merchant, instead of dislodging his young tenant, told him not to worry and ordered two portraits; his son Charles and his son-in-law John H. Gray. Sittings began the next day, and George Healy found himself as much at ease with the son as he had been with the father. All hesitancy, shyness, or awkwardness vanished when the youth became absorbed in his work. One thing only counted—to re-create in line and color the model before him and give it life.

Mr. Tucker talked of his travels to a very willing listener. Young Healy wanted to hear of other great cities besides Boston. His sitter was familiar with New York and Philadelphia and with Washington, the national capital, which always held a special fascination for Healy and which he would learn to know so well in the years to come.

The Tuckers' interest in the young painter grew as the work progressed. They were amazed at the amount accomplished while talking. His uncanny rapidity enabled the artist to hold the freshness of a first impression so that he gave not only the likeness but the character of his model. Friends came occasionally to watch the painter at his work, and when later the two portraits were exhibited at the Athenaeum, Healy tasted the first fruits of real success. By this time the Tuckers considered G. P. A. Healy as their discovery and recommended him widely. This success marked the beginning of a long and brilliant career. Years later, long after the death of his kind and understanding landlord, George Healy was commissioned to paint the portrait of a Tucker descendant, the first American woman millionaire, the famed recluse Hetty Green. That portrait, sold after her death, is now the property of a later Tucker descendant, Mr. Loring.

New sitters occupied the model's chair. Among them Healy particularly enjoyed a young and attractive naval officer, Lieutenant Gershom J. Van Brunt. One day Healy confided to this friendly sitter his great desire to paint beautiful women.

"Nothing easier, I assure you," Van Brunt remarked. "All women want to see themselves in paint, especially if they are really beautiful. If you were to paint Mrs. Harrison Gray Otis, the young one, I mean, all the society women would flock to you for their portraits, too!"

"You mean the Mayor's daughter-in-law? The one whose husband died so suddenly?"

"Of course. Elizabeth Boardman, Otis. She's a great society leader, and all her friends would follow her lead and want their portraits."

Healy laughed ruefully. "But I don't even know her."

"That's easily remedied," said his sitter. "Just give me a pen and paper." George handed him the quill and a sheet of paper, and hastily Van Brunt wrote a note, which he handed to Healy, saying: "Take this to her."

The bold lieutenant would have laughed had he seen the manner in which his young friend carried out his advice. George Healy was still very shy. Like all Bostonians he had heard a great deal about the noted Otis family—the able statesman, lawyer, and mayor of Boston and his gracious and distinguished wife, whose invitations were always eagerly sought. The younger Mrs. Otis, a widow with two boys, was a social leader, her receptions the nearest thing to a French salon, Van Brunt told Healy. The next day he went to Mrs. Otis' house, but turned back without even going up the steps on Beacon Street. The following day he tried again, and this time, just as he reached the top step, the door was opened by a maid. With all the dignity he could muster, young Healy said, "Please tell Mrs. Otis that a gentleman wishes to see her on business."

The lady of the house heard and saw and, amused, came forward.

"What can I do for you, young man?" she asked, leading the way into the house. Healy, flustered, blurted out:

"Madam! I want to paint a beautiful woman. Will you sit for me?"

Throwing back her head, laughing, Mrs. Otis heard the youth exclaim: "Oh! That's the way I want to paint you!"

Amused, the charming Mrs. Otis questioned the young artist, extracting much of his story and hopes. The note of introduction from Van Brunt remained in Healy's pocket—unpresented, forgotten.

The next day Mrs. Otis was at Healy's painting room. Curious to see if he really had talent, she looked about the room. There was a portrait of his mother, an unfinished sketch of his sister, as well as others of local people, some in the form of sketches, others in finished form.

Exclaiming at the charm of Healy's portrait of his mother, without more ado the Boston belle walked to the armchair on the model's table and seated herself. And so, in 1831, hardly a year after he had hung his sign, chance favored the artist, and he began to paint.

This first portrait of Mrs. Otis, painted in the fearless audacity of inexperience, brought a stream of commissions. No longer could Healy complain that only men visited his painting room. And as the friends of Mrs. Otis and of the Tuckers came to sit for their portraits, he learned from them much of Boston's virtues and prejudices and a great deal of American history in the making. Romanticism caught him, for these were the days of sentimental heartaches, undying love, eternal vows, and easy tears. Nevertheless, the young artist kept his feet on good solid Yankee ground, combining realism with social manners and idealistic faith.

This year, 1831, marked the turning point in George Healy's career. All doors opened to him. His models came from all walks of Boston life. At the waterfront, Healy painted his father's friend, Father Taylor, who busied himself with seamen's souls; then Samuel Dorr, the India trade merchant; Moses Pond, also a merchant of prominence; David Henshaw, the Massachusetts politician and future Secretary of the Navy in Tyler's cabinet, and others of greater or less importance. Samuel Appleton, the noted Boston merchant and philanthropist, commissioned Healy to paint the portraits of his two daughters—Mary, the future Mrs. MacIntosh, one of the most beautiful girls in a set where beauty abounded; and Frances, the future Mrs. Henry Wadsworth Longfellow. The father, himself, later sat for his portrait. It can still be seen in the Athenaeum.

Mrs. Otis urged the young artist to go to Paris, London, Rome, and to other cities in Europe rich with the art of centuries. Healy's mother was very proud, not only of his talent and success, but of his deep sense of responsibility as the eldest child of a family of five. She encouraged him to save his money; she prodded his ambition to go abroad to study and paint.

In April, 1834, after he received payment for his successfully completed portraits of the Appleton sisters, Healy prepared to leave for France.

Chapter IV

TRAGEDY AT THE ATELIER

APRIL, 1834. In New York, Healy called at the Washington Square studio of Samuel Finley Breese Morse. With something of the excitement he had felt on meeting Thomas Sully, young Healy looked forward to meeting this man, who, in the flush of youth, had boldly proclaimed his ambition to emulate the genius of a Raphael, a Michelangelo, or a Velasquez and to shine with a light brighter than theirs! Morse, starved for art, had organized a "Drawing Association" in which all would-be artists shared the expense of light, heat, and the models. After his successful portrait of Lafayette in 1826, Morse had helped found the National Academy of Design. But now he was forsaking art for some strange mechanical invention that seemed to fascinate him.

Unlike Thomas Sully, Morse did not encourage his young visitor. Instead, he told him that art was a "cruel jilt," that painting never nourished its man, that people were not interested in beauty. He sounded bitter and skeptical. Healy did not attempt to show the sketches he had brought; he merely talked of his hopes, his great desire to learn. Morse, shaking his head, remarked:

"Young man, you'll not earn salt for your porridge!"

"The very words my grandmother used, sir," sadly acknowledged Healy, but he added: "Yet, for three years my work has supported us, and, if I have to, I shall eat my porridge without salt!"

Morse laughed. Then, more amiably, asked: "What ship are you sailing on?"

"The *Sully,* sir."

"Oh. I shall give you a note to Captain Pell."

Encouraged by this kindness, Healy asked Morse if he would favor him with a note of introduction to Lafayette, the great French hero. The older artist unbent and graciously complied.

Healy left New York with a sense of bewilderment, not un-mixed with apprehension. But he blamed New York for Morse's pessimistic attitude—a strange nervous city whose atmosphere seemed charged with struggles, with sparks, like Morse's tele-graph, vibrant and noisy from constant building, feverish in its perpetual search for new ideas, new beliefs.

On the *Sully*'s deck, the wind in his face, his eyes following the blue, white-capped waves, the artist shed his oppression. The rhythm of the ship's motion, the sound of the wind in the sails, the sea, restless as his soul, filled him with a sense of progress. It would ever be so. Healy's innumerable crossings offered the only content he ever felt away from his work.

The *Sully* made a fast journey over. Within a week it was far enough into European waters to enable the passengers to make out the Normandy shore line when using strong glasses. Then the wind died and the vessel was becalmed for ten interminable days. At last Le Havre came in sight, and young Healy was caught in the confusion of landing. He did not speak French, and the quick, staccato exchange of words around him made him dizzy.

With other passengers, Healy boarded the rickety diligence bound for Paris. It was a lumbering old four horse-drawn coach, high, noisy, and slow. As the vehicle rolled along the twisting bends of the Seine, Healy noticed the yellow and brown thatch roofs that picturesquely topped old white farm buildings set on hillocks or in the midst of green fields. A hot spell had opened red poppies swaying beside the white daisies and blue bachelor buttons. "My flag!" thought the American, forgetting the French tricolor. Girls in white *coiffes* feeding the chickens attracted his attention. He wished he could sketch their graceful gestures.

Then, all at once, they were in Paris.

As Healy stepped down from the high-slung coach, he felt stiff and cramped, but no sooner had he deposited his belongings in the room of a modest hotel recommended by a fellow traveler than he rushed out to stretch his legs and to fill his eyes with the new scenes of the Paris he had tried so long to imagine.

May is the loveliest of months in Paris. Cobbled, crooked, narrow streets were no novelty to a Bostonian, but the beauty of the wide boulevards and the flowering chestnut trees with sun-splashed pink and white blossoms, the ancient arched bridges across the Seine, the magnificent buildings grayed with age gripped the artist's soul with intense delight. The spell of Paris was on him.

The next morning, however, brought a double disappointment. Mrs. Otis had already left for Switzerland with her two boys, and, with sorrow, he learned that Lafayette lay dying in his Paris home. So the American's dream of telling his hero his unbounded admiration was unrealized.

On May 22, 1834, from the Paris sidewalks crowded with the mourning populace, Healy watched the funeral procession of his hero. Under guise of military honors, the hearse was surrounded by a formidable array of troops, arms glistening in the sun, and only from afar could the spectators see the tricolor placed at the four corners of the catafalque. Lafayette was buried at Picpus, the cemetery founded by his royalist wife.

Had the young artist but known it, at about the same time his father, Captain William Healy, was being laid to rest in a Boston cemetery—but he would not hear of this for weeks. Mails were slow in 1834.

The first thrilling month in Paris was not wasted. Always quick in his decisions and active in carrying them out, Healy, using all available information gathered in Boston and New York, made the rounds of the studios and, in due course, was accepted as a student, by Baron Gros himself, the noted French painter.

Gros and Ingres were the leaders, not only in painting, but in all forms of art in France. Disciples of the great David, who, said the wits, had "guillotined" eighteenth-century French art, even as the Revolutionists had guillotined royalty, they inculcated stern principles in their pupils. Ingres had just been named director of the French Academy of Art in Rome, which left Gros the undisputed master in Paris.

On a hot June day in 1834, one of those lazy days when sunlight makes surrounding colors shimmer, Gros's pupils cast longing glances through the windows. A model slumped momentarily with fatigue, and Healy tried to catch the movement. At his easel, a short, stocky young man, brown-eyed and wild-haired, watched the newcomer's efforts with commiseration. Without so much as a by-your-leave, Couture, a name later to become famous in French art, strode over to Healy's easel, shoved him aside, saying, "Give me your seat!" At first stiff with indignation, then keenly interested, the new student watched him. This foreshortening, he thought, is easy, a trick, but as he started to express his thoughts in his halting French, Couture, who had already put down the charcoal pencil, returned to his place without a word, merely acknowledging with a nod Healy's hesitant *"Merci!"*

From his teacher and his comrades Healy learned a great deal. His pencil became bolder, surer, his color brighter and more transparent. He practiced the mechanics of composition, that art which came to him instinctively, yet required a knowledge of balance and proportion that the old master, Gros, could explain.

With others Healy soon established friendly relations. The strictly reared Boston youth found French studio life exciting. Little cafés, incredibly cheap; the gay *midinettes* and models so friendly, so co-operative; the jokes perpetrated on solemn bourgeois—all this opened a magic world, a world where laugh-

ter and dreams, ideas and ideals, counted for more than drab
reality.

The shyness Mrs. Otis had tried to cure in Boston left young
Healy completely; his five feet eight inches no longer occasioned
the term "little Healy" used by lanky six-footers at home. His
nationality gave him a friendly importance; his comrades initi-
ated him in the salty, colorful argot of the ateliers.

Breathing the Paris air, Healy found it quite natural that
audiences should fight with fists and canes to decide on the merits
of a play. He thrilled at the love affairs of George Sand and
de Musset, of Franz Liszt and the Countess d'Agoult. He
broadened his outlook on life and art; he steeped himself in this
new atmosphere, forgetting the stiff New England middle-class
prejudices so firmly rooted in his own fiber. He belonged to
the Romantic vanguard.

There is a self-portrait of Healy painted at this period—a young
face with a small mustache and lively eyes. He wore a dark, high
cravat in vivid contrast to his clear complexion. His brown hair,
parted at the side, is abundant; the heavy brow gives power to his
face. Delacroix's famous self-portrait, painted two years later,
presents an interesting similarity with this self-portrait of Healy
at the age of twenty-one.

In addition to his course at the atelier, Healy also spent as
much time as he could at the Louvre, copying old masters. The
guardians there soon came to know him and brought him his
easel and paints when he appeared. One day, absorbed in his
copy of Correggio's "Mystic Marriage of Saint Catherine," he
heard English voices and noted a man and his wife sauntering
leisurely in evident enjoyment of the masterpieces that adorned
the walls. Even spoken in that accent peculiar to those from across
the Channel, the sound of English made Healy's heart beat
faster. The couple stopped at his side, and as Healy looked up,
the man remarked, "Good! That's an excellent copy!" Healy
thanked him, and in the conversation that followed, the Ameri-

can found himself explaining that he hoped very much to visit and work in England before returning to the United States. It was a pleasant meeting, but no names had been mentioned and when the visitors were gone Healy regretted it, but it was too late. A full year had passed since Healy's arrival in Paris. He wanted to study longer in this treasure house of art, but he also felt the pull of family life and perhaps of family needs, for he was still spending, though occasionally he could sell a picture. At home he would really again be the bread earner!

Then tragedy occurred at the atelier. Gros had been the butt of severe attacks by the Romantics, as they called themselves, and one particularly harsh critic had closed his tirade with the remark: *"Gros est un homme mort* [Gros is a dead man]"! His pupils laughed at the absurdity of such a thought. They loved Gros and appreciated him, both as an artist and as a man. They were dumfounded when the painter greeted a visitor with the bitter remark: "So you have come to see the dead man in his grave?" It was so unlike the forceful, active man who showed himself such a fine master.

But the next day, when the master, always punctual, did not appear, the students became concerned, and one of them went to his home to inquire. Yes, Monsieur le Baron had left that morning as usual. As the hours passed, anxiety mounted. The search was continued. It was only the next morning, June 26, 1835, that they found him at Bas Meudon, drowned in three feet of water. The artist, who knew and loved every bend of the river Seine, had come there to end a life he could no longer endure.

Chapter V

FRIENDS, NEW AND OLD

THE tragic death of Gros ended Healy's year as a student, his only extended period of training under a teacher. The atelier closed its doors, and the pupils scattered, some to seek a new master, others to search for an easier and safer way of life than that of an artist, and a few, believing in their talent and a kind fate, to strike out for themselves.

Healy was at loose ends. At a reunion of fellow artists in the studio of one of the more prosperous they spoke heatedly of this master and that; discussions threatened to degenerate into bitter quarrels, and Healy, still unfamiliar with most of the theories expounded or of the personalities under scrutiny, felt his isolation. Suddenly his eyes met those of a quiet, smiling man, older than himself, who was studying him from across the room. Instinctively they went toward each other. The Frenchman addressed him:

"A stranger here?"

"American," Healy responded and explained that, like their host, he was adrift since the death of Gros.

"But you are not returning to America now, are you?" asked the other, after introducing himself as Edme Savinien Dubourjal, miniaturist.

"I would like to remain," Healy started to say when all at once dizziness overcame him; he would have fallen had not Dubourjal seized his arm and led him to a nearby seat. The spell did not last; young Healy felt humiliated as his companion brought a glass of wine and pressed it on him. But Healy, because he had not eaten, refused the proffered glass.

The two men slipped off to Dubourjal's nearby painting room. The fresh air restored Healy. He relaxed in an atmosphere of comfortable companionship. The Frenchman brought out food, and they ate as they talked. By evening there was little of his life that Healy had not confided to this new-found friend. Dubourjal urged him to remain in Paris and try his luck.

"Among the many Americans who come over at this season," he said, "you ought to find sitters or buyers for those landscapes you say you painted all summer."

"The difficulty is finding a dealer to handle them," objected Healy.

"Oh, no! Not through a dealer," countered the older man, "not at first, anyhow. You must have your own studio and show your work yourself." He stopped a moment. "I know of one near here," he suggested, "that has just been vacated. Would you like to see it?"

Rested and seized with a new surge of enthusiasm, Healy agreed. Together, the two artists walked to a little court nearby at the back of which stood an old building with high windows. The American liked its picturesque approach, and when the concierge showed them a well-lighted room, Healy decided to take it.

Before night he had brought over his few belongings, had bought the couch, easel, and two chairs left by the former tenant, and, with Dubourjal's help, soon transformed the room into a presentable studio. The next day his new-found friend brought a handsome piece of brocade to throw over the couch. He then led the way to a secondhand shop where Healy acquired a bright red screen, a table, mirrors, and a rug. Portraits and sketches hung about the room furnished all the decoration needed. The room looked cheerful and inviting.

In the winter months that followed, young Healy settled down to serious work. Gradually his reputation filtered through the neighborhood. In the course of the winter, he acquired his first serious pupil, an American, Oliver Fraser, a few years his senior, who had studied under Jouett and Sully before coming to France. Old patrons from America sent him sitters. Healy was not experiencing the quick success he had tasted in Boston, but he kept busy and he earned a living. Dubourjal, whose miniatures sold less easily, became more and more convinced that everything American turned to gold.

Healy, who liked long, easy strokes, disciplined himself to do miniatures when a sudden vogue created a demand. There is one of Frances Sargent Osgood done in 1835; but usually Healy directed miniature seekers to the studio of his friend Dubourjal.

It was toward the end of 1835 that Healy undertook the long-anticipated trip to Italy. By stage, he crossed to Mont Cenis and reached Alexandria on the frontier, expecting to go on through Italy on foot. His luck followed him. As he alighted before the busy little inn, the first persons he noticed were the pleasant English couple who had spoken to him at the Louvre. The husband was coming toward him, hand extended.

"This is Mr. Healy, isn't it?" he inquired.

"Why, yes!" replied the astounded and flustered youth. "But how did you know my name?"

The mystery was soon explained. In Switzerland, the couple, Sir Arthur B. Faulkner and his wife, had met their friend Mrs. Otis and had told her of the young American artist copying in the Louvre.

"Why, that must be George!" she exclaimed and proceeded to tell them of the way she had posed for him in Boston and of the great hopes she and her friends held for his success.

The Faulkners invited young Healy to dine with them. He felt himself transported again into that delightful atmosphere he had first breathed at Mrs. Otis' friendly gatherings. His hosts were enchanted with Healy's bubbling enthusiasm, and before the meal was over, had invited him to join them in their roomy carriage for the trip through Italy. They planned to visit several of the important cities and to tour art museums. Healy could hardly believe his good luck. Words failed him, but his expressive face gave the answer, and thus began for Healy one of the important friendships of his career.

Color, color everywhere—a sky bluer than Healy had ever seen, white and pink marbles, tinted bricks, flowers that bloomed in all seasons, dotting the landscape with brilliant red and yellow, orange and purple—every turn of the carriage revealed some new wonder.

Stops were made in Turin and Milan; Venice with its black gondolas on blue waters, its singing boatmen, fascinated the young New Englander. In the tours through the museums Healy studied the marvelous Titians, and in Florence the power of Michelangelo burst upon the young painter, who wished he could stop long enough to make at least one copy. They saw the leaning Tower of Pisa, visited innumerable churches, all in leisurely comfort. Truly, a fairy had waved her wand, and George Healy wondered when the midnight hour would strike.

The Faulkners did not regret their kindness; for them Healy's enthusiasm renewed ancient things and familiar places. Their journey turned into an adventure.

In Rome they stopped long enough to steep themselves in its magnificence while Healy made sketches in the Colosseum and at the Arch of Titus. He made copies of a few Raphaels that appealed to him. The backgrounds in primitive paintings fascinated him.

But for the young artist, it was essential that he earn something. And so at Turin, Healy parted with his friendly hosts, they to return to England and he to go to the frontier, where he stopped before returning to Paris. Before parting with the Faulkners, Healy accepted their cordial invitation to visit them in London.

In Boston, Mrs. Healy's reaction to her son's success was

twofold. With him, she rejoiced that he had made important English friends and might soon be visiting them in London. Most of the important American painters owed much of their fame to England—Copley, Stuart, Peale, Allston, Morse, Sully. In her letters to her son she detailed the doings of the family and their delight over all his news. "We hope you will have many commissions in England, but not so many that you cannot return to us by next summer," she wrote.

But the winter of 1835–36, so momentous for her son in Paris, brought Mrs. Healy great physical distress. However, she continued her cheering letters. For his sister Agnes' birthday in January, 1836, Healy sent one of his Italian sketches. His next letter brought news that Mr. James John Cox, of Philadelphia, in Paris with his family, had ordered a painting of a family group —his sister, Mrs. Sitgreave, himself, and his son, with his two daughters, Julia and Florence, seated at the piano.

This ambitious attempt stirred the artist and delighted his family. But in the midst of this happy labor, Healy received the crushing news of his mother's death. The slim little woman had not long survived her seafaring husband, who, from her fourteenth year to this her thirty-sixth year, had filled her heart. Healy was crushed. She, the tower of strength to which they all had clung, gone before he could bring her the fruit of this new success.

Only Dubourjal, the faithful, understood all the young man went through and somehow managed to make him realize that his advance in life, his promises of the future, must have meant even more to her than the sadness of his absence. When the young American heaped abuse upon himself for having put his career ahead of everything, Dubourjal could point out to him that not only had he done what his mother wanted him to do, but that his success had enabled the family to live in reasonable comfort— a meager consolation to young Healy in the face of the devastating sorrow of death.

"And now," Healy questioned, "what must I do?"

"Keep on working," was Dubourjal's practical advice.

They argued as they sketched. And then one evening, in the spring of 1836, as he returned to his studio, Healy found a letter from Sir Arthur Faulkner inviting him to come to London as his guest and to paint both his own and Lady Faulkner's portraits.

Chapter VI

GROSVENOR SQUARE

THE lumbering diligence to Calais seemed luxurious to young Healy compared to the one that had brought him from Le Havre to Paris two years before. He looked quite elegant in his tight-fitting redingote, long clinging breeches, high collar, and dark cravat. The expressive mouth with its little mustache, the deep blue eyes, and a youthful air of expectancy made his fellow travelers instinctively eager for conversation. As usual, George responded sociably, yet soon fell into a brown study, questioning himself. Should he not go back to Boston instead of accepting this tempting invitation to London?

Peering through the dusty coach windows, Healy scanned the country's serene aspect under a warming sun and his spirits rose. The anticipation of a London season set his nerves atingle. At Calais he walked up the gangway with a jaunty step, glad to set foot on the boat that would soon bring him to the English side of the Channel.

The landing at Dover in the midst of a dense fog did not dampen his ardor, but in the scramble of debarkation Healy failed to get a porter and found himself standing alone with his unwieldy bags; he could see nothing, hear nothing, did not know which way to turn. The stories he had read and disbelieved about English fogs rose in his mind as a passer-by bumped into him. Laughing at his own confusion, young Healy found his voice to ask, "How do I get to London?"

"I say!" answered a friendly, very English voice. "You've just missed the coach!" But the good-natured Englishman took him by the arm, adding, as he pointed to a faint light that seemed far away, "Come over to the inn; it's just across the street."

Bewildered but grateful for this aid and for the light and warmth he found at the inn, Healy watched the group of travelers from whose damp clothes a mist rose with strange, shadowy effects. "What a picture," thought the artist. It reminded him of some black and white sketches by a young Frenchman, Honoré Daumier, whose caricatures and lively drawings were attracting the attention of Paris critics. This was no time to get out his sketchbook—he had to get on to London. The American looked around the room, and seeing a jovial, bald-headed, red-faced, typical John Bull walking from group to group, surmised that he was the innkeeper. To him Healy promptly put his request for some means of transportation to London.

"Impossible now, sir." The answer sounded very final, but young Healy's insistence finally goaded the landlord to gather several other London-bound guests and to suggest that together they hire a hackney coach.

They had barely finished their early dinner when the coach, drawn by its four horses, clattered noisily to the door. The travelers climbed into the coach, the driver cracked his whip, and off they went.

Had he been able to pierce the mist, Healy would have enjoyed every mile of the Dover road, of which he had heard and read so much, but even his keen eyes failed to penetrate the yellowish, cottony sheet that enveloped the whole landscape. The coach passed Canterbury without his knowing it; at dawn in Chatham, while the horses were changed, Healy swallowed a hot, tasteless breakfast. The coach finally reached London. Each passenger was deposited at his given address. At Grosvenor Square, the fog lifted. A friendly house stood revealed; an immaculate footman answered the bell pull; another took Healy's bags. His host's hearty greeting brushed away the fog, the cold, the fatigue.

George was happy to feel Sir Arthur Faulkner's warm handclasp. He looked with sincere admiration at the erect, slender figure of this man of fifty-seven who spoke and moved with the vivacity of youth and the dignity of a vigorous middle age.

Knighted in 1815 for his services to his king and country, Sir Arthur Brooke Faulkner was an alert physician, progressive, curious, ever ready to experiment boldly, which he did with amazing success. He had won fame at Malta when the plague, brought from Alexandria by infected ships, invaded the sunny, cheerful island. King George III appointed him physician to the Duke of Sussex, a constant sufferer from gout. Whether at Cheltenham, a fashionable summer resort, or at Grosvenor Square, the Faulkners' home presented English life at its best. Formality reigned supreme, with constant respect for court etiquette.

The inexperienced, unworldly American found it a harrowing experience as he stood in the guest room of this stately Jacobean house, a valet unpacking his bags, another bringing hot water for shaving and bath, their voices discreet, their steps subdued. Healy felt as if he were in a cathedral, ignorant of the rites and moving under amused eyes. When at last the servants silently closed the door, leaving the young American to his own devices, Healy heaved a sigh of relief.

Stepping before a painting by Sir Joshua Reynolds, Healy examined the rosewood writing desk that stood beneath it. On the desk were a quill and drying sand, some pencils and papers, and a drawing tablet. In these satisfying surroundings Healy relaxed, suddenly conscious of fatigue, and stretched out for a short nap, from which he rose quite refreshed and in high spirits.

Luncheon with Sir Arthur and his wife—a plentiful meal that made the traveler realize he was starved—renewed for them all the happy mood of their Italian journey. Lady Faulkner promised to begin her sittings in the morning. "I have chosen a well-lighted room in which to do your painting," she remarked, and noticing Healy's smile, continued, "You'll find plenty of sunshine in London in May. Such fog as we had yesterday is exceptional at this season."

In a letter to his sister Agnes, Healy pictured his arrival at Dover, the Faulkners' warm reception, and their order for portraits. He also asked his sister to write full details about everyone and everything at home. He understood that his friend, Francis Alexander, was painting her portrait. Would he send him a sketch of it? In her last letter Agnes had repeated her plea that her brother make no change in his plans. With his financial help they could manage at home, and she wanted Healy's English visit to be a real success.

The next morning Lady Faulkner sat for her portrait. As the young painter worked, he shyly asked this gracious new friend to help him avoid blunders in a country he knew but vaguely through American history and prejudices. "I know nothing of titles, rank, and position over here, and I would hate to disgrace you. But, truly, I understand very little about the Georges in England."

Lady Faulkner briefly sketched the various relationships. She also mentioned the young girl, Victoria, and her old uncle, King William IV, who seemed determined to live until she attained her majority so that her mother, whom he detested, could not become queen regent. Young Healy listened to all of this as if it were some spicy story, entirely out of his ken, while trying to remember connections and names.

But of her husband's patient and patron, the Duke of Sussex, another of Victoria's uncles, Lady Faulkner spoke affectionately. Later, when Healy saw the big, towering Duke and his diminutive wife, Lady Inverness, in the intimacy of their home, he marveled at the simplicity of their life and of their romantic love.

When Sir Arthur came in, he told his wife it was time for their guest to see something of London, and after studying the painting, he complimented Healy with, "You've caught the characteristic tilting of the head. Very good!"

As the two men walked out, Sir Arthur reminded his wife that he would take Healy to lunch at his club.

As they passed Buckingham Palace, the changing of the guard offered a colorful display. The doctor pointed out homes of noted Britishers and little narrow streets with famous names.

That evening the Faulkners entertained informally. By the clothes laid out for him, Healy realized that, however informal, entertaining in England required full evening dress. Save for his usual trouble in remembering names, the artist steered an easy course through the outspoken and rude personal remarks that startled him, particularly as applied to the royal family. However, no one was shocked. Next morning, during the sitting, Healy expressed surprise at some of the things he had overheard, particularly about the Duke of Cumberland. "I know," answered Lady Faulkner, "he's either hated or adored."

Several days later, as young Healy and his host walked along the street, they met Aaron Vail, who had been in charge of the American legation in London until a successor could arrive. Sir Arthur remarked, "This is most fortunate. Here is Mr. Vail, just the man you ought to know." As the three men walked on together, Vail told his companions of the appointment of Andrew Stevenson, of Virginia, lately Speaker of the House of Representatives, as the new United States Minister to England. "He is due to arrive in June." It was thus that Healy first heard of the man who was to play an important part in his future.

Chapter VII

ENGLISH ROMANCE

DURING this short and intensely worldly London season, George Healy fell under the spell of English life at its brightest; he became quickly attuned to the old-world atmosphere and found people more hospitable than he dared hope.

New patrons, owners of mansions that held the portraits of generations, demanded of his talent that he continue the tradition; he painted portraits, thrusting aside his ambitious dream of more inventive pictures; his work grew absorbing, his life too full and exciting for regrets. He took for granted the privileges accorded him, naïvely attributing them to English liking of their transatlantic cousins. He modeled his clothes and manners on those around him, wore without a murmur the high, choking collar and cravat that used to elicit his commiseration. With a new social ease he moved and spoke as swiftly as ever, and his wit remained spontaneous, his accent American.

A letter from Agnes startled him; she wanted to become a nun! What a life for his sprightly, charming sister! His answer was a vehement protest, but sometime later another letter reassured him on the subject—though not in a very satisfactory manner. "The Grey Nuns of Quebec do not want me," she wrote sadly; "they claim I am not strong enough for the hard life and I feel desolate...." Not strong enough... poor little Agnes! George worried. "Too much responsibility on her shoulders," he murmured. Well, he would have to go back. So George decided to work harder than ever.

41

The Faulkners brought him an interesting and important sitter—the philanthropist Francis Place.

Power showed in every feature of this self-made man, typical of true English democracy. London born, a baker's son brought up in a poor neighborhood, Place had acquired an education while working as a tailor's apprentice. It meant dogged perseverance and the burning of midnight oil—or more probably candles—but he accomplished it; breeches may have been his trade; books remained his avocation. From books he moved to action, organizing the breeches makers' strike when he was twenty-two, and two years later, in 1794, at the time Thomas Hardy was arrested for labor activities, young Place obtained the latter's post as secretary of the London Corresponding Society. He always strove for reform without violence; yet in the strong lines of his face, in the brilliant eyes there still shone, even at sixty-five, a fearless determination to fight if necessary.

His conversation with the Faulkners, who often joined them during those sittings, showed George what influence this "tailor" had with noted statesmen. Many plans for reform had been discussed, his sitter claimed, while he measured breeches for leading members of Parliament.

Long ago, back of his tailor shop, Francis Place had installed a library, and there around 1812 James Mill brought his six-year-old boy, Stuart, who looked wide-eyed at his father's friends. Joseph Hume, Burdett, Brougham, and others came, eager to push through a Reform Bill, which finally was passed in 1832, after twenty years' effort. In that modest sanctum James Mill wrote many an article for the *Encyclopædia Britannica,* and Hume collected data for his tremendous political activities. Place recalled the time Burdett had been imprisoned in the Tower for subversive writings; Faulkner interrupted:

"Burdett's no longer a fire-eater; it's too bad! But then," added the Doctor, "as sure as a lobster turns red in boiling, a Whig goes Tory when long in power!"

"Don't let him hear you say that!" laughed Place. "I'm afraid it's true, though. He's giving up politics to live in his garden...."

"Yes, he wants to be more with his family, especially his daughter," said Faulkner.

"Lady Augusta worships her father," went on Place.

Years later Healy met that immensely wealthy philanthropic lady, of whom King Edward VII said, "After my mother she is the most remarkable woman in the kingdom!" Lady Burdett-Coutts proved that her father's teachings had not fallen on barren ground.

In the midst of all this talk the American painter inwardly thanked his early Boston sitter, David Henshaw, who had familiarized him with certain aspects of British politics. When Francis Place quoted some of Bentham's most noted theories, "The end of all government must be utility, the good of the governed," or, "the greatest happiness of the greatest number," Healy promptly claimed, "That's American!"—a remark that brought a quick smile to the sitter and for the artist a chance to capture his expression. The Faulkners were delighted. This portrait, shown to many friends, brought compliments and urgent advice to young Healy to enroll as student at the Royal Academy.

The Faulkners, as the London season drew to a close, planned a journey, while George debated whether to return to Paris or go home to Boston. The last weeks were filled with constant entertainment.

One evening at a party, the young American heard a hearty laugh and loud Eh! Eh!'s that warmed his heart, for his own noisy laughter often embarrassed him; at first he could not see the owner of that laugh, hemmed in by a bevy of chatting women, but Faulkner took his arm, saying as they went forward:

"Come, I want to present you to the Prime Minister, Lord Melbourne."

Extremely good-looking, affable, and charming, Lord Melbourne immediately captivated the artist. His appearance fitted the aura of romance that surrounded his life. His brilliant youth as William Lamb had been more social than imposing, and the many scandals associated with his vivid eccentric wife, Lady Caroline, one of Lord Byron's adorers, might have wrecked Lamb's political career had she not died—insane, it was rumored—before he was entrusted with the reins of government.

Lord Melbourne's picturesque language startled the American, not used to talk sprinkled with so many damns. Noting his amazement, Dr. Faulkner quoted Lord Ossington when he asked Melbourne for information about the Poor Law: "Go see my brother," the Minister had said. "I've seen him," Ossington replied, "but he damned me and damned the bill and damned the paupers!" "Well, damn it!" burst out Melbourne. "What more could he do?"

An outraged husband, George Chappell Norton, was then suing Melbourne, but because of insufficient proof the case was dismissed and a new scandal averted.

At the Royal Academy the American discovered a spirit more akin to his own. Leslie, the artist, never forgetful of his American origin, received him charmingly and presented him to Sir David Wilke. When George asked to meet Mr. Turner, whose work seemed to him most inspiring, Leslie warned him: the artist was peculiar; he did not like foreigners; nevertheless, Healy's sincere enthusiasm apparently pleased the older man, who showed him his latest paintings of the French coast and of Venice. This, the young man thought, was worth many a lesson in any atelier.

Joseph Mallord William Turner, then sixty-one, had no friends. Small, unattractive, born poor, the son of a barber, he had not risen from his surroundings with the bold courage of a Francis Place. His talent for drawing was encouraged from the start by Mr. Turner *père,* the boy's first works being exhibited on the walls of the Maiden Lane barbershop. No doubt some of the patrons bought sketches, but none took this very seriously. Some magazines ordered illustrations, and young Turner finally enrolled as a student at the Royal Academy. There his genius was recognized, but it took the general public much longer to accept his brilliant color and the feverish movement of his land- and seascapes.

Devoted to his son, the father came to live with him when Turner bought a house on Queen Anne Street where he could paint in peace. The old man seemed to be his only companion, and when Mr. Turner died the artist retired entirely into his shell; he admitted no one but the housekeeper to his cheerless home, became more eccentric than ever, and cultivated frugality to the point of miserliness.

At the Academy, Turner's influence among the younger generation of artists produced a new school of landscape painters. He grew famous and in his will carried on the distrust he always seemed to feel toward strangers, leaving his big fortune to "poor artists born in England, of English parents and legitimate birth." He always treated George Healy cordially, and the American never failed to visit him each time he returned to England, though the house on Queen Anne Street remained grimly closed, and once when Healy went there, having failed to find the artist at the Academy, he had the door practically shut in his face.

Turner, he heard, would disappear for months, leaving his housekeeper and his solicitor in a fever of anxiety. The painter would reappear without explanation and with a wealth of new pictures. His mind clouded; at the end he hid in a Chelsea boardinghouse, seeing only the children of the neighborhood who knew him as "Admiral Booth." The day after his housekeeper finally discovered his hide-out, Turner died.

In 1836 George, with two other artists, started on a tramping tour through Switzerland and France. It was an invigorating leap from that English social whirl to fields and mountains and the simple life. They walked, talked, painted, slept in barns or under the stars, ate anywhere, anything, and, steeped in the joy of nature, the trio of artists achieved sketches filled with vigorous realism.

Once, as they were painting, an oldish individual stopped to look at their work; he spoke of art with delight and unexpected knowledge. The young men, curious, entered into an animated discussion, and as time passed, the man invited them to dinner at his place. They picked up their paintboxes and accompanied him, startled beyond words when their host led them to a superb old château. His rough country garb had not prepared them for such good luck, and the meal, with choice food and wines of old vintage, further loosened their busy tongues. As they parted, they all declared this was the most perfect evening of their trip.

During that summer of 1836, while Healy tramped the French countryside, London seethed with gossip. Letters from friends brought the artist echoes of the great uproar at Windsor Castle— a terrific scene between the King and his sister-in-law, the Duchess of Kent, at the banquet given in honor of William IV's birthday. In the presence of all his guests, the King had given Victoria's mother a cruel tongue-lashing, accusing her of insolence, defiance, and unbecoming conduct toward the Crown, of listening to foreign advisers (a dig against her brother, King Leopold of Belgium); and poor little Victoria, turning red, then white as a sheet, forced back her tears while her infuriated mother haughtily ordered her carriage. An absolute break seemed inevitable after years of more or less controlled hostilities. The King wanted Victoria near him; he alone, he felt, could prepare her for the role of English queen; the girl would not be of age until May of next year, and the mere thought that the Duchess of Kent might become regent gave him fits of fury and made him hold on tenaciously to a tenuous thread of life. Queen Adelaide, good soul, once more patched up the quarrel, and Victoria's mother remained. The marriage of Lady Augusta on August 26 revived all the old Jordan scandal. It was an outrage, said the simple folk, that His Majesty should endow all these children with large fortunes and high-sounding titles—think of calling them Fitzclarence! And had not the old skinflint let the woman who gave him those children and supported him for years die in abject poverty? It was high time His Majesty rejoined his ancestors and left the throne to a simple, pure, honest girl.

Healy imagined the lovely English voices airing these views and recounting spicy episodes, but he kept his answers guarded. He had found out that the British who vituperated with such amazing frankness against their government and the royal family never tolerated criticism from an outsider; besides, American jokes about "high-ups" struck no responsive chord in England; Yankee wit differed radically from dry English humor and took time to penetrate.

But the young artist wanted to return to England; the Royal Academy's stamp of approval seemed to him indispensable for his success at home, and he hoped that some of the portraits vaguely spoken of during his stay with the Faulkners would materialize. In the absence of his good friends he dared not risk a move to London without some tangible assurance of work. Joseph Hume, he heard, had liked his portrait of Francis Place very much. After much hesitancy he wrote to Mr. Place telling him what it would mean to him to have another year in England, and asking if Mr. Hume could be induced to order his portrait at once.

In a little town on the Loire, the Englishman's reply reached George Healy. Place had sent a note to the Radical Member, who, busy as he was with new elections coming up, promised to have his portrait done by Mr. Healy if the latter could arrange to be in London between the twenty-first and thirty-first of January next....

Back in Paris, the American hurried the work in hand, and, helped by Dubourjal, made ready for his second English experience.

Promptly on January 22, 1837, he arrived in London and immediately paid his respects to the philanthropist.

"My boy," exclaimed Francis Place, "this is fine! Mr. Hume

will appreciate your diligence. I know you must, you shall succeed!"

The choice of a suitable painting room was George's first step. He remembered a charming spot to which Dr. Faulkner had called his attention during one of their morning rides—a regular Mecca for artists, Fitzroy Square. Now bleak with the grayness of a cold January day, it had then been gay with green trees and masses of colorful flowers, but its present bareness brought out even better the harmonious lines of those Adam houses that bordered the square on three sides. George looked in vain for "to let" signs and was turning away disconsolate when, at 28 Grafton Street, almost on the corner, he noticed the wished-for card in the window. He ran up the steps, and a pleasant-faced woman who answered the bell told him as he made his request:

"You're lucky. I have a good room, vacant only since yesterday!"

The room was well lighted and contained enough necessary furniture so that with his easel, his sketches tacked on the wall, and his few belongings it would be ready to receive Mr. Hume the next day. Arrangements completed with his kind landlady, the artist walked away happy, to call upon his sitter-to-be.

As he passed Charlotte Street, he noticed signs of life in the John Constable house and wondered if the ailing artist had returned from Hempstead, where he spent most of his time since the death of a much-loved wife. George admired Constable and Turner above all other English landscape artists; he felt tempted to stop and ask if Mr. Constable would receive him, then decided to wait until someone could present him. That time never came, as two months later Constable died.

On his way back to the city, Healy stopped a moment at the old Whitefield Chapel and saw the tomb of Toplady, the author of "Rock of Ages"; it reminded him of past excursions through London with Sir Arthur and again he felt the chill disappointment of the Faulkners' absence. Well, he consoled himself, when they return they'll find me pretty securely established, and they'll like that!

Joseph Hume approved the young artist's exactitude.

"This was the only time I could give you, Mr. Healy," he said. "Election year, I must be back and forth constantly...."

The vivid Scotsman might not be easy to paint, thought Healy as he studied his features; he was never still! His pungent words would light up the whole face—a difficult characteristic to render on canvas, but the challenge put the painter on his mettle.

They arranged to have the first sitting on the morrow, and early in the morning George was at his easel, preparing the canvas, testing the light as he moved his model's chair in various positions.

Joseph Hume then stood at the peak of his parliamentary career. Known as a Radical, he had begun by voting Tory, but the needed reforms stirred his human sympathies as well as his common sense, and he soon found himself among the fighting Whigs, counted now as one of their important leaders.

Like Faulkner, Hume had studied at the Edinburgh College of Surgeons and been attached to the colonial army in 1797; he was then twenty. His extraordinary gift for languages got him the post of Persian Interpreter to the Army, which soon included an incredible number of Indian dialects. He remained in India in that capacity from 1802 until 1807 and his canny Scotch financial acumen enabled him to build up a large fortune for himself while he also improved the resources of his branch in the service.

Back in England in 1808, Hume gave up military life for politics. He took up his new duties with great zest when Weymouth returned him to Parliament. After his marriage to wealthy Maria Burnley in 1818, he was returned to Parliament by the Aberdeen burghs, where Maria's father, a high East India Company official, wielded great power; in 1830 it was the County of Middlesex that sent him as its representative. Now Kilkenny called him,

and he was due in Ireland shortly. In Parliament as in India, his
sense of finance brought him to the fore; he delighted the Opposition by challenging every expenditure of the Government.

"You'd better be careful when you speak of money before Mr.
Hume," Francis Place had warned the artist. "The waste of a
penny is to him a heinous crime."

George promised to avoid the thorny subject and asked what
other *faux pas* he must eschew.

"Don't speak of the Duke of Cumberland as a criminal plotter,"
added his mentor. "Mr. Hume is counted as one of his partisans."

"Oh!" The American appeared truly shocked. "But the Duke
is a terrible person!"

"Not to his friends," countered Place. "Mr. Hume would
probably show you a very different Cumberland from the one
we imagine."

But in that first sitting, to Healy's amazement, Joseph Hume
began by flaying the Royal Academy. The artist bristled. That
distinguished institution, associated in his mind with Benjamin
West, aroused in him a sort of national pride.

"It's costing the Government a lot of money," Hume grumbled.
"If taxes pay for it, the people should get the benefit."

"But they do!" exclaimed Healy. "And I was told that the
Academy received a special grant—"

With an impatient gesture of the hand Hume explained that
he wanted the summer exhibit open free to the public at least
once a week; the president, Sir Martin Archer Shee, claimed
this would reduce receipts and cut down student classes. "I've
taken the debate to Parliament," concluded the testy politician.

George changed the subject. It would never do to paint an
irritated gentleman! Speaking of the grand doings at Saint
James's Palace in honor of Victoria's coming of age and disre-
garding Place's cautious advice, he brought up the name of the
Duke of Cumberland. Hume's face lighted.

"A fine man, a strong man!" he exclaimed. "No indecision

about him; our government would function differently under his rule...."

Then suddenly he closed his lips in a tight line; it was unwise to flaunt his views at this time, but Healy pursued with a pertinent question:

"Could the Duke prevent strikes and labor disputes?"

"Mr. Healy, the people always profit under intelligent rule. The first Hanoverian allowed intelligence to control his policy, and even my native Jacobite burgh of Montrose followed the Georges, though the old Pretender had sailed from our Scottish port."

This awakened a new curiosity in the American, who, carefully skipping any allusion to the Orange plot, in which some said Hume was concerned, asked how he, a Scot, could represent an English county.

"A burgh, county, or city," explained Hume, "elects its member among those who have its interest at heart."

"Yes, but in my country a representative stands for his own state."

"Great Britain is not a conglomeration of states," replied the politician. "This year I shall represent Kilkenny."

"Ireland!" The artist showed his amazement, then with a smile added, "Kilkenny is not far from my father's home," and seeing the gleam of interest in Hume's eyes, young Healy gave a sketchy account of the Healys from Dublin.

"Well, you must have a lot of cousins among my constituents," remarked Hume, but Healy explained that the three Healy boys— his father and two brothers—had left Dublin in 1798 and never returned to their native land.

On subsequent sittings, as the artist watched for revealing traits while his model spoke, he became more impressed with the warm, human side of this apparently dour Scot; Hume's keen financial genius had not dulled his generosity or his rich fund of humor; in tiny lines around the eyes and a slight quirk of the mouth Healy tried to suggest this quality. Francis Place noticed it immediately when he came in one day.

"My boy," he told him, "you certainly go deeper than the skin! I congratulate you and I think we are both fortunate, Hume and I, in our portraits."

Joseph Hume declared himself so well satisfied that he promised to have his wife's portrait painted later.

It was always "later," George thought sadly when spring came and he found himself without a cent. The money he faithfully forwarded to Boston, besides his rent and living expenses, ate up all he earned. What should he do? George again turned to Francis Place, and the philanthropist quickly proved how he had acquired his reputation. Scarcely had the young man presented his predicament when Place stopped him:

"Don't worry, my boy, don't worry. You are doing very well and success will come, but it takes time," and as George seemed ready to interrupt, "Yes, I understand; you haven't a farthing. Well, here's twenty pounds. And count me as your banker for two hundred more if you need it, but keep on as you are doing now; it may take two or three years before people recognize your talent—but they will, they will...."

Somewhat embarrassed by young Healy's deep gratitude, the older man took him out to dinner, talking the while of possible sitters.

This marked the turning point of Healy's fortunes. Whether through Place's good offices or Hume's flattering remarks, George received an order for a small full-length portrait of the Master of Grant. This was bound to draw attention to his work.

Sir Lewis Grant, tall, extremely handsome, and much younger-looking than his seventy-one years, was a figure of romance. He had become chief of the clan in 1811; the virtues of a Scottish master won for him the loyalty and devotion of every branch of his clan, and women considered him irresistible, even at this advanced stage of his career.

The picturesque costume with stripes of green and red, its solid red panel and central block of dark green traversed by black and green lines, gave the artist full scope, and the rich colors brought out startlingly his model's fair hair over tanned features; the blue eyes still held their fire. Healy made a replica of the small picture to hang in his studio. A few months later the Master of Grant suddenly died. Almost immediately the artist received an emissary from two ladies of very high rank who ordered a copy of the portrait, exacting a pledge of secrecy; the painting was to be sent under lock and key. Healy wondered what thrilling romance of the past hid under this curious request —whether these great ladies cherished merely tender memories of the gay Scot or if some deeper drama of illicit love underlay the secrecy; he never revealed the ladies' names—or solved the mystery.

Miss Flora McLeod of McLeod, Lady Faulkner's sister, who had come to London for the season, also ordered her portrait. George seemed to move among the Scots, and he grew very fond of them. From all she had heard about the American, Miss McLeod felt favorably inclined toward him, and in a short time they became good friends; but though he squired her occasionally, George Healy at this time fought shy of society, which absorbed too much time and caused inevitable expense.

At about this time, the celebrated singer, John A. Braham, whose daughter married Lord Waldegrave, had his portrait painted by G. P. A. Healy; this was the first portrait the singer had ever ordered—a strange circumstance for one so much in the public eye. He declared it "a successful likeness," and his praise brought other sitters from the stage world.

George wrote in elated mood to his friend Dubourjal, suggesting that he join him quickly in London—there was plenty of work for both of them.

"I miss you greatly," he wrote, "and I know you will like the nice friends who have helped me through some very difficult days. Now there is sunshine ahead, and I want you to share it with me."

Dubourjal came. His painting room was on the same floor as George's, and the two men worked, talked, read, went out together in happy comradeship. George had not exaggerated; with the vogue for miniatures at its height Dubourjal's delicate work soon was in great demand.

Before winter set in, a momentous change occurred in George's life—he fell in love. He and Dubourjal had become socially popular; the Frenchman's ready laughter, his pleasant round face with its refined features and liquid brown eyes so expressive and affectionate, assured him a welcome everywhere. As for George, many already called him the "Lawrence of America." The adjoining studios filled after working hours with friends who dropped in for a cup of tea and a look at the new paintings and to discuss books, the theatre, etc.

Among the Americans introduced by Mr. Stevenson came a Mr. James Hanley, an inventor, whose English wife seemed particularly happy to find herself back in her native city. One afternoon Edme Dubourjal, usually so quiet, rushed into George's room talking rapidly and excitedly:

"*George! Mon ami,* listen! You remember Mrs. Hanley? I've just been with her and her sister. She's lovely, *exquise!*"

George raised his eyebrows. "Mrs. Hanley?" he asked, with a clear recollection of a woman in her late thirties but far from fascinating.

"*Non, non!*" exclaimed Dubourjal. "The little one—her sister. Her name is Louisa Phipps, and she's promised to sit for me!"

"Humm ... she seems to have made quite an impression."

"Wait till you see her!" Dubourjal added, "I've asked them both to come to your studio...."

A few days later George was running down the stairs, in a hurry as usual. He had just locked his studio door. Two ladies were walking up. Taking off his hat, the artist effaced himself to let the ladies pass, but the older one stopped, saying in a disappointed voice:

"Oh! Mr. Healy, are you leaving?"

George looked startled, then fortunately recognized her.

"Mrs. Hanley! I am so sorry...I have an appointment."

His eyes wandered toward her companion.

"My sister, Miss Phipps, Mr. Healy; Monsieur Dubourjal had promised us a visit to your studio."

The artist immediately proffered the key, which was still in his hand.

"I wish I could return with you but I am late....Dubourjal will show you the pictures, but," and he looked at the young girl as he spoke, "please come back soon when I may have the pleasure of receiving you...."

Bowing, George Healy proceeded on his way while Mrs. Hanley and her sister continued upstairs. From the lower step, he watched them turn on the landing to his friend's door, and as he looked, Louisa Phipps leaned over the banister. His eyes met hers; their blueness sparkled at him from under her demure poke bonnet, then she lowered her eyelids and rejoined her sister —but the mischief was done.

Alas for poor Dubourjal! He lingered over the little water-color portrait; he painted with tender hands the girlish oval of her face framed by light brown ringlets and the parted hair topped by the fashionable high comb. In the wide-spaced blue eyes lurked a disturbing mixture of innocence and amused archness; the small mouth and chin could assert themselves in suddenly stubborn or severe lines; her slender neck and white sloping shoulders emerged from a low-cut dress with puff sleeves. To the sitter, Dubourjal's face became an open book; she liked its telltale admiration, which, however, left her untouched, whereas the quick steps of his friend, that American artist with his foreign look and his mustache, made her heart turn somersaults.

The Frenchman, torn between a very deep friendship and this

sudden unexpected feeling of love, suffered. It was he nevertheless who suggested that they adjourn to George's studio for tea;
it soon became a daily practice. Forgetting how he had teased
Dubourjal, Healy promptly fell under the same spell. Since that
glimpse on the stairway Louisa had darted frequent glances in
his direction; unconsciously drawn together, the two young
people let Mrs. Hanley and Dubourjal entertain each other.

"Do you sing?" Dubourjal asked her one day.

She admitted that she did, and Dubourjal begged her to sing
for them; but they had no spinet. Mrs. Hanley invited both men
to her parents' home, and there they found Mrs. Phipps, a capable,
rather dry, sharply busy woman, who watched with eagle eye
every step her invalid husband took. He was tall, gaunt, wasted
by illness, but in him George discovered the gay spirit that so
attracted him in his daughter.

In a clear, sweet, true voice Louisa sang for her visitors the
songs then in vogue; after her first shyness, warming up at their
evident delight, she took up Irish ditties; they thought her
brogue irresistible; then she sang in excellent Scottish such as
her mother had taught her "Auld Robin Gray" and "A Highland
Lad," and prettily asked them to join in the favorite "Auld Lang
Syne."

They were lustily singing the last notes when a visitor arrived
—a tall, blond Englishman, punctiliously dressed, a friend of her
brothers, whom Louisa greeted with seeming gladness. It set
George's teeth on edge; signaling to his astonished comrade, the
American seized his hat and made his adieus. He did not like
the dancing gleam in Louisa's eyes as she bade him good-by
with an amused, "Oh, so soon? Must you go?" The scowl did not
leave his face as they walked silently home. Dubourjal sighed;
George would not take love lightly....

Chapter VIII

AUDUBON IN LONDON, 1837

LATE in 1837, George Healy was called one day to the house of the Countess of Essex, a most charming old lady, an invalid who requested the artist to paint her portrait in her home. It was not an easy task, but he managed to imbue the likeness with her feminine appeal by softening the lines of age and illness.

After the death of her first husband, Edward Stephenson, she had married George, Fifth Earl of Essex, known as Lord Coningsby when he inherited his grandmother's title and estate. He was now approaching his eightieth birthday—a lively old gentleman. Age had not deprived the Countess of her many friends, and it was Healy's good fortune that she took a fancy to him. On New Year's Day, 1838, he was surprised to find at the door of 28 Grafton Street Her Ladyship's carriage and to receive from the plush-breeched flunky a note asking him to take the little portrait and a letter from her to the Duke of Sutherland. So it happened that 1838, which proved such an eventful year for him, opened with a call at Stafford House.

His Grace's patronage meant almost as much to an artist as that of the Queen herself; it was well known that the Duchess of Sutherland, Lady Georgiana Howard, was Victoria's closest friend. On arriving, the young American discovered that the Duke's private secretary was a man whose acquaintance he had made in Paris the year before; they were very congenial, and his presence lent a certain informality to this first visit. The Duke complimented Healy on the portrait, which he found excellent, and recommended him for membership in the Royal Academy the goal of so many Americans.

The study of a head he submitted to the Academy faculty admitted him at once; it was judged "painted with a firm free pencil, good tone and color." When would he be able to add the desired R.A. to his signature?

Before his admission to the Royal Academy his amiable model, the Countess of Essex, died. In her will she left her last portrait to the Duke of Sutherland.

Meantime, George was conducting his courtship with all the impetuosity of youth as he urged Louisa to embark fearlessly on matrimonial seas, unknown and adventurous. She was afraid. Her practical mother inclined toward the English suitor whose safe and calm life appealed to her more than that of an unpredictable American artist. Her eldest daughter's marriage to an inventor overseas, though happy enough, was not particularly brilliant.

That winter was filled with excitement; travelers came from every part of the world. Apartments rented at exorbitant prices for the coronation period. Mr. Andrew Stevenson, the United States Minister, informed George that Thomas Sully was coming and had been commissioned by the Saint George Society to paint the Queen's portrait. Her Majesty had graciously consented to pose, but not until the spring....

Stevenson's father, the well-known rector of St. Mark's Parish in Culpeper County, Virginia, James Little Page Stevenson, now minister of St. George's Church in Fredericksburg, also came on a visit, and George painted his portrait. This and several others, including those of Hume, Miss McLeod, the Countess of Essex, Audubon, and the children of Tyrone Power, were shown at the 1838 exhibit of the Royal Academy.

On a day in November, 1837, Healy burst into Dubourjal's studio with the excited announcement:

"Audubon is here! I've just seen him!"

"Audubon?" questioned his friend, pronouncing the name correctly. "A Frenchman?"

"No. Don't you know? The great American bird artist."

"Oh! the one whose book is appearing now? Yes, it's beautiful work.... And you say that with that name he is an American?"

"French born, I believe," answered Healy, vaguely, pursuing his own thoughts. "I'm going to call on him and ask him to let me make his portrait."

For a shy man, thought the miniaturist, his American friend had a good deal of nerve, but when he turned to tell him so, Healy had already disappeared into his own painting room, changing his high collar and cravat. In a short time Healy presented himself at No. 4 Wimpole Street, the address Mr. Stevenson had given him, a house chosen by Audubon in a pleasant street a few doors away from the Barretts' home.

The older artist looked somewhat startled on seeing again the young man he had met only a few hours earlier, but with his unfailing courtesy he ushered Healy into his library, where the bird plates lay spread on a large table. They were truly beautiful, and the young American expressed his admiration but lost no time in coming to the point. Half boldly, half diffidently he addressed his host:

"Mr. Audubon, sir, please let me paint your portrait!" Voice and eyes pleaded naïvely.

Audubon had sat to other artists and to his sons and had also painted his own portrait more than once; he was totally absorbed at this time in the publication of his 435 bird plates; so with gentle politeness he refused. Healy's crestfallen attitude, however, urged him to add:

"The only time I am free is at night, and that would hardly do, would it, Mr. Healy?"

But the young man jumped at the chance.

"The very thing, my dear sir! I shall paint by gaslight and it will make an original picture!"

Caught, the great man capitulated gracefully.

The face Healy was so eager to paint seemed chiseled in light golden bronze, for the woodsman hunted his birds in all weathers, through the marshes of Florida and Louisiana or through dense western forests; his wild appearance contradicted the aristocratic beauty of features and courtly manner; the high forehead, prominent nose, the thin, sensitive mouth, and willful chin were illumined by deep-set blue eyes, so intense and piercing that the painter immediately compared them to eagle eyes. Long, dark curls touched with gray fell to his shoulders. When, on his first visit to Scotland, Audubon had been advised to conform a little more to fashion and cut his very long curls, he had written his wife a sad letter bordered in black in sign of mourning for his shorn locks, saying it reminded him of the French Revolution, "when the same operation was performed upon all victims of the guillotine...." Audubon chose to pose in his hunting clothes: a loose white shirt open at the neck and crossed by an embroidered leather shoulder strap, a gun under his left arm, the barrel held in his shapely nervous hand, the feel of his gun seeming to awaken that untamed look so characteristic of the man; and Healy imagined him peering through the trees or scanning the horizon, moving quickly and silently, Indian-like, stalking birds, picking out the most beautiful, killing them, and bringing them back triumphantly with their blood-stained plumage, which his deft fingers would reproduce on paper in exquisite detail and beauty of color.

Mrs. Audubon occasionally joined their conversation. As she came in, "Ah! Mr. Healy," exclaimed Audubon with Gallic exuberance, "there is the most wonderful woman in the world. Can you believe it? She left a fine, comfortable Louisiana plantation to follow me—and we have known hard days...."

Lucy Bakewell, devoted English wife, had turned teacher in order to enable her husband to continue his hunting and painting and to finance his journey across the ocean. It shocked Healy as

it had shocked other American men, but the women understood
—indeed many of them envied Mrs. Audubon.

A son came in to watch Healy's progress, and his young wife,
expecting a baby, sometimes brought her sewing by the lamp.

Strange that George Healy should consult so self-absorbed
and impractical a man as Audubon on his own problem, but
somehow he confided to him his love for Louisa and his qualms
because of present responsibilities and still inadequate earnings.
Audubon gave him his enchanting smile.

"An English girl?" he said encouragingly. "Why, man, they
make the best of wives. You ought to marry. . . . Money? Money
is not essential. Don't waste these precious years. No happiness is
greater than a good marriage!"

Mrs. Audubon looked somewhat quizzically at this devoted
husband who left her, years on end, to carry most of the burden
and watch over their two boys while he pursued his own work
wherever it called him. . . . But she shared his views on love and
nodded confirmation when the young artist turned questioningly
to her.

George promptly repeated their advice to Louisa; however,
Audubon's Latin enthusiasm only intensified her fears. He
sounded like a very impractical man, and Louisa had been
brought up among the genteel poor, for the Phippses' independent spirit kept them away from aristocratic relatives who
might have helped them. Louisa wanted security. This impetu-
ous, gay, hard-working American who never kept still, in mind or
body, at times terrified her.

A mystery surrounded Audubon's origin—many believed him
to be the lost little Dauphin. Adopted by Captain Jean Audubon,
he was taken by him from Saint-Domingue to Brittany, then at
eighteen sailed to America. Sometimes, George said, he would
exchange covert glances with his wife or else shut himself in a
dramatic silence. Once he hinted at a vow of secrecy. The legend
has expanded with time. Was he Louis XVII, smuggled from the

Temple Prison in Paris to the colony of Saint-Domingue and brought back later to his native France with the connivance of the French mariner Audubon? Partisans of this view like to point out that his passionate interest in birds sprang from the memory of his only companions in captivity, the caged birds so cruelly put to death by the guard Simon.

But at fifty-three years of age, Audubon considered himself absolutely American. With his strong French accent he would expatiate on the greatness of *his* wonderful America! And George Healy joined him in extolling the glory of his native land. The two artists egged each other on, and the portrait gained in sparkling naturalness. This quality struck Thomas Sully when he saw it.

The moment Healy heard of Sully's arrival, he called upon him at Hatchett's Hotel, where the artist and his daughter Blanche stopped before they found a suitable studio at 40 Great Marlborough. There, in March, 1838, the Queen gave Sully her first sitting, but long before that the Philadelphian made his promised call at Fitzroy Square.

As he entered Healy's studio, his eyes arrested by the new portrait, Sully exclaimed:

"Ah! My old friend Audubon! That's excellent." And as he approached nearer to examine the detail, they spoke of the talented and eccentric woodsman to whom Sully had given lessons years ago. "Did you know, Mr. Healy, that Audubon sat for the figure of Vanderlyn's General Jackson?" asked the artist.

"So Mr. Audubon told me, sir; he said that hunger in those New Orleans days made him thin enough to become the ideal model."

The visitor gazed long and earnestly at Healy's paintings, showing the same interest he had manifested for the boy's efforts in Boston seven years before, and as he was leaving, with great sincerity and his most gracious smile, he said to the young man:

"Mr. Healy, you will never regret having followed my advice in your choice of a career."

To the twenty-four-year-old artist, these words seemed like the consecration of his work. When he repeated Sully's words to Louisa, she was thrilled that an artist chosen to paint the Queen should be so praising of George.

Throughout the winter, preparations for the coronation formed the main topic of conversation. A Queen's legend was shaping, born of the people's desire to see virtue at court. Women had worn the English crown with glory; many hoped there might rise a Victorian era no less potent than the Elizabethan age. Never had a new sovereign been more sincerely acclaimed, and among the young girls who watched adoringly her every move, none was more enthusiastic than Louisa Phipps. It amused the American artist to hear her proudly compare her height— five feet—her age—nineteen—her slender figure, her looks even (though she was really much prettier) with those of Her Majesty.

Accustomed to open criticism of royalty from radical Whigs, George brought to Louisa amusing tales of the Queen's entourage heard from his sitters; there were quips about her rigid adherence to every form of etiquette. But where he expected Louisa's sense of humor to respond, instead of the laugh he loved to hear, he saw her eyes grow icy, her mouth set, and one night she exploded with a furious:

"How dare you speak of Her Majesty so disrespectfully!"

Aghast, George vowed he had meant no offense and suddenly realized how peremptorily the new Victorians viewed their allegiance. To make his peace, he willingly agreed that the young Queen was perfect. . . . Later he would find in Louisa also that "vein of iron" Lady Lyttleton spoke of in regard to Victoria.

Healy's newest patron who was to become a lifelong friend was the eldest son of Lord and Lady Holland, General Charles

Richard Fox. By normal rights he should be the heir to lands
and titles, but his beautiful, gifted mother was still in name Lady
Webster, traveling in Italy, when Lord Holland fell in love with
her. She had not yet been divorced when their son was born in
1796. Lady Webster married Henry Richard Vassall Fox, third
Lord Holland, in London, on July 6, 1797.

Illegitimacy, Boston had taught him, invariably brought shame
and disaster, and George could not adjust himself to the cheerful
way in which English aristocracy regarded its complications.

When he sat for his portrait, Charles Richard Fox, sanguine,
vivid, with his ruddy complexion, his pleasant face, and animated
countenance, was a most attractive man of forty. He was aide-de-
camp and son-in-law to King William IV.

General Fox's great hobby was his remarkable collection of
coins. The painter cared little for coins. What affected him was
the almost fanatical intensity of the collector, which he wanted
to reproduce; that meant drama to a painter. When he caught a
reflection of the soul, painted a strong emotion, or awakened in
features, by line and color, the true character of his model—
then portrait painting became as thrilling as an inventive composition. The concentration he brought to his study of the face
before him and the power he injected in the hand that directed
the brush made him feel like a runner gathering every ounce
of vitality to win the last lap of a race. It left him exhausted.

Noticing the young man's fatigue, Fox rose.

"Let's rest a bit, Mr. Healy," he suggested. "Your friend Edme
Dubourjal will soon be here and dinner must be about ready.
Come, my dear Velasquez!"

General Fox enjoyed dubbing his friends with great names of
the past, and Healy became in turn Murillo, or Rubens, or
Raphael, while in later letters Fox unconsciously revealed his
love of life by signing himself Volpone or some other vigorous,
full-blooded character who had tasted life to the full.

At dinner, Lady Mary presiding, they talked familiarly of art and travels, of Paris where the General and his wife spent part of every year, and in this warm atmosphere the artist found the same comfort and uplift he had known with the Faulkners.

That year George painted a group picture of Tyrone Power's children, and Louisa helped to keep them amused with stories or reading. The painting had been ordered as a surprise from Mrs. Power to celebrate her noted husband's return from an American tour and was exhibited at the Royal Academy in May, 1838. The great Irish actor had just made his first appearance across the ocean. Mrs. Power brought to George's studio the two younger boys Frederick and Harold and three blue-eyed girls gifted with Irish charm. The eldest son, William, was to be knighted and live in Australia; his brother Maurice would become an actor, like his father. Healy thought them a fascinating family. A few years later a shocking tragedy brought gloom to this happy group. On his return from another American visit on the *President,* Tyrone Power and his shipmates were caught in a terrific gale at dawn, March 14, 1841. Neither ship nor passengers were ever heard from again.

Chapter IX

THE CORONATION

Healy's days became a kaleidoscopic succession of portraits, visits, functions of all sorts, late hours, and early rising. Dubourjal could not follow that pace; he contented himself with a few interesting contacts and sufficient work.

Through Sully they came to know the poet Leigh Hunt. Still wearing the Byronesque collar, Italian cape, and wild mop of hair, Hunt exuded an aura of romanticism; he had known, befriended, and encouraged such geniuses as Byron and Shelley and always surrounded himself with young writers or artists who benefited by his judgment.

At Hunt's home in Chelsea, No. 10 Upper Cheyne Row, a few doors from the great Carlyle, Healy and Dubourjal met Elizabeth Barrett of Wimpole Street who wrote fine verse and collaborated with Hunt; she was charming, ethereal looking, a passionate girl with bladelike spirit. There also they saw Robert Browning, whose "Paracelsus" had just appeared. The poet's fluent French (he had been brought up by French tutors) relieved Dubourjal from the necessity of twisting his tongue into English sounds.

Years later, in Florence, Healy saw again these early London acquaintances; Elizabeth Barrett and Robert Browning had then become a very celebrated couple, the axis of an intellectual and artistic English center.

As spring approached, Louisa began to complain of George's "neglect." He was working every hour of light and spent most of his evenings among new friends, with or without Louisa. Her

pique delighted him, and he was not sorry to tease her occasionally—especially after some encounter with the faithful Englishman at her house. Noticing a jealous glint in her eye when he
mentioned Lady Buller, he expatiated on her charm, her fascinating hint of a lisp.... Louisa tried to appear indifferent. George
told her how the day before a total stranger had stopped Lady
Buller in Piccadilly to ask if the new number of Master Hum-
phrey's Clock were out yet! Dubourjal interrupted:

"How could anyone have courage enough to speak unasked to
so dignified an old lady?"

"Old!" exclaimed Louisa. The cat was out of the bag, and
George was forced to make amends for his teasing.

A month before the coronation, the launching of a new steam-
ship, the *British Queen,* was scheduled to coincide with the
Queen's birthday. Everyone made much of it—a new queen, a
new ship, a promise of new times. The ceremony brought out
crowds as May 24 shone bright with what the people already
called "the Queen's weather." At the dockyards of Messrs.
Curling, Young and Company, visitors milled around, while
above the usual British tones one could hear shrill American
voices exclaim, "The greatest ship afloat!" "Longer than a battle-
ship!" "It carries two hundred passengers!" And already many
fought for passage on the first crossing; the fare rose exorbitantly
and was paid, nevertheless by the eager passengers.

Healy and Dubourjal arrived early to witness the christening
of the ship, their arms numb from lifting their hats continuously
as on the way they seemed to have met everyone they knew in
London. The sound of American voices, the sight of this brave
new ship aroused in Healy a fierce desire to cross the ocean and
return home. As he glanced toward the new liner his eye caught
the familiar figure of Andrew Stevenson. With him stood a tall
man, powerfully built—heavy neck, large features, very tanned.
Healy approached them, and as soon as he saw him, the American Minister exclaimed:

"I was just speaking about you, Mr. Healy. Let me present you to General Lewis Cass, our Minister to the Court of France."

While Healy and Dubourjal paid their respects to the American, Stevenson added:

"I want you to paint Maréchal Soult for me. He represents King Louis Philippe at the coronation, and the Duke will be his host. Think of it! Wellington and Soult—rather exciting, isn't it, after all their encounters on the battlefield!"

Healy was enthusiastic; they spoke for a while of the two great generals, and Cass added to the artist's pleasure by saying that he had heard so much of his talent he would like him to paint his portrait as soon as he returned to Paris.

At a reception in the American legation for Mrs. and Miss Cass, Mr. Stevenson gave his young compatriot two tickets for Westminster—an unhoped-for privilege in view of the great demand for admission. That night George rushed over to the Phippses' home, and Louisa danced with excitement as he showed her the tickets. She would actually see her Queen being crowned!

But on June 27, there came to Healy's studio a flattering and peremptory invitation from Lady Agnes Buller to join the Northumberland party on the morrow for the coronation at Westminster. This was almost a royal command—the artist could not refuse. . . . To Dubourjal, George handed his two tickets, saying:

"I'm glad at least that you can go, only please, please make Louisa understand."

But Louisa, hurt and highly offended, refused to see George and for days flaunted her English admirer, who assiduously accompanied her everywhere. London was in an uproar. Never had it known such noisy crowds, such confusion.

Visiting celebrities flocked to London. President Martin Van Buren's son John, Secretary at the American legation, whose daily hobnobbing with high titles caused the opposition newspapers at home to call him Prince Long Shanks and hint that perhaps the President hoped to make him Prince Consort, and other Americans gathered around Stevenson—Sully, always gracious; Morse, who praised and congratulated Healy on not having followed his advice; and Colonel Thorn of New York with his dazzling daughters. General Cass and his family were often seen with King Louis Philippe's representative, Maréchal Soult. There was no thought of sittings from the Napoleonic hero at this crowded time. The Maréchal's presence created a stir wherever he appeared; it was curious to see persons of every rank and the common people in the streets cheering him; during the Court Procession, shouts and applause greeted Soult and Wellington as those two military giants who had fought each other so furiously in Spain and at Waterloo appeared together.

In her gold coronation coach the Queen smiled at the throngs and behaved with magnificent composure although she constantly whispered, asking what she was supposed to do. When the orb was placed in her hand, she looked at it askance.

"What am I to do with it?" she asked.

"Your Majesty is to carry it if you please in your hand."

"Am I? It is very heavy."

But she suffered in silence, even when the Archbishop insisted on putting on her fourth finger the ruby ring adjusted to her little finger. It hurt. She was obliged to bathe her finger in ice water to remove the ring.

From his vantage point with Lady Agnes Buller, Healy studied the various figures as they took their place in Westminster Abbey. The Duke of Sussex in his black velvet cap struck a strange homely note amid the gorgeous conventional dress of the Queen's party. Prince Esterhazy stood out conspicuously in his white Magyar uniform, while the Turk, Sarim Effendi, was heard to murmur, "All this for a woman!" Ambassadors, said Greville, suffered from the honor of joining the Royal Procession. It meant costly equipages and other expenses that most governments could not or would not meet. In the audience Sir Arthur in full regalia and Lady Faulkner exchanged friendly signals of greeting with Healy.

The festivities continued on through the summer. When not at work, Healy joined many a party, and Louisa, forgetting her resentment in all this excitement and forsaking her English cavalier, went out again with George.

The autumn lull permitted both artists to remember orders awaiting them in France. For once Louisa lost her composure; was she letting happiness slip by? To Healy nothing seemed so important as his love.

"George," Dubourjal remonstrated, "don't marry too soon. Marriage will interfere with your work—you take your duties so hard!"

"I would marry this minute if she'd only have me," sighed the sentimental wooer. "We'd manage, I know...."

"Keep your freedom a little longer, *mon ami*. Have you forgotten your project of work in Belgium and Holland?" asked his friend, whose admiration for the English girl did not blind him to the hampering exigencies of married life.

When they left, Louisa exacted from George the promise of frequent letters. He wrote from Paris, Brussels, the Hague, and Amsterdam, where he was steeped in the glory of Rembrandt's power and Rubens' luminous color; he confided to her his artistic dreams, and in her prim little answers he could read a sympathetic understanding of his aspirations.

On his way back to Paris, at Antwerp, where he copied Rubens' "Descent from the Cross," he received a letter from General Cass forwarded by Dubourjal. Maréchal Soult, too busy as Minister to the King, could not yet give the requested sittings; but he and Mrs. Cass were ready for their portraits as soon as Mr. Healy returned to the city. The very next day, George reached Paris where his friend had already found the necessary studio, and soon the artist was at work on a full-length portrait of the General.

The bronzed outdoor face with big features and eyes that

looked straight at you from under dark brows inspired the painter—a virile model despite the rather long, wavy hair parted on the side since fashion condemned men to the curling iron unless nature favored them with a natural curl.

"Mr. Healy," asked the sitter, "where would you prefer to live, in France or England?"

"In America," promptly replied George Healy, and Lewis Cass laughed.

"Good for you, young man!" His eyes appraised him. "I see they haven't quite turned your head in London...."

The rugged pioneer was an intelligent educated man, lawyer, soldier, statesman; an ardent patriot, he had fought in the War of 1812, breaking his sword in anger and shame when General Hull surrendered to the British. His captivity no doubt accounted for Cass's lasting distrust of England, whereas the Indians whom he had defeated in 1814 found him a most sympathetic governor when the Territory of Michigan was placed under his command.

As he painted, Healy and his subject talked much of Cass's past and of his frequent hopes and interests.

"Someday," said Cass to the artist after one of their séances, "I hope to have you paint for me a portrait of the King."

George flushed with pleasure—this meant that the American liked his work. Cass admired Louis Philippe; he believed in the sincerity of his democratic views; he approved the simple family life at the Tuileries. Cass's own life in Paris was anything but simple; his fortune enabled him to maintain sumptuous apartments, which, like Franklin, he considered necessary to American prestige abroad. His drawing rooms were constantly crowded and his dinners famous.

The daily reminder of America swept George into a new wave of nostalgia, and he wondered why he did not take the next boat home. Then the image of Louisa rose before him, and he knew he must win her before returning. One thing, however, he could do now that orders came more easily: he could send for Thomas, let the boy enjoy those early advantages he had missed. So, at eighteen, Thomas Healy arrived in Paris.

"Oh, oh!" thought Dubourjal when he saw him. "What a fascinating young fellow! And how good looking! I wonder if George realizes what he has on his hands now...."

Exuberantly happy in their reunion, the brothers talked as if they were running a race against time; they were much alike, Thomas' eyes were more sparklingly audacious, George's showing a depth of thought and feeling the younger one might never reach. Both had "the gift of the gab" and Irish wit and tenderness, but Thomas' insouciance, which had troubled their mother, was a matter of temperament, not of age. George saw only the gaiety, the charm he remembered, and felt convinced that proper training would make of him the great artist that he had always believed was Thomas' destiny.

They spoke of the family; William, said Thomas, was in a fever of impatience to leave Boston; he wanted to live in Baltimore with their sister. John liked his quarters in Lowell, but looked thin with that transparent complexion their mother had.

"His lungs are weak and he works too hard," complained Thomas.

Dubourjal helped them choose a room in the Latin Quarter, while they talked at random of galleries, the Beaux Arts and its teachers, of art students, their life, and the dangers of ateliers.

During their first dinner at a little French restaurant George told his brother about Louisa; Thomas became very excited at the prospect of a sister-in-law.

George Healy returned to London for the portraits he had promised to paint that summer; as he left Paris, he exacted Thomas' promise to work hard, not only at his painting, but also at sculpture, which would strengthen his line in drawing.

At Fitzroy Square once more Louisa came to pour tea for George's guests and read aloud to some of his sitters. They were so happy together that the artist thought he could at last break down her fears, but another obstacle presented itself. She would not have a Catholic marriage; he pleaded that since their God and their faith were the same, she might give him the comfort of accepting his church.

"No," said Louisa. "I shall be married at Saint Pancras or not at all." That age of innocence could show stubborn firmness, and the deadlock continued.

Then in July came a letter from General Cass announcing that the King was willing to sit for his portrait! George in his jubilant enthusiasm finally drew from Louisa the fateful yes.

On the morning of July 23, 1839, George Healy and Louisa Phipps were married at Saint Pancras Parish on Euston Road; James and Mary Ann Hanley signed as witnesses; a few friends accompanied them. The bride wore her traveling dress, as they were to start immediately for Paris. George had celebrated his twenty-sixth birthday the week before; Louisa was twenty.

That evening when the English admirer, back from a short journey, presented himself at her door, Mrs. Phipps was faced with the unpleasant duty of telling him that her daughter had been married that day and was on her way to France. To her dismay, the blond giant fell in a faint at her feet.

Gaily the couple started off for Dover, Louisa clinging to her handsome husband, hiding her blushes under the poke bonnet, wrapped in her beautiful traveling shawl though the sun made a wrap unnecessary. George kept looking with proud and hungry eyes at his dainty bride. All seemed perfect until they stepped on the boat—and that brought Louisa's defeat. Never was there a poorer sailor! Too sick even to feel the blow to her pride, she let her distressed husband carry her from the gangplank to the rickety diligence that drove them through the night to Paris. What a climax to all her romantic expectations of a honeymoon! At the hotel she tumbled gratefully into bed, and fortunately the sleep of exhaustion soon dried her tears.

A magnificent traveler, George could not understand; he felt

unhappy and guilty. Such trials, however, are quickly forgotten.
The next day Louisa, rosy-cheeked again, smiling, eyes filled with
adoration, was ready to find Paris and the whole world enchanting. As soon as she declared herself willing to see them, George
sent word to Thomas and Dubourjal of their arrival. The young
brother-in-law was immediately captivated by this new member
of the family; as for Dubourjal, he had definitely let friendship
win the battle over love.

In the rue de l'Ouest near the Luxembourg—a street better
known later as the rue d'Assas, which sheltered so many artists—
the Healys found an apartment that became their home for
nearly a year. No kitchen, few of those improvements Americans
craved, but it had light, a good studio, a cozy atmosphere. Louisa
enjoyed the beautiful park close at hand, and she learned French
by reading aloud to George while he worked. She labored over
Alexandre Dumas's new play *Mademoiselle de Belle-Isle,* which
George translated for her, and which they afterward were able
to enjoy together at the theater.

Louisa's new existence thrilled her; she tried to feel shocked
at this haphazard way of living, compared with her orderly youth
in London, but she loved it! They ate at restaurants; they sat at
little tables on the sidewalk to drink pretty colored and innocu-
ous syrups as they watched the crowds go by. She could not
understand a word of the first play George took her to see, but
she liked the acting and the responsive audience. When they came
out, the night was warm, the boulevards bright; they stopped at
a café. Louisa looked particularly attractive, and a daring dandy,
smoking his big cigar, leaned over their table, trying to catch a
glimpse of the face under the bonnet. His cigar smoke cast a haze
over her, and George, the indignant new husband, seized a glass
of water, which he threw in the face of the dandy, spilling the
water all over him and over Louisa's bonnet. Then in the most
gracious manner he rose, excusing himself by saying:

"I thought my wife's hat was on fire."

Delighted laughter rang from the neighboring tables as the discomfited dandy quickly departed.

Another instance of young Healy's occasional fits of jealousy occurred some time later at a ball while Louisa danced more than once with a French officer who seemed to be whispering in her ear. With an unwonted gleam in his eye, George came over to her.

"Dearest, I think it is time for us to go."

Louisa looked up, surprised, but seeing his expression she answered him with a merry twinkle:

"After this dance, dear. I have promised one more to my partner."

George contained himself with difficulty. Must he create a scandal? Stiffening, he waited, had her wrap ready when she returned to him, but in the carriage on their way home the couple remained silent. Finally, as Louisa looked at him sideways, he asked her in sarcastic tones:

"What did that Frenchman have to whisper so tenderly?"

"Oh! Do you really want me to tell you?"

George faced her in anger—she was mocking him. But immediately contrition filled her voice as she realized his hurt.

"Nothing to worry over, my darling," she told him. "He wanted to learn the new step; I showed him, and he was counting very carefully, *'Un, deux, trois—un, deux, trois....'*"

Chapter X

KING LOUIS PHILIPPE, 1839

A LOUD pull at the studio bell startled George Healy; palette in hand, he went to the door. A messenger handed him a letter, mumbling, "Very urgent." George saw the U. S. Legation seal and in sudden excitement opened the note.

General Cass informed him that King Louis Philippe expected them both at the Tuileries Palace at two o'clock; George must bring several sketches, his paints, and canvas. Quickly the artist dashed his answer, closed the door on the messenger, and rushed to Louisa's room. She was at the window and turned suddenly, surprised at this unaccustomed break in his work. George was all excitement as he put his arms around her.

"Darling," he exclaimed, "I'm to meet Mr. Cass at two at the Tuileries and see the King!"

As happy as he, she helped him choose the sketches he would show, and on the dot Healy met the Minister at the Palace. Louis Philippe received them most cordially and examined Healy's work with evident approval, saying that he liked his portrait of General Cass very much, and, said His Majesty, they might as well start at once. To Healy's great relief, General Cass remained; an officer, a minister, and a chamberlain were also present.

Absorbed in his model, Healy studied intently Louis Philippe's fine features and the straight carriage of this elderly man. His was a kingly figure, though it recalled but faintly the handsome, romantic youth of revolutionary days.

Measuring compass in hand, the painter moved toward his model. Immediately three men sprang forward—they had seen the flash of steel between his fingers—but the King merely laughed as he stopped their progress.

"Gentlemen! Mr. Healy is a republican, yes, but an American —not a killer of kings!"

Recovering from his amazement, Healy explained that he always measured the head before blocking in the figure. They smiled their relief, and the sitting continued.

The King spoke fluent and excellent English, for he had lived in England and in America during his long periods of exile. With Cass and the artist he talked about Philadelphia, where he and his two brothers made their home for many months, and of the little room above Hovey's store in Boston, where he lodged while teaching French to ladies of the Boston aristocracy; he told them how cordially General and Mrs. Washington received them at Mount Vernon and helped map out the brothers' projected expedition down the Ohio and Mississippi to New Orleans.

"Do you know, gentlemen," he said with a twinkle, "that I almost became a medicine man for a village of Cherokee Indians?"

Chuckling over the incredulous look of the two Americans, he explained that during that hard trip, having fallen from his horse, he doctored himself, and the Indians, intrigued by his skillful bloodletting, begged him to visit their old chief, who was very ill. The Duke of Orléans treated this old man, who got better and offered him the post of doctor for his tribe! Louis Philippe managed to avoid the honor by stressing the necessity of his return to his own tribe, but he could not refuse the chief's greatest proof of gratitude, which was to sleep in his tent between the two most noble and venerable women of the tribe—the chief's grandmother and great aunt!

"How my brothers teased me!" laughed His Majesty, but his

laughter ended in a sigh, for both brothers, Beaujolais and Mont-
pensier, whom he loved dearly, were now dead.

"We had many varied experiences," he continued. "In Philadelphia, Mr. Healy, we had the privilege of watching Gilbert
Stuart at work on a portrait of Washington."

"Mr. Stuart is our greatest painter, Sire."

"A great painter anywhere," answered the monarch, launching into a discussion of art and artists.

The sittings continued, and to Healy one day Louis Philippe
spoke of Versailles; now that the Palace, turned into a museum,
was constantly visited by the masses, he meant to create a gallery
of historical pictures that would popularize great deeds not only
of France but of other countries, such as England and America;
he wanted their great men represented—the builders and defenders of a democratic civilization. No project could have appealed
more to the artist, who wished he might be given a share in this
work.

Every sitting brought new interest, and the portrait advanced
rapidly. Now it was over. Everyone in the royal family seemed
pleased with it, and General Cass promptly hung it in his great
drawing room; neither Ingres, nor Scheffer, nor Delaroche, he
claimed, had rendered so realistic and living a presentation of
the King.

"It is wonderful, George!" Dubourjal exclaimed. "Just think—
at twenty-six, you have arrived!"

When his smiling young wife, important and happy, nodded
her agreement, George, embarrassed by all this praise, turned
to her.

"Now, dearest, we can really hope to go to America before
long!"

To him this meant real success; to her, the unknown that she
dreaded; but she said nothing—they certainly could not afford
that long journey yet....

While orders came faster, the money melted rapidly; George

still supported his family in Boston; he was paying for Thomas
in the Latin Quarter, and at home he felt that nothing was ever
quite good enough for his dainty wife, who constantly had to
check his extravagance.

Exulting over his brother's achievement, Thomas basked in the
reflected glory and boasted a good deal about George to the comrades who now invited him on parties and outings.

"All this does not help his work," Louisa complained to her
husband.

"He's so gifted, dearest," George protested, "and Paris is exciting.... Give him time. When he settles down, I believe he'll
paint better than I do!"

"Nonsense!"

Louisa resented her husband's constant praise of others; his
effervescent enthusiasm over the work of other artists sounded
to her like self-depreciation, and belligerently she stood ready
to assert his superiority. George's quick sense of appreciation was
in reality quite independent of comparisons; he counted a fine
painting a treasure in itself, the highest form of beauty, and he
seldom resisted the impulse to buy his comrades' best sketches.

Among the men George admired particularly was his ex-com-
rade from Gros's atelier, Thomas Couture, and Louisa wondered
how two such different temperaments had ever been attracted
to each other. She knew their common love of art and respect for
artistic integrity, but this seemed to her pretty abstract as a basis
of friendship.

After that day at the atelier, in 1834, when Couture had unwit-
tingly given the newcomer a practical lesson in drawing, the two
students never spoke to each other. Then a couple of years later,
walking in Paris with an English friend, Healy, as they passed
Desforges's art shop, stopped suddenly, attracted by an oil
painting in the window.

"Look, Topplis," he exclaimed. "That's real painting!"

"That Venetian figure, you mean?"

"Yes." Healy's excitement grew. "Notice the powerful line—how ruggedly true—it's masterly!"

"By Jove, you're right, Healy." And after studying the picture a while longer, the English artist added, "Let's go in. I must get my brother to buy this."

The sale was arranged, and Desforges gave them the artist's address; the name Thomas Couture recalled nothing, but as soon as the artist answered Healy's knock at the studio, the American had a retrospective vision of that summer day at Gros's and of the Frenchman pushing him from his easel to draw the tired model.

"Oh! I'm so glad it's you," he blurted to the nonplused stocky man, who looked just as rumpled and shaggy as he had in their student days. After enjoying for a few moments the artist's mystification, Healy reminded Couture of the incident and asked what he had done since then.

After Gros's death, Couture had entered Delaroche's studio, he said, but irked by the limitations of schools, he had broken away and decided to walk alone. He still found the trudging a little hard. The bond of shared memories and the frank admiration George showered on his comrade developed into an active friendship, and Couture was one of the first artists George presented to his wife.

She shuddered at the loud fellow; he seemed uncouth, so unlike her adored husband or their gentle friend Dubourjal!

Dubourjal's admiration was more restrained than Healy's.

"Yes, he's a real painter," he admitted, "but with all his early training and sureness he has not the utter naturalness of your self-taught painting," and laughing, he added, "American candor, I might call it." George thought this sheer partiality.

Over the problem of his brother Thomas, George and Dubourjal put their heads together; they did not want Louisa to know of the boy's escapades. There had been an extraordinary scene at the atelier, where the hot-blooded young American was reported to have pulled a gun and set the place in an uproar. Then he was such an easy prey for scheming young women! It was decided finally that Thomas had better return to America, open his own studio either in Boston or in Lowell, where his brother John seemed to be doing nicely. Louisa was not sorry; she would have George more to herself! George felt they had acted wisely when Thomas's letters came, full of hope concerning the growing city of Lowell and his first American sitters.

In Paris the young couple's life continued full of contrasts. When General and Mrs. Cass invited them to a grand dinner at their beautiful home in the rue Matignon in the Élysée quarter, George ordered for his wife a dress of white satin and chiffon that swallowed up the price of more than one portrait—but she looked so lovely in it! Miss Isabel was charmed with the bride's looks and her charming timidity.

"You had not told us, Mr. Healy, that you married a little girl," she teased.

Indignant, Louisa swiftly turned, but as her eyes met the warmth of Miss Cass's smile, she joined in the laughter. At first, the presence of formidable liveried footmen behind their chairs intimidated her; her natural English poise, however, saved her from showing any embarrassment. The evening proved most successful.

Now Louisa busied herself with baby clothes. As the time approached, George decided that it would be easier and safer for Louisa to be at her mother's. Advised by the Faulkners who had promised to stand as godparents to the newcomer, they reached London in February, 1840, and in mid-March little Arthur Faulkner Healy made his appearance.

George left his wife and child in the care of Mrs. Phipps and returned to his work in Paris.

At long last the eagerly awaited opportunity to paint Maréchal Soult presented itself. In March, 1840, his ministry had fallen, and now that he was out of office, the ex-Minister remembered his

promise to Cass. He invited the General and the American artist
to visit his picture gallery.

"A rare privilege, Mr. Healy," the United States Minister informed his young countryman. "The Duke of Dalmatia guards
his treasures jealously and seldom lets anyone see them."

As they admired the priceless collection, they understood the
reason; many of these old masters came from Spain. "War loot,"
whispered General Cass at a moment when Soult, busy with a
messenger, could not overhear.

Before a particularly fine "Immaculate Conception" of Murillo
—the one now so familiar to visitors of the Louvre—the Maréchal
remarked:

"That picture saved a man's life," but vouchsafed no further
explanation.

Healy that evening mentioned it to his English neighbor at
dinner, and the latter told a strange story. This painting, he said,
had been demanded of the monastery to which it belonged. The
prior denied any knowledge of its whereabouts. If by sundown
he had not found it, he was informed, he would be hanged "on
yonder tree." By sundown Soult had the picture, and the prior
did not hang.

There were innumerable stories about Soult, whose political
career, to say the least, lacked unity. A Bonapartist in his youth,
Soult became a royalist after the Vienna Congress. Under King
Louis Philippe he became an Orleanist. In 1832, Louis Philippe
called on Soult to head a new cabinet, and the Maréchal thought
himself safely in power for many years to come. But in his cabinet two noted men of more liberal trend, though opposed to each
other in politics, united to defeat him and succeeded. They were
Thiers and Guizot, both historians and statesmen.

Years later, Thiers, who had replaced Soult in the early spring
of 1840, told Healy of an incident of that year. He and his new
ministers were waiting at the Tuileries while in an adjoining
room of the Palace the King informed his Maréchal of the sad

necessity to part. They waited a long time; the ministers grew fidgety, and then they saw the door opening very slowly and quietly as Louis Philippe's head appeared an instant to whisper:

"A little patience, gentlemen; we are weeping together."

Superb in his gold-embroidered uniform, white-plumed hat in hand, Maréchal Soult presented a fine figure for Healy's brush. It was fitting that the artist should paint him standing in military regalia with all his medals. The portrait, ready for delivery to Mr. Stevenson in London, was to be exhibited at the Royal Academy. At this same time Healy's portrait of Mrs. Cass obtained a medal at the French Salon, and the artist was called to the Tuileries.

Louis Philippe surprised the painter with a most unexpected and welcome request.

"Would you make some copies of English paintings for my Versailles gallery, Mr. Healy?" he asked, and noting the artist's pleasure, added with a smile, "Yes, I know. Mrs. Healy is there, and I congratulate you both on the birth of your son. I thought it would be a good time for you to work in England...."

George wanted wings to fly to London and tell Louisa the good news—but he waited a few days for Queen Victoria's answer to the French King's letter. It arrived shortly with the assurance that Her Majesty would be pleased to let the young American painter and his wife stay at Windsor while copying the pictures. Baroness Lehzen would receive them and attend to their needs.

Chapter XI

AT WINDSOR CASTLE, 1840

So IT happened that in 1840 George and Louisa Healy with little Arthur enjoyed two idyllic months at Windsor Castle under the maternal care of Baroness Lehzen. This good lady, left to superintend repairs during the Queen's absence, was delighted with the rare treat of young companionship. While Arthur slept contentedly in his pram, Louisa spent restful hours on the sunny terrace, listening to accounts of the Queen's virtues and to minute descriptions of Victoria's marriage. Good Lehzen praised highly the handsome German husband, little suspecting that within two years Albert, irked by her influence over his wife, would engineer her return to Germany.

Louisa gloated over the fact that the Queen's marriage had coincided with her birthday—February 10; everything in her life, she said, seemed to connect in some way with the Queen. Healy's Americanism bristled somewhat at what seemed to him a childish veneration for royalty; Baroness Lehzen on the other hand fully approved of it.

Occasionally, with or without the baby, Louisa accompanied George into the gardens or the surrounding woods where the artist sketched various views of Windsor. Fascinated by its history, they listened avidly to tales of the historic castle. In the midst of an ancient forest, solid and steadfast as Britain itself, Windsor Castle with its many towers seemed to keep watch over the Thames flowing leisurely at its feet. The past revived as the visitors looked at Arthur's Round Table, heard of the great feast of

St. George held there, were told that Froissart and Chaucer had sung its glory, and that two great royal poets had been interned here—James of Scotland, who wrote the "King's Quhair," dreamed of his mountains under these trees, and Charles of Orléans, taken prisoner at Agincourt, tried here to re-create in jewel-like verse the spring season and gay flowers of France. Because the ladies liked the Frenchman too well and might help his escape, he was removed to more inaccessible fortresses while impoverished France labored twenty-five years to gather his huge ransom. At Windsor also, King Charles I had spent his last Christmas and after his execution was brought back for burial at St. George's chapel....

Parts of the great domain had then fallen in ruin, but as game abounded Windsor became a hunting lodge, scene of much revelry. With German love of home, the Georges made the apartments livable, ordered new gardens with a long shaded walk leading to the forest. Queen Victoria and her consort continued these improvements. In the upper court, divided from the lower court by the famous round tower, architects remodeled state and private apartments that contained innumerable treasures, which Victoria, good housekeeper, ordered properly catalogued. The Chapel and Deanery, the Knights of Windsor's apartments, the Queen's Mews, stables, dairy, and aviary completed the domain. To the couple who had lived in one room and studio, it all seemed rather fantastic.

Rosy-cheeked, rested, and healthy, Louisa with little Arthur left for London before the Queen's return. One morning while George Healy was at work in the Waterloo Gallery, the royal couple appeared. Quickly, the American rose, waiting to be addressed. But he had not been personally presented and Victoria believed in strict etiquette. Turning to her husband, she said:

"Ask Mr. Healy if King Louis Philippe contemplates further changes at Versailles?"

Prince Albert shot his wife a curious look, then in all seriousness

repeated questions and answers until, glancing at the copy of
Lord Bathurst by Lawrence, the Queen, with a slight bend of
the head no doubt meant to be gracious, expressed her appreciation with a short remark, "It is very like," and walked away,
followed by the Prince.

How different from the Tuileries! thought the outraged
American as he made valiant efforts to control a mounting storm
of angry laughter while the royal footsteps died in the distance.

It distressed Louisa when her husband mimicked the scene.
She wished it had not occurred—but the Queen could do no
wrong. Following this experience, the homely familiarity of Victoria's uncle soothed the artist's ruffled temper. The tall, stately
Duke of Sussex at last gave George Healy the long-promised
sittings, and his sprightly wife, the Duchess of Inverness, received
him charmingly.

At Kensington Palace, between sittings, Healy saw the work of
many contemporaries, for the Duke of Sussex was an art patron
and president of the Royal Society. Among American artists he
had favored Webster's friend, Chester Harding, and now
sprinkled his conversation with stories of painters and sculptors
always fascinating to the young artist.

As a husband this immensely tall, gouty, portly gentleman
became jovial, tender, delightful. He would take up his guitar
and sing sentimental ditties to his diminutive wife, who thoroughly enjoyed these romantic moods. Healy would have liked
to paint this picture instead of the more conventional portraits
agreed on. However, his painting obtained favorable comment
and some Londoners repeated a remark made before: "G. P. A.
Healy, ah, yes, the Lawrence of America."

His pictures for Versailles crated and on their way, Healy still
remained in London to finish the portraits of Lord and Lady
Waldegrave. He had never seen Strawberry Hill, Horace Walpole's historic domain inherited by Lord Waldegrave. His sitter
suggested an excursion there for the artist, his wife, and several

of their American friends. It was a day they never forgot, a lesson in history so living that it would ever remain with them. Walpole's letters were being published, and this gave Strawberry Hill actuality. They saw the printing press of which Walpole was so proud and some first editions published under his supervision. Healy spent most of his time studying the priceless collection of pictures, while the others ambled through the magnificent grounds, those famous gardens where Walpole wrote some of his wittiest letters to the wittiest woman in France, the Marquise du Deffand. A festive lunch was served, and mountains of succulent chops vanished so fast that even impassive British servants could not hide an incredulous smile.

Summer had come and gone; the Healys, back in Paris, settled on the *rive droite* in a studio apartment 50 rue Saint Lazare, a quarter more suitable to a rising artist and more comfortable for a baby's needs. In a life more complex also, Louisa showed herself a competent manager as well as devoted wife and mother. Dubourjal resumed his role of faithful, helpful friend, eking out their insufficient silverware with his own when guests came to dinner, or—a gourmet always—added some special delicacy to the menu. One night he brought two bottles of old Burgundy as the high point of the feast. From a carefully wrapped bottle the maid solemnly poured its red liquid into glasses that the guests held to the light, admiring the ruby color, sniffing the bouquet, and pronouncing the wine delicious. Two days later George Healy, to his chortling delight, found in the kitchen Dubourjal's precious bottles untouched—their unappreciative maid had served ordinary wine.

Chapter XII

BACK IN PARIS

As 1841 opened, the Healys could look back with pride on two full and successful years; his medal at the Salon for the portrait of Mrs. Cass; his paintings shown at the Royal Academy favorably received; Louis Philippe's portrait and his orders for Versailles; the Duke of Sussex' kindly patronage—all this surrounding the happy event of baby Arthur's birth; truly Providence smiled upon them, and the new year was to fulfill many happy promises.

It began with a portrait of François Guizot painted in 1841 in Paris, which offered a marked contrast with that of Soult painted the previous year—the latter martial, authoritative, high-born, flamboyant; the other, distinguished and severe, the product of Calvinism, cold, but gifted with its logical penetrating eloquence. Both statesmen impressed Louis Philippe with their strength, but whereas Soult quickly aroused opposition and had to be dismissed, Guizot retained power throughout the King's reign.

Guizot possessed the Protestant's lasting virtues in complete antithesis to his other political rival, Thiers, who, a native of the sunny ancient city of Nîmes, was endowed with all its southern effervescence. After the fall of Soult, Thiers had sent Guizot to England as ambassador, but on his rival's return Thiers himself was dismissed and Guizot placed at the helm.

Healy studied his model curiously—an austere face with chiseled features, a spare figure indicative of abstemious habits; the man's evident intellectuality and known integrity seemed utterly at variance with the touching story of his first marriage and especially with his rumored present attachment to the noted Princess Lieven. After Metternich and after various shooting stars of the political world, Guizot now reigned supreme in that intensely French salon of a Russian princess, even as the aged Chateaubriand still reigned over the salon of Madame Récamier. It would have seemed more natural for the romantic Chateaubriand to associate with the lover-laden princess, while ascetic Guizot might have breathed a purer atmosphere in the chaste Juliette's company, but love is contrary and both lions—the poet and the historian—presided over their curiously chosen circles until death broke the strong ill-assorted ties.

It was murmured that when Madame de Chateaubriand died a friend asked Madame Récamier if she would marry her idol. The wide-eyed Juliette, a tender smile hovering on her lips, answered, "But where would Monsieur de Chateaubriand go then every afternoon?"

When an indiscreet caller asked Princess Lieven why she did not marry Guizot, she laughed, saying: "Can you imagine my being called Madame Guizot?"

Like the King, the Minister spoke English with the painter.

"Lady Holland is delightful as you know, Mr. Healy," he remarked, "but what a temper!" One evening Guizot was giving a dinner in honor of Lord and Lady Palmerston, newly married; his guests were late, and Lady Holland, starved, for she had missed her lunch, insisted on not waiting for them. "I could not do that," the Minister went on, "but she stormed and ended the scene with a fainting fit. It was awkward."

"She corrected my English," continued George's sitter. "It seems one must not speak of hell in English—only Milton and the Bible may mention it. *Que diable!* That seems funny to a Frenchman."

The mixture of stoicism and worldliness in Guizot intrigued the painter; he spoke of it with Dubourjal, who had told him

about the Minister's early romance. As a young writer on Suard's
paper *Le Publiciste,* Guizot had noticed a series of articles signed
Pauline de Meulan; they stopped suddenly, and the writer heard
that Pauline de Meulan was ill and in dire need. With Suard's
assent and promise of secrecy he wrote the articles under her
signature. Finally Pauline learned who her savior was; she was
forty, he twenty-five, but their marriage turned out most happily
until her death fifteen years later in 1827. Their son, for whose
sake Guizot married again, had died some four years back, and
now Guizot, once more a widower, counted on his mother to
bring up his daughters and the eight-year-old boy of his second
marriage. In later years, one daughter, Madame de Witt, was to
write charmingly of her father's life. Sympathy easily swayed this
man called hard by his political adversaries, for it was Princess
Lieven's sorrow over the loss of her two youngest sons that first
aroused his feelings. No one knew what Guizot's virtuous and
dignified mother thought of this new attachment; proud of her
son's achievements, she remained close to him to the end, sharing
his exile in England, where she died.

Looking around the studio during one of their sittings, Guizot
noticed Couture's "Prodigal Son."

"Who painted that, Mr. Healy?" he asked.

Delighted to have his friend's work singled out, Healy spoke
eloquently of Couture's talent. The Minister became interested.

"A Prix de Rome? The Government should follow the careers
of its promising laureates. I shall speak of him to the King."

"If only you could spare the time for a visit to his studio, sir, it
would do much to restore his faith in the future," urged Healy.

The promise was given—and kept. On the bare wall of
Couture's monastic studio, when they entered, they saw the artist
brushing in vigorous strokes the outline of his "Roman Decadence." Guizot liked it, not unaware that this Prix de Rome had
no canvas big enough for his composition and probably could not
afford one. He asked if there was an order for this picture.

"*J'attends*," replied Couture with characteristic and somewhat bombastic independence. Learning that the painter had worked in Delaroche's atelier, Guizot said:

"I shall have great pleasure in speaking of you to him." Unfortunately there was no love lost between the old and the young artist, and the King listened to Delaroche's criticism of his ex-pupil. This was not the only time that Couture lost an opportunity for official patronage. Some years later, under the Second Empire, he was chosen to paint the christening of the little Imperial Prince, but Napoleon III made so many suggestions that finally the exasperated artist exclaimed:

"Who is painting this picture, Your Majesty? You or I?" and that was the end of an important commission.

Nevertheless, Couture's famous picture "Roman Decadence" caught the judges' attention at the Salon of 1847 and the following year was placed at the Luxembourg Palace.

Meanwhile, at Versailles in the previous year, 1846, Healy had surveyed the placing of his English pictures. His visit to this historic palace reminded him of stories Guizot told about Franklin's fruitful years in France; in the gorgeous throne room he tried to picture Franklin at the Court of Louis XVI; the idea took shape, and he mentioned it to the King.

"Splendid, Mr. Healy," agreed Louis Philippe; "the very kind of picture I want. Make me a sketch, and we'll see...."

Guizot encouraged the artist.

"You'd better see M. de Rémusat," he counseled; "his mother was the niece of Franklin's friend, Vergennes, who worked so hard for the Franco-American treaty of alliance."

Not only did the Comte de Rémusat furnish George Healy with details and personal touches that gave him the atmosphere of those bygone days, but he procured authentic costumes in which the painter's models seemed to revive the ghosts of that last brilliant French court.

The original picture executed in the throne room measured

36 by 24 inches, and to make sure that he had the right proportions and perspective Healy asked one of his friends, an architect,
to accompany him and verify his first blocking in of the composition. Vivid in color and action, the picture, now over a hundred years old, still retains its freshness. Louis Philippe approved
it and gave the order for a large canvas with life-size figures for
the walls of Versailles.

Day after day, Healy went to Versailles; wrapped in his work,
he returned to Paris at sundown exhausted but supremely happy.
Louisa felt the pangs of jealousy. She knew that while she missed
him throughout the long day he remained too completely
absorbed to give her or the baby much thought. Could it be that
his work surpassed his love? At first oblivious of any tension, the
artist finally became aware of his wife's distress and loneliness.
He then brought home much of his paraphernalia and worked
on innumerable drawings in his studio while little Arthur played
or slept and Louisa read aloud all they could find concerning
Franklin's long years in France. The artist based his figure of
Franklin on several contemporary portraits and also on those
little porcelain or wood figurines, so expressive and characteristic,
that flooded Paris in Franklin's day. As he painted the high forehead, the wide-open probing intelligent eyes, the quizzical mouth
with its upturned corners, a spirit of early Americanism seemed
to permeate the studio. That solid figure with its plain longish
white hair and simple clothes—knee breeches and long coat—
gave an impression of dignity and power that overshadowed the
crowd of fashionable courtiers.

Dominating the picture, Franklin holds in his right hand a
paper setting forth his plea for the cause of America. In the
brilliant setting of the great paneled room with its rich red throne
and dais, Healy has him centered on the second blue step leading
to the throne, above the General Assembly, thus bringing his head
on the level with that of the enthroned King. Louis XVI in his
satin coat and Marie Antoinette in her white dress look charm-

ingly young but lack vitality; their royalty failed to inspire the artist; it belonged to a dead past. More natural is the grouping of courtiers as they stand, sit, turn, talk, or whisper; to the right, in the foreground, a quartet of men in conversation remind one of Daumier's dynamic animation.

The large picture made from this earlier one suffered a checkered career; the revolution of 1848 changed its destination; completed in 1855, it obtained at the Universal Exposition in Paris the highest honor yet bestowed on an American artist; brought to America, it was exhibited throughout the States, where so many schoolbooks reproduced it that it became very familiar to a whole generation of young Americans, but in the end it vanished in flames during the Chicago fire of 1871. The first painting, however, remained always with the artist in his various studios on both sides of the ocean, a cherished reminder of happy days; it escaped the fate of so many other Healy paintings destroyed by fire and attests to the qualities that won him fame while still in his twenties.

With the end of that busy winter Louisa, who expected her second baby, pleaded to return to England; in January, 1842, reluctantly George tore himself from his work and once more he and his wife saw their London friends while little Arthur claimed all the attention of his doting grandmother. Healy met his old comrades, visited galleries, went to the Royal Academy, where Charles Leslie spoke feelingly of Sir David Wilke, whose death at sea the preceding summer had saddened the artist colony. Turner, said Leslie, was working on a picture of that burial at sea. Taking a studio for a few weeks, Healy set to work; among the portraits he painted then was one of Charlotte Everett, the future Mrs. Augustus Wise, a daughter of Edward Everett, who had succeeded Andrew Stevenson as minister to the Court of St. James's.

On February 16, baby Agnes, named after George's sister, made her bow to England with indignant cries against the damp cold she would hate all her life. Leaving his family in Mrs. Phipps's competent hands, George hastened back to France and his work at Versailles. Once in a while, to rest his mind and change his outlook, he would leave the great hall and sketch out of doors various bits of that magnificent park.

One day in the spring of 1842 a summons from the Tuileries drew him back to Paris. As soon as he appeared, the King asked:

"Mr. Healy, where did you copy your Washington? I was seen last night, it seems, in very good company at General Cass's —between Washington and Guizot, both painted by you."

The painting, Healy explained, was made from a print, but familiar as he was with Stuart's tones he had been able to reproduce the color from memory. Louis Philippe had set his heart on a copy from the portrait Gilbert Stuart was painting for Mrs. Bingham when he visited the studio in Philadelphia over forty years before.

"That is the one I want," he insisted. "As soon as we discover where it is, I would like you to do it for me."

A few days later, rueful at his lack of success but proud of his colloquial achievement, the King greeted him:

"We are dished, Mr. Healy! The portrait I want is in Russia, and at present I can ask no favor of the Russian government. What other portrait of Washington would you suggest?"

At the mention of the one in Faneuil Hall, the King shook his head; no military uniform. Washington should be represented in civilian clothes as the greatest citizen of a great country.

"See what you can find over there," concluded the Monarch; "and while you are in Washington, you might paint Mr. Webster, President Tyler, Mr. Calhoun perhaps...."

Healy left the Tuileries in a daze of happiness; he was to go back to America—and under what glorious auspices!

Chapter XIII

AT THE WHITE HOUSE, 1842

IT WAS April again—April, 1842—and George Healy once more stood leaning against the rail of a ship, plunged into memories of the past while his eyes turned oceanward toward the future. Louisa had not accompanied him to Liverpool—eager though she had been to see him settled in his cabin on the *Caledonia*—because the new baby required her continued presence in London. So George had left her with little two-year-old Arthur and two-month-old Agnes in the care of her mother.

Healy's thoughts turned to those earlier Aprils, momentous milestones in his exciting twenty-eight years of life. In 1830, twelve years before—was it April, that month of nature's promise that so often presaged new unfoldings in his career?—Mr. Sully was in Boston to paint Colonel Perkins, and Healy, only sixteen then, had opened his heart to the older artist, whose encouragement had hastened the day of George's great decision.

Then in April, 1834, after his success with the Tuckers and lovely Mrs. Otis, he had found himself on his way to France: his first view of New York, his first ocean crossing, Paris, a new life, new comradeships, and art as he had dreamed it.... Two years later, in April, 1836, he was in England with the Faulkners. And now, in 1842, after an absence of eight years Healy was on his way back to America—on a mission for the King of France.

Eight years! Much had occurred in that time: his father's death soon after he left; then two years later his mother's; and lately the loss of his brother John, who had not let them know how ill he was in Lowell, and who had slipped out of life at the age of twenty-four. Thomas, back from France, had arrived just in time to soften his last moments.

The old home in Boston would probably be occupied by total strangers since Agnes had moved to Baltimore; William, also studiously inclined, had followed her south. George must stop in Baltimore, of course, yet he could not tarry long before presenting the King's letter to President John Tyler. In Washington Healy hoped to find the Stevensons, who had left London the previous October.

So his thoughts ran, leaping from the past to the future, anticipating the joy of a family reunion, and figuring already on the portraits he would paint for Versailles. It might mean several months in America. How he wished Louisa were with him! Up to now their partings had been short, and for distances that a few hours could bridge, but this time George was proud of the manner in which this timid young woman had taken their separation. "English wives don't fuss when their husbands leave for the colonies, do they?" she had replied when he praised her courage. As the ship pulled away, she waved farewell without tears.

The salt air that filled Healy's lungs brought vivid memories of his early Boston days; a rising eagerness to reach the other shore surged from his soul. Never had he felt so American! His Paris life, his English marriage, his European ways became gifts he was bringing home, and his mission a recognition by the oldest European court of America's growing importance. It seemed incredible that less than a century ago Voltaire had dismissed Canada as an unimportant expanse of snow, and that only a little while back Napoleon dared sell the vast territory of Louisiana for a few millions!

Healy held many a conversation with Captain Lott, who, though he had never met him, knew a good deal about Captain Healy. They talked of the old trade vessels, of the first experiments with steam, and the *Savannah*'s ocean crossing, of the

successful though dangerous journey in '39 attempted by the *Chile*
sent by Brown's of London to South America; the ship had run
aground, short of fuel and dangerously stranded, when the Captain's cabin boy, who had been reading Charles Darwin's *Voyage
of the Beagle,* discovered on the island the "mountain of coal"
mentioned by the author. That coal saved them and made history
in steam shipping.

The Captain mentioned the storms in January when Mr. and
Mrs. Dickens came over on the *Britannia.* The writer, it appeared,
never wearied of recounting the horror of seafaring, and the
Captain laughed heartily.

"But the danger is real," he added more soberly. "Do you remember last year? The packet *President* was never seen again...."

"I know. Mr. Tyrone Power, the great actor, was on her," murmured the artist, as he recalled the pleasant days when Power's
children sat for their group portrait.

The passengers were friendly; a Miss Duncan spoke of having
her portrait painted; a Dr. Fisher mentioned acquaintances
George had met in England and in Paris; Commodore Josiah
Tatnall was interested to hear that Lieutenant Van Brunt had
sat to Healy some ten years before; he was now at the Bite of
Craney Island, experimenting on a naval gun carriage that seemed
promising, and the following January George Healy heard that
a commission appointed by the Secretary of the Navy had brought
back a favorable report.

To Louisa, George wrote daily accounts of deck friendships
and conversations, little intimate details such as he would have
told her at home after a sitting or a visit.

The *Caledonia* stopped at Halifax, and with other passengers
Healy stepped off long enough to catch a glimpse of the city, a
busy bustling port. But he was glad when they lifted anchor; a
fever of impatience goaded him; he longed for Boston—Boston
with all its memories, its familiar faces, and the Yankee atmosphere he so often missed. At last, on May 5, under a brilliant sun

Healy caught the distant shore and the docks' outline; the ship's slow approach stirred in him an agony of suspense.

There was Thomas, cheery, bright, waving wildly; in no time the two brothers were together, hurrying toward the Tremont House.

"Yes, you must go to the best hotel, George," laughed Thomas in answer to his brother's protest; "an artist sent by the King cannot do less! Besides, Louisa would like you to stop at the hotel Mr. Dickens chose!" The brothers talked in an unending stream of exchanged family news; Thomas was doing well in Lowell, the growing town that owed its sudden expansion to the Appleton industries. That very day, they called on Mr. Stephen Appleton and were charmingly received.

"I understand, young man," said their host addressing Thomas, "that you are having success; Lowell considers you a very enterprising and social-minded gentleman. Keep it up, my boy, keep it up!"

As they walked down the steps the young man gleefully explained to his brother that he was painting the six beautiful daughters of Mr. Hildreth on one canvas, each in an oval.

"What a strange idea!" laughed George. "Why not group them?"

"That's the way they want it, and anyhow I haven't your gift of composition." Thomas's enthusiasm over the charming models showed that he had not changed much; apparently the artist had fallen in love with each one in turn; to him, life was still a great festival.

"Careful, Thomas, careful," warned George. "Remember Paris."

"Oh! This is America—and these are ladies...."

They said no more on the subject. With all their exuberant Irish temperament, New England reticence still held them.

Together the brothers visited their parents' graves; George experienced a surge of religious feeling mingled with a sense of guilt. He, a Catholic, was letting Louisa bring up his children as Protestants; his mother-in-law, whose little sharp eyes saw much, but saw things as she wanted them to be—or made them so—was responsible; Arthur and Agnes would learn the same Lord's Prayer he had lisped at his mother's knee, but they would not hear the penetrating chant of his church, the mysterious Latin words, or watch the symbolic rites he found so beautiful. Thomas glanced at his brother's troubled face. "Poor old George," he reflected, "he's so beastly conscientious! After all—they're good Christians just the same...."

Thomas wanted George to meet his Bohemian friends in Lowell, but Washington called.

"On my return, I will," the traveler promised. "Now I must see Mrs. Otis." The artist found his great friend at home. She would not hear of his remaining at the hotel and immediately, as her guest, "little Healy" resumed the Boston mantle he had shed abroad. Old friends came in shoals, and many expressed a desire to have their portraits painted. It was tantalizing to postpone all this and risk a change of heart on the part of would-be sitters—yet he must first accomplish his mission.

A visit to the Tuckers filled him with sorrow. Mr. Richard Tucker, his earliest patron, had died suddenly in January; Charles Tucker, John Gray, and the aunt, Miss Sarah Chandler Tucker, received George with open arms, made him tell of his marriage, his success, his years across the ocean, avoiding Boston recollections that rendered more poignant their present loss, but despite the foreign talk it was Boston that filled his heart.

As he "took the cars," that jolty new train that could go several miles an hour, Healy was already planning to make Boston his real home. The journey to Washington with stops in New York, Philadelphia, and Baltimore thrilled him.

In the Quaker city, George called on the Sullys, delightfully hospitable in their brick mansion on Sixth Street just above Chestnut, a house built for the artist in his more prosperous days by Stephen Girard in answer to Sully's need for painting and exhibition rooms.

"It is good to have you back in your own country, Mr. Healy," said the older artist. "I hope you will remain with us some time."

Healy explained the King's commission and his difficulty about the Washington portrait.

"I cannot believe it's in Russia," Sully told him; "as far as I know, it was never sold, and if it went to Lord Lansdowne as Mrs. Bingham intended, it must be in England."

George made a mental note to inquire in London on his return, but meanwhile he would copy the one at the White House.

"Not one of the best, I fear," Sully warned him. "However, you are familiar with the master's coloring and I am sure you'll give a fine reproduction."

The two men launched into a discussion of Stuart's human quality and agreed that at his best he could not be surpassed.

"My father liked him personally," said George, "and we all admired his talent tremendously. I remember once in Boston catching a glimpse of his back when a boy cried out: 'There goes old Stuart!' I wanted to run after him so as to see his face, but felt too shy."

Sully laughed.

"His face would not have pleased you as much as his work; it had coarsened with age, and if you'd blocked his path, he would have cursed you roundly!" At Healy's surprised look he added, smiling: "His language often shocked people, but you can discount many of the stories told against him ... a great man should have no foibles," sighed the artist.

George protested, "Miss Stuart spoke of her father with veneration."

"Yes, after his death," remarked Sully dryly. "His family found him hard to live with; he could, if he wished, show himself the most courteous of men, but he was too outspoken for his own good; the only person who always unconsciously silenced him was

Washington. Even the irrepressible Stuart felt awed by the President's dignity."

George looked with delight at Sully's unfinished sketch of Queen Victoria and warmly congratulated him on his recent election as President of the Pennsylvania Academy of Fine Arts. He then told of his own work on "Franklin at the Court of Louis XVI."

"Why, that's splendid, Mr. Healy!" Sully exclaimed, his eyes shining. "That is the sort of thing you must enjoy."

And as the young man waxed enthusiastic over the historical research he had to do, saying that he learned the history of his own country in trying to depict it for the French, Sully replied that he himself had always wanted to paint large murals of American history.

As he left, Sully advised the young man to see Mrs. Madison in Washington and ask permission to copy her husband's portrait, which the Philadelphian considered one of Stuart's best.

In Baltimore, George visited Agnes; the meeting after eight long years affected them deeply. They had so much to say that these talkative Healys in their emotion remained tongue-tied.

Washington startled Healy. After London and Paris, the newness of the city struck him; he could not help noticing the muddy, unpaved roads, the vacant pieces of land like big gaping holes between fine houses. His artist eye saw it as a huge unfinished canvas, very crude, yet showing tremendous possibilities. The plan was there with its central point and radiating sections, its carefully balanced symmetry, its promise of classic beauty and infinite extension—a promise that would take a century to realize. Louis Philippe had spoken to him of Major l'Enfant, a Frenchman, who designed the capital. "Another link between our nations, Mr. Healy," he had said with his smile that conveyed so much.

The returned American imagined Washington as a magnet for other nations, becoming spiritually as well as materially the symbol of world understanding, strong as the structure of its republican principles. He began to wonder if Washington would not be a fitter place to live in even than Boston.

Newspapers heralded Healy's coming. The *Daily National Intelligencer* made much of the artist's arival in Washington and of his mission, calling it "a pleasing instance of honor to genius and the fine arts...a compliment to our pride of country," for Louis Philippe chose "a young native of our own country...." Other cities also felt pride in the French King's choice of an American, and the Philadelphia *Public Ledger* on Wednesday, May 18, announced that Mr. Healy of Boston had been sent by the King of France to copy Stuart's portrait of General Washington and that the artist was then at the President's House. Ten days later the *Niles Register* told Baltimoreans as they took their breakfast and at the same time digested the weekly news that Mr. Healy was in Washington painting the first President's portrait for the King of France.

When by appointment he reached the President's House, its harmonious lines, its stately entrance made him instinctively straighten his shoulders and attune his manner to the dignity of the mansion. President Tyler's graciousness did much to increase that first feeling of well-being. After an exchange of polite greetings and some conversation about the King's commission, a room was placed at the artist's disposal. There he painted his reproduction of Washington's portrait.

On May 30, 1842, the artist received from the National Institute a commission to paint the portraits of President Tyler and of Senator Preston, who was shortly to leave Washington and political life. In June the *Niles Register* gave an account of the placing of Guizot's portrait at the Institute, quoting the text of President Tyler's letter to Mr. Poinsett on the subject.* And the

---

* Sir:

A full length portrait of Monsieur Guizot, Prime Minister of France and biographer of Washington, executed by Mr. Healy, an American artist, upon subscription of certain

National Intelligencer informed its readers that Mr. Healy had been engaged "since his arrival upon other work for public institutions and private individuals."

President Tyler's refined features, in spite of the big nose he deprecated and often mentioned, offered an excellent subject with his light hair, piercing blue eyes, and tanned outdoor complexion. In his portrait Healy showed the thoughtful yet determined character of the man who happened to become President when General Harrison died within a month of his inauguration.

Strong-willed, the unexpected President had soon come to grips with the Whig party, whose leader, Clay, meant to run the administration. The Harrison cabinet resigned in a body—except Daniel Webster, who considered the conspiracy unworthy and unjust, and remained to carry out the foreign policy planned between himself and Harrison—a policy Tyler wished continued and which was at that moment bringing to a satisfactory conclusion the Webster-Ashburton Treaty. In spite of Webster the President was "read out" of the party, and since he had incurred the Democrats' displeasure by his association with the Whigs, John Tyler became that strange individual in American politics, a "man without a party."

Healy found the Virginian an extremely pleasant sitter; both men liked to tell stories and a humorous twinkle in the President's eye would frequently soften his rather austere appearance. The artist's faculty of making friends quickly proved itself once more;

---

citizens resident in Paris has been consigned to my care with a request that I should give it a place in some one of the public buildings of this Capital. After full consideration of the best disposition to be made of it, as well in honor to the distinguished statesman and man of letters whose person and features it is said most accurately to delineate, as well to meet the wishes of the citizens who have made me its repository, I have concluded to tender it through you to the National Institute.

May I ask, Sir, that you take measures to give the portrait such place in the Institute as may exhibit it to the best advantage and thereby gratify the wishes of many of our fellow citizens whose desire is to see it. A work of art, apart from the high consideration in which the original is justly held, it may favorably be compared with any similar work to be found in the United States....

JOHN TYLER

several of the Tyler children came in; he painted a portrait of Miss Alice and was allowed the privilege of presenting his respects to charming Mrs. Tyler, an invalid whose strength drained away day by day. She delegated most of her social duties to her daughter, Mrs. Semple, and her daughter-in-law, Mrs. Robert Tyler, the "fascinating Fairlie" of Washington Irving. Only once that winter Mrs. Tyler graced with her presence a reception, on the occasion of her daughter Elizabeth's marriage to William Waller.

Healy had but a short glimpse of her, yet it left a lasting impression, and when that September Mrs. Tyler died, he grieved with the nation over the first tragic loss that threw a pall on the President's House.

Chapter XIV

THE AMERICAN SCENE, 1842–44

D EAREST," wrote George, "do you know that over here they call a portrait 'a counterfeit representation'? How do you like to think of your husband as a counterfeiter?" And in London as she read this Louisa chuckled delightedly. She devoured these weekly journals, trying to follow George from afar in his hectic journeys. During the warmer season of calm seas the mails arrived quite regularly; but the ocean, Louisa knew, could be very erratic and terrifying. In spite of his resolution not to frighten her, George had been unable to resist the temptation of quoting Dickens's description of his stormy crossing when, said the Englishman, "the horizon seemed drunk and was flying about in all directions."

"Your beloved Boz is being lionized beyond comfort," continued George. "In New York, it seems, he tried to escape invitations that poured from every house and almost every street corner.... I happen to reach the cities he has visited a few weeks too late to meet him! People have little to say about Mrs. Dickens."

In subsequent letters he told Louisa of Dickens's sudden friendship with Cornelius G. Felton, the learned Greek professor who possessed a keen sense of humor. In comical contrast the two men could be seen swinging along Broadway—the ponderous, hugely carved, soberly dressed, but whimsical American and the little, active, dynamic Englishman in his startling red waistcoat. They walked, talked, laughed so loud that passers-by turned to look at them, and according to Sam Ward's letters to his friend

Longfellow, they often stopped to eat oysters and drink champagne. "Nothing but the interference of Mrs. D.," added Ward in a missive that later made the rounds of the select Boston Saturday Club, "prevented their being attached to each other like Siamese twins, a volume of Pickwick serving as the connecting membrane."

Louisa remembered this some years later when, living in Cambridge, she found herself seated next to Felton at a dinner of famous men. Awed by so much learning, she took refuge in the familiar subject of Boz, and from that moment her host had ears but for her as they spent the evening in a spirited exchange of Pickwickian sayings.

The newspaper clippings George occasionally sent his wife spoke eloquently of his success and popularity; the artist was swamped with orders, and his working days lengthened outrageously. How, wondered Louisa, could he write so much and so gaily before five in the morning when he had spent his evening at a reception, or a party, or theater, or else making innumerable calls from the moment twilight forced him to lay down his brushes? She worried. Next time, she would accompany him; the sea voyage lost its terror in her fear of his overwork.

Meanwhile the Yankee artist was meeting many Southerners and finding them utterly charming. Among them, Senator W. C. Preston, whose portrait he was now painting, vaunted constantly the beauties of South Carolina. An ardent Southerner though born in Philadelphia, William C. Preston had represented South Carolina in Washington since 1833, always clamoring for free trade, inviolable States' rights, and even nullification. Listening to him, Healy suddenly realized the bitterness of political factions and sensed a growing danger to the Union. His personal convictions made him wonder how such a fine man could defend gag laws, slavery, and class distinction, and still proclaim the United States Constitution.... But Preston, great nephew of the eloquent Patrick Henry and himself past master of dialectics, presented his arguments so plausibly that the painter felt bewildered if unconvinced.

In Paris in 1841 American subscribers had ordered from Healy a full-length portrait of Guizot that they had presented to the United States. President Tyler recommended that it be placed "to the best advantage" in the National Institute, of which Joel R. Poinsett, diplomat, ex-Secretary of War under Van Buren, a much-traveled and highly educated South Carolinian, was president.

In accordance with the presidential request, Poinsett had the painting placed in close proximity to the full-length portrait of George Washington, whose biography Guizot had recently completed. It aroused the public's curiosity and incidentally promoted the sale of Guizot's book. The papers in publishing the list of donors made a point of the fact that Captain James Funck of the *Oneida* refused any pay for the trouble and expense of bringing over the picture.

Charles King wrote an enthusiastic notice about the Guizot portrait in the *Daily National Intelligencer,* calling it a masterpiece and signing himself, "a fellow artist";* flattered and pleased, Healy sought out this amiable confrere, and the two artists saw much of each other.

Born in Newburyport in 1785, the veteran painter had studied in London with Alliston and Leslie; comparing notes about the

---

* I have seldom had the pleasure of seeing so beautifully perfect a masterpiece as the splendid, full-length likeness of M. Guizot by the distinguished young artist, Mr. Healy. So noble, calm, simple and characteristic is the posture of the Minister, so chaste and correct the drawing, so natural and harmonious the coloring, so rounded and full of bold relief is the whole figure without either harshness or rigidity, and so tasteful the disposition of all its parts, that it is impossible to view with an artist's eye this noble production of the pencil without feelings of exquisite delight and unqualified admiration. Certainly, nothing equal to this have I yet seen from any native artist; and one knows not whether most to applaud the skill of the painter or the magnanimous liberality of his Royal Patron. Louis-Philippe's generous attentions to Mr. Healy have set an example, patronizing merit, regardless of the accident of birthplace.

A FELLOW ARTIST

Washington *Daily National Intelligencer.* June 15, 1842.

Royal Academy, King and Healy marveled at the influence still exercised over the institution by Benjamin West, long dead.

"Personally," volunteered Healy, "I consider Stuart a greater painter than West."

"So do I, my dear fellow," agreed King.

Both felt that Stuart's influence through his many pupils as well as in his own work was more definitely American. As they walked, King showed Healy a less-known part of Washington, picturesque with its swarm of Negroes, men, women, and children, who lazed around, singing in their rich warm voices, happy-looking in their squalor, a gleaming white-toothed grin slashing their shiny faces.

It seemed difficult in this atmosphere of insouciance, with many undeniable signs of devotion between the Negroes and their white masters, to conjure up the horrors of slave ships and slave markets and the fundamental inhumanity of slavery. But Northerners were loud on the subject, and Healy's inner conviction as well as his New England upbringing agreed wholly with their views. The inhumanity, for him, was not effaced by individual kindness.

Saturday afternoons there was music outdoors, on the grounds of the White House—an innovation sponsored by the Tylers and universally approved by Washingtonians.

At this time Daniel Webster also sat to Healy and listened with pleasure to the artist's early memories of his oration at Bunker Hill in 1825. The American statesman felt flattered that King Louis Philippe should order his portrait and recounted with gusto the various conversations he had had with the Monarch during this famous journey of 1839. He laughed over the necessity of arraying himself in a makeshift court costume.

"Mrs. Webster liked it," he remarked with a twinkle.

Webster had been in Paris in the latter part of 1839, but Healy, newly married and just settled with his bride in Paris, had not seen him, though he had received at his studio a visit from Mrs. Webster and Mrs. Bates, who came to view his paintings, particularly his portrait of Mr. Joshua Bates, which was to be shown at the Royal Academy the following spring.

"Indeed, sir, I well remember their pleasure in your work," Webster assured him.

The superb figure, the majestic head of Webster made an inspiring model, and Healy, who had painted Maréchal Soult, Guizot, the Duke of Sussex, and King Louis Philippe, felt that he never had faced a more imposing and compelling personality. He worked feverishly, for Webster, constantly engaged from dawn till late at night, resented the time given to sittings. Despite this, the two men grew very friendly, and later, at other sittings, Healy was to see Webster on more intimate terms. Mrs. Webster accorded him a gracious reception and rejoiced with him when the British Minister, Lord Ashburton, at Webster's request, consented to sit for his portrait.

Healy found the Englishman, then negotiating the Webster-Ashburton Treaty, agreeable and interesting; they had many friends in common. Webster, perhaps feeling that someday these portraits might commemorate the treaty and perpetuate its authors, ordered duplicates for himself of his own and Lord Ashburton's portraits.

Back and forth went the artist, working, talking, visiting, enjoying his varied activities though he longed for the company of his wife and children and felt somewhat guilty at leaving them so long. He painted Daniel Carroll, of Duddington, and his daughter Maria Fitzhugh, fascinated by all the tales they told of an earlier Washington, for in those bygone days the Carrols owned almost a third of the land that would become a capital. Mrs. Moulton and her son Henry, of Virginia, sat for their portraits as did Mrs. Corbin and her son; Miss Noel of Baltimore; Mrs. John Cruger (nee Van Rensselaer) of New York and Thomas B. Wales of Phillips Exeter. In Boston in February, 1843, Healy painted Colonel Charles S. Greene of the *Boston Post,* a grandson of the revolutionary General Nathanael Greene, whose portrait by Peale Healy had copied for Louis Philippe. He also painted William Hickling Prescott at his beautiful home on Beacon Street. Everyone was praising the historian's *Conquest of Mexico,* about to go to press and already familiar to many Bostonians. A close friend of Edward Everett, whom Healy had painted in London, Prescott spoke of him and his family, of Charlotte Everett, whose portrait the artist had also painted and who, as Mrs. Henry Augustus Wise, was to play a prominent part in Washington life; later her husband's Virginia relatives would resent and blame her for Augustus Wise's antislavery attitude.

Prescott liked to recall his stay in England. Pointing to a frame with brass wires that held a carbonated sheet of paper on which he wrote with a stylus, the historian said:

"It was in London in 1815 that I discovered this noctograph and I have used it ever since; it saves my eyes."

In his student days at Harvard, Prescott was almost blinded by a crust of bread that hit the pupil of his eye; but in spite of his impaired sight and painful spells of illness, the New Englander never lost his bubbling spirits. Handsome, tall, erect, eminently hospitable, he shed gaiety and charm wherever he went. His enchanting house contained a study built over the drawing room and reached by a winding stairway through a secret door hidden by a bookcase. There hung the swords used by his two grandfathers, who fought on opposite sides during the American Revolution, and there he would receive delightfully the more intimate of his friends.

From Boston Healy went to Providence, where he saw relatives of Henry Wheaton, who, though minister to Berlin, often visited Paris, where he had lived many years.

So went the weeks and months, until Healy, finally aware that Louisa's patience was reaching the breaking point, packed up, made his adieus, and sailed for London, having promised to return the next year.

A joyful reunion in England inspired him to paint a romantic picture—"Happy Moments"; it was exhibited at the Royal Academy. Mindful of Sully's remarks about the Washington portrait, he searched and finally found it in London in the collection of John D. Lewis and obtained permission to retouch his copy, thus carrying out the King's express wish. He also made for Versailles a copy of Queen Elizabeth's portrait by Zuccaro, in the Marquis of Salisbury's collection.

At the Tuileries, Louis Philippe gathered a number of persons to view the American artist's work; they all admired his copy of Washington; Calhoun's and Tyler's distinguished clear-cut features impressed the audience; Lord Ashburton was no stranger to them, but Webster attracted most of the attention. Standing before that compelling head, one of the court ladies asked if he had ever visited France. When Healy answered in the affirmative, to the intense amusement of others, she exclaimed in anguish:

"To think that I missed seeing him!"

Healy promised that if Webster came again, he would arrange for her a personal encounter.

The King wanted to hear everything about Healy's American sojourn. He asked news of the families he had known in his days of exile, was tremendously interested in the development of Washington and the cultural progress of New York with its new Board of Education and infant Philharmonic Society; Boston's increasing trade aroused his wonder. With a twinkle Louis Philippe asked the artist if Boston ladies still quoted metaphysics and literature over their teacups.

"More than I remembered, Sire," answered Healy. "But some of them seem quite revolutionary in their views. There is a Miss Fuller who writes remarkably well and uses her talents to plead for women's rights!"

"Oh, so you have your George Sand," smiled the King, and as Healy seemed ready to protest, added, "of course, allowing for differences in genius and Puritan point of view." It always amazed the American to discover how well informed the King remained on the subject of the United States.

Louis Philippe listened to Healy's idea of a picture representing the Senate scene of January, 1830, when Webster made his celebrated reply to Hayne.

"It is such a typically American scene, Your Majesty," the painter explained, describing the orator's commanding figure as the center of a picture, the senators grouped around him, and above, in the Senate gallery, crowds of pretty women from the fashionable world of 1830. "A homely setting, yet an unforgettable day with Webster's ringing words: 'Liberty and Union... now and forever....'"

The King pondered, moved as Frenchmen always are by the galvanizing power of words.

"It could be," he murmured, "a companion panel to our Franklin at court. But how about those portraits, Mr. Healy?"

George, realizing that he had interested the Monarch in his idea, explained:

"Portraits from life, Your Majesty. Most of these men and women are still living. I am sure they would all be pleased to see themselves on the walls of Versailles, and none of them would object to having twelve or thirteen years taken from their features!"

"I'll think it over, Mr. Healy. We'll speak of it again."

George's elation communicated itself to Louisa, who had been busy settling their studio apartment at 10 rue de la Paix. Dubourjal and Couture watched him sketch his new project. As in the Franklin picture his hero must dominate the scene, but the Senate chamber lacked the vividness of a Versailles throne room. To correct this, he might fill the balcony circle with attractive women in colorful clothes. Over the speaker's desk the American eagle symbolically spread its wings.

Orders multiplied, and the children thrived while Louisa expected another addition to the family. George worked faithfully at his Franklin pictures; he had some difficulty in finding original portraits of Silas Deane and Arthur Lee, who had been with Franklin at Versailles on that March day of 1778; Rémusat gave him pictures of Vergennes and also of Cardinal de Rohan, whose red robe made a dashing splotch of color in the background. As he worked, the artist realized how different these two paintings would be. In the American setting Webster must furnish the whole dramatic effect. It held a challenge; Healy would picture the rugged quality of American leaders. When the King, greatly pleased with the progress of his Franklin canvas, suggested that he complete this picture before undertaking the other ambitious project, the artist again urged the tremendous advantage of painting the American portraits from life, instead of waiting until the participants in that scene of 1830 had grown too old or died; he won his point.

That winter in Paris, on December 8, 1843, a girl—Mary—was born to the happy couple, but her advent again prevented Louisa from accompanying her husband on his second return to America. So, once more, the following spring of 1844, Healy prepared to cross the ocean without his wife.

Before leaving he saw eight of his portraits (Baron and Baronne Theodore de Vareigne, Mrs. Moulton and her son Henry, the writer Oliver Gibbes, Major Poussin, Charles Draper, and Mr. Deacon) well placed at the March Salon in the Louvre; and as he once more installed his family in London with Louisa's mother, he sent five paintings—King Louis Philippe, Lord Ashburton, Mr. Stevenson, Miss Everett, and Master Corbin—to be shown at the May exhibit of the Royal Academy.

"Don't stay away too long!" begged Louisa. "I wish Dubourjal could go with you."

"That's a marvelous idea! I'm sure I can secure enough orders for him. Do you think he would join me in Boston?" he asked.

"I am sure he would," answered Louisa, confident that a little note from her to their devoted friend would decide him to cross

the ocean. She was right. In June, 1844, the French artist's name
appeared on the passenger list of the *Argo,* sailing westward
toward Healy's native land. On July 1 the breath-taking view of
New York harbor burst upon Dubourjal, who soon caught sight
of George waiting for him at the wharf. After the dazzling
effect of the sunny bay, the wide ribbon of the Hudson shimmer-
ing under a blue sky, it was a shock to the Frenchman to find the
landing docks rickety, dirty, and noisy, and the surrounding
streets anything but inviting. However, as soon as the customs
officials let him go, George installed Dubourjal with his bags in
an open landau; they left the shabby quarter, and the whole
aspect changed. It was very hot, but not unbearably so, thanks to
an occasional breeze. At the hotel Dubourjal exclaimed with
horror when George proudly offered him ice water, which a
bellboy brought in.

"You want to kill me?" he asked his friend, who expatiated on
the virtues of iced drinks in hot weather. Indeed little "Madame"
had been right, thought Edme; her husband needed a guardian!

In spite of merciless summer heat and dangerous iced water,
Dubourjal soon became acclimated and grew to love "the land
of the free." His close companionship with George grew even
closer in a congenial atmosphere.

"Americans are simpler, easier to live with than the English,"
he confided to his friend.

Boston took Edme Dubourjal into its rigid bosom with the
same kindliness London had shown him. Bostonians liked his
charming manners, his quaint French accent, his unfailing sense
of fun, and sparkling brown eyes. More to the point, they liked
his work—miniatures, pen and pencil sketches, precise and refined. On board the *Argo,* he had sketched several passengers,
among them the French-American Tancred Savageau, whose
family has carefully preserved the delicate portrait.

The work already accomplished by George for the Webster
composition amazed him; sketches were piled all over the studio,

some of them bare outlines, others almost finished portraits. In Washington, several of the men who well remembered that epoch-making scene gladly sat to Healy when the artist explained the King's desire to place this American picture at Versailles. Healy took great delight in introducing into the picture Charles Tucker, whose portrait had been his first exhibit at Boston's Athenaeum.

Webster's opponent in the controversy, Senator Robert Y. Hayne, had died in 1839, but his widow furnished data, and his son sat for the coloring. Webster, in spite of cutting remarks about pestering artists, willingly posed again. He appreciated the honor of seeing one of his most significant moments preserved for history, and added many details to those Healy already knew about the debate and the persons present.

It was good to find that in this new democracy political fights did not always end in estrangement.

There was the story of a woman admirer who immediately after the debate pressed forward toward Webster, gushing:

"Oh! Mr. Webster, you had better die now and rest your fame on that speech!"

But Hayne, who heard her, protested at once.

"You ought *not* to die! A man who makes such speeches should never die."

And that same evening at the President's reception the two men greeted each other in friendly manner.

Webster's closing words, "Liberty and Union, one and inseparable, now and forever," seemed in the artist's mind to illumine the projected picture. Healy went to several meetings of the Senate, absorbing the atmosphere. In the picture, John C. Calhoun as Vice-President occupies the chair on the rostrum—a conspicuous spot for his handsome figure. Between Calhoun and the standing orator sit a number of senators; in the front row, though somewhat back, Robert G. Hayne, full face, listens intently to the man bent on tearing down his arguments of the preceding day. Near him John Tyler with his warm outdoor coloring offers a startling contrast to his other neighbor, the white-haired and white-collared Tazewell, that ardent advocate of States' rights who always spoke of his native Virginia as "my country." Their portraits Healy painted in Washington, and now in Boston he was painting many Northerners.

"George," Dubourjal reproached him, "you are putting in more people than were there!"

"More?" Healy laughed. "I could not possibly crowd in all who were present! But in the gallery I can take a few liberties and include some of our friends."

"Was Mrs. Otis among the listeners?"

"Of course. She was always there when anything important happened," replied the artist with conviction.

Dubourjal smiled. This most honest of men was quite capable, he believed, of stretching the truth a little for the sake of the picture; Mrs. Otis and her friends in the balcony would undoubtedly lend a brightening note. Dubourjal admired the lady but thought her somewhat overpowering. American women seemed to him to lord it over men and society more even than the most exacting French coquette!

"You would like the South," George assured him. "It has an old-world chivalry. There also the women expect everything from gentlemen—and get it, but in a more subtle way than our Boston ladies."

Dubourjal worried about the terrific expense this huge picture entailed; it would take years. . . .

"I know," answered the American, shaking his head as if to throw off the bothersome question. "But I shall continue taking orders for portraits and sell some landscapes."

As Healy hoped, many of the sitters ordered their portraits as painted in the picture, and many ladies appeared at his studio dressed in becoming 1830 costumes resurrected from their attic trunks.

As the fall of 1844 approached, Dubourjal, amazed at himself, promised to return with his friend the following year; both men had orders ahead that might occupy several months, and Healy hoped that on this next visit his wife would at last be able to accompany him.

In London, they saw many friends and spent companionable days with the Faulkners, storing up happy memories that they treasured all the more when to their great sorrow a few months later Sir Arthur, apparently vigorous to the last, suddenly died in an epidemic of cholera.

Back in Paris with the family, they took up once more the busy life George enjoyed. Louisa had her hands full with three growing children to be soon followed by a fourth. Her husband made constant demands upon her time; he loved to listen to her reading as he worked, and in this way they kept well abreast of current publications. Every new Dickens novel enchanted them, and among the French writers they chose the romantics: George Sand, Alexandre Dumas, Eugène Sue. Balzac they thought engrossing but too somber. History appealed to them and was necessary as a background for George's projected paintings. They read Alexis de Tocqueville's book on American democracy and consulted Guizot in the choice of other serious reading.

Thus the winter passed, and the beginning of 1845 saw Healy deep in his two great compositions, turning from one to the other when either threatened to grow stale; the contrast was vivifying. Louisa felt that they had reached the security she desired when another change occurred.

Chapter XV

A SITTING AT THE HERMITAGE

FROM London came word that Louisa's father had died in his sleep, and though death for him was a blessed release, it left his widow rudderless. The Healys persuaded Mrs. Phipps to return with them to France; she who had ruled her home so many years found it hard to live even with her favorite daughter. To make the change more complete they moved out to Versailles where the grandmother and the children might enjoy country air, sit under the trees, or run through the shaded avenues of that beautiful park. There they spent most of their day while Healy worked at the Palace or in his studio, Louisa reading to him, able now to remain with her husband without worry about the children.

Meanwhile Mrs. Phipps, more domestically inclined than her daughter, busied herself with homely occupations; she solaced her inner loneliness with practical activities that proved she could still be of use in this world. She would not, however, learn French, though the children refused to answer in her own tongue. It created at times amusing incidents when Arthur and Agnes (baby Mary's cooing had as yet no language) made friends in the park with two little French boys, Tiburce and Albert de Mare, and their mother, who refused as stubbornly to speak anything but French. The two ladies, except when Louisa joined them, found themselves communicating by signs or through baby interpretations! Nature's healing process made Mrs. Phipps more contented, and the children soon learned to twist around

their little finger this severe-sounding Grandmama with humorous eyes. George and Louisa made her feel that her presence
rendered their life easier and pleasanter.

That spring of 1845 at the Paris Salon, Healy exhibited a new
portrait of the King and another one of General Cass; he also
showed a particularly fine child's portrait—that of young Corbin.
The notices about his work became more flattering; he was
making a place for himself in the French capital as he had in
London. The Healys felt more secure than they ever had, and
life seemed to settle into the routine Louisa thought that she
craved.

Then most unexpectedly the artist received a hurry call from
the King.

At the Tuileries, Louis Philippe greeted him with:

"Mr. Healy! It seems that General Jackson is very ill. I must
have his portrait! Can you start at once for the Hermitage?"

The artist gasped, and meekly said, "Yes, Sire."

Louisa received the exciting news with consternation. Her
husband found it difficult to persuade her that his absence would
seem shorter now that she had her mother with her and that
they lived in the country.

"It's terribly lonely here, dear...."

"If you prefer living in Paris—" But she protested at once.

"Oh, no! Not without you. We shall really be very comfortable
here, with summer coming."

"And happy?" asked her husband.

Louisa swallowed hard.

"I'll try," she murmured.

So Healy left in April. Another crossing, another rapid journey,
another separation. He gave himself no time for regret. On the
other shore he did not even take an extra day to see his sister in
Baltimore; he must reach the Hermitage in time....

News of Jackson's grave condition stirred the capital. Newspapers reported the constant inquiries received about the ex-

President's health, and even his bitterest enemies had no word against him now.

George Healy sped straight on to Nashville as fast as train, boat, and horse could carry him. In the Tennessee city he obtained a fresh horse and, shown the way to the Hermitage, rode on.

The old covered bridge that spanned Stone River led to a blockhouse where, his informant told him, Jackson and Coffee kept store in the early days. There they had contracted to build boats for Aaron Burr. Intent on reaching his goal, the artist scarcely noticed Clove Bottoms in ruin, but he glowed at the luxuriant growth of trees—how wonderful it would be to pitch an easel here and paint! The country seemed wild, for the thousand acres that comprised the Hermitage were only a little more than a third under cultivation.

At last, after following a well-worn path that wound in and out among the trees, Healy came to a long, superb, tree-lined, private road leading to the large, white-pilastered, and porticoed house that was the Hermitage. His heart thumped. He had at last reached the goal set him by the King.

Negroes gathered as the rider stopped his horse at the entrance. While one helped him alight, another took down the bag that held his paint and canvas, yet another led the horse away, and he was ushered through a stately hall adorned with busts of Cass and Jackson himself into a large sitting room. On a sofa, propped by a bolster while a Negro boy waved a peacock fly brush to shoo the flies away from his head, a gaunt old man was resting. With an abruptness that his inner shyness often brought on, the painter blurted his request. The General looked up, then said bluntly:

"Impossible, sir, impossible," he said. "I'm a sick man, a dying man. Can't sit, not for any king in Christendom!"

"But, General, His Majesty wishes to place your portrait by the side of Washington's and—"

"Sorry, sorry. Can't do it. Good day, sir."

Baffled, angry, hurt, and amazed, for he was unused to rebuffs,

Healy left the Hermitage, mounted his horse, and rode wearily back to Nashville. A dismal ride; he had failed. All that hurry in vain. On his journey from France, for a little over a month, he had dreamed of this meeting with "Old Hickory" and pictured it in a hundred different ways, but not once like this. Irascible old gentleman! Never gave him a chance to explain! Surely, there must be some way....

Back at the hotel, somewhat restored by a hearty meal, the artist pondered. Suddenly he remembered Justice Catron of the Supreme Court, whose home was in Nashville.

"Is Judge Catron in the city?" he asked at the desk.

"Yes, sir. His house is just a few minutes away."

Following directions, George lost no time in presenting his name at the door of Judge Catron's house. There with true Southern hospitality his host expressed delight at seeing him, installed him comfortably, had drinks brought, and then listened sympathetically to the traveler's tale of woe.

"Well, Mr. Healy," he offered, "perhaps all is not lost, and you are in luck, because Mrs. Jackson is staying with us. If anyone can ever make the General change his mind, she can. Wait here, please, sir, while I go and tell her."

In his absence Healy tried to remember all he had heard of "young Mrs. Jackson," as the residents called the wife of Andrew Jackson, Jr. The beautiful and adored wife of Jackson, Rachel Donelson Robarts, had died December 22, 1828, just a month before the General entered the White House as seventh President; they had no children of their own, but the artist remembered hearing that a baby nephew, one of twins born to Rachel's brother, Severn Donelson, had been adopted at birth by the General and Mrs. Jackson. He was Andrew Jackson, Jr., and must now be a man slightly older than Healy, though naturally enough treated as a boy by all these old-timers. Mrs. Jackson, Jr., entered with the Judge—a pleasant-faced woman who looked at him curiously.

"Judge Catron tells me you have come from the King of France to paint Father's portrait, Mr. Healy?"

Healy bowed.

"I am evidently a poor messenger," he admitted ruefully. "The General would not listen...."

Both Mrs. Jackson and the Judge smiled; they could easily imagine the helplessness of a stranger before certain moods of the stubborn man.

"Father," she explained, "is sometimes a little suspicious of foreigners."

"Foreigners!" exclaimed Healy, stung to the quick. "But I am an American!"

Healy blushed then at her frank examination of his clothes, his mustache, and sighed. Yes, he probably looked foreign out here, in these far reaches of Tennessee. A little stiffly he drew from his pocket the King's letter and with a bow presented it to the lady, while the Judge looked on, amused. He had already told Sarah of Healy's mission and success in Washington three years back. This was no adventurer, no impostor.

The letter with its royal stamp, its official tone, and the praise for the American artist G. P. A. Healy, whose brush could only do honor to America's great hero, General Jackson, impressed her immensely.

"Did you show this letter to Father?" she asked.

"He gave me no chance!"

Judge Catron then added his encouragement. If the General felt that it would please his "dear child," as he called Sarah, he might relent. And the artist, slightly comforted, returned to the hotel, where excitement and anxiety kept him awake most of the night.

Each time his eyes closed with fatigue, some new picture of an irate fighting general would rouse the sleeper, and sitting bolt upright on his uneasy bed, Healy would see the terrifying old man passing through a hundred different phases of his adventurous life—the young frontiersman, the soldier, the captain, the General sweeping his way through New Orleans, ignorant of the fact that peace was signed, humiliating the English, who hated him. And then an amusing note would slip in, the great actress Fanny Kemble crossing to America in 1832, hearing the name so often that in exasperation she exclaimed, "Hang General Jackson!" though a year later she was to impersonate him proudly and be painted thus by Earle. For by that time General Jackson was President of the United States after a thrilling career as a fighting judge in Tennessee; after also—but Healy was vague on this subject in his diary—some scandal about his marriage.... Before morning, Healy felt as if he had lived centuries with this dynamic idol of America.

The French also considered Jackson a colorful hero. Louis Philippe had thought enough of Jackson to make Healy stop all he was doing in order to reach the old warrior in time, and wide awake now, the artist prayed that Judge Catron might be right, that Mrs. Jackson would obtain those sittings. He could not go back defeated.

At ten the next morning, Andrew Jackson, Jr., drove up to the hotel with the assurance that his father would pose, and together they drove out to the Hermitage.

A very different reception awaited him, and George Healy was given a taste of Jackson's charm, though the outspoken old man once more chided him with this admonition:

"Young man, always show your credentials."

The artist's evident amazement at the thought that anyone could distrust him immediately won them over, and from that moment, he was made one of the household. The Negro servants looked on him with awe—a man sent over by a king to paint their beloved "Massa"! Never had the American known service so admiringly and devotedly tendered. Yet imagination must have worked actively in one of the slaves, Alfred, who years later in the Hermitage, transformed into a shrine for tourists, would

point to the Healy portrait of Jackson and tell how the artist
threw himself on his knees before the General and wept, implor-
ing him to sit for a last portrait! Perhaps George Healy felt
desperate enough, but the actions described certainly a romantic Negro's imagining. Long after Healy's death, two of his
very dignified daughters heard the old Negro's incredible version
that shocked them into silence. Alfred died at the Hermitage, in
1901, aged ninety-nine, and had become quite a feature of the
place. Once Judge de Witt asked him if he thought General
Jackson got to Heaven, at which the old Negro replied, "If General Jackson takes it into his head to git to Heaven, who's gwine
to keep him out?"

The sittings, tiring though they were to the dying seventy-eight-
year-old hero, brought out vivid accounts of past events, sometimes only a murmur from the shapely lips, but to his last breath
Jackson retained his gift of picturesque speech. Earle, Vanderlyn,
Jarvis, Sully, and many others had painted him—a tempting
model for any artist, with his long, strong face and burning eyes,
his thin, tall figure and proud bearing; his love of horses naturally
encouraged equestrian presentations, and later, when Healy was
commissioned to paint a portrait of Jackson for the Capitol, he
also painted him standing by his horse—using for the animal
George Healy's own favorite rider.

This, however, was to be but a head—picturesque with the
long white hair parted framing startlingly the gaunt visage and
deep, luminous eyes.

To Healy's amazement, visitors came daily to see the "Chief,"
and to all he showed the same kindness and courtesy though he
must have longed for rest.

"No," countered Andrew Jackson, Jr., "Father won't rest; it
isn't in him to do so! He'd never forgive us for turning away his
old friends."

Yet each day brought new concern about his health. Healy
worked at high speed, an inner prompting telling him that he

must hasten this final record of an indomitable spirit and that it must prove worthy of the model.

So pleased was the family with the result that Sarah begged for a replica for herself and even obtained from the old General the promise of more sittings. After this Jackson wanted the artist to paint his "dear child"—but Healy's commission included a portrait of Henry Clay, and Jackson's political rival was supposed to be in Nashville. Healy felt he must go.

"Always do your duty, young man," was Jackson's only comment as George Healy left his host with a heavy heart. Chance, however, came to his rescue. In Nashville, John Bell informed him that Clay's boat had run aground on the Ohio, and gladly, his conscience clear, the artist went back to the Hermitage. They received him as the prodigal returned, and the painter set to work.

Between sittings Jackson showed him a pair of pistols given by Lafayette to Washington, which he intended to leave in his will to George Washington Lafayette; he spoke of Lafayette's stay with his son at the Hermitage in the spring of 1825; and Healy, visualizing again the Boston pageant, thought he heard across the years Webster's rich, penetrating voice. Webster ... the contrast between those two men struck the artist constantly as he listened to his model and watched the mobile face still so expressive though marred by coming death. How different from the scholarly New Englander!

Had he searched among America's great leaders for totally opposed types, Healy could not have found two more striking examples than Webster, the steady, logical Northerner who worked up to enthusiasm and carried his listeners by art and force of argument, and Jackson, the fiery Southern soldier, always in action, leading his party as he had led his soldiers to battle. Webster, man of the world, used his eloquence in lawyerlike fashion; Jackson, blunt, forced obstacles out of his way; both showed an amazing capacity for making and holding friends, and in both willful, forceful men, personal consideration gave way before their love of America and their faith in the United States. During that famous Hayne-Webster debate in the Senate in 1830, in spite of himself, Jackson had recognized the truth and power of Webster's stand for union and disagreed with his friend Hayne's willingness to see the States fall apart.

The artist spoke of Lewis Cass, Jackson's devoted friend. With all his European polish Cass possessed much of the ex-President's pioneering spirit as well as his love of rugged vast spaces. The minister was still fighting bitterly what he called Webster's pro-British attitude since the Webster-Ashburton Treaty; never would he accept the logical and inevitable rapprochement between the United States and Great Britain.

There were days when the General could neither pose nor talk; Healy, with his host's permission, made a copy of Jarvis's portrait for his own collection. Around him were varied artists' conceptions of Jackson's striking personality, and such was the model's character that even a poor painting became arresting.

From the talk of friends and the naïve expressions of devoted Negroes, the artist understood how Rachel Donelson's spirit still pervaded the whole place; he formed a touching picture of the wife so loved and so maligned, who now reposed in the Victorian tomb erected on the grounds by her stricken husband. She it was who brought such a profusion of flowers to the Hermitage, who added color and cheerfulness to the severe green and white background. Her love had sustained Jackson through difficult years, but both suffered from the vindictive cunning of her first husband, Robarts, who meant to ruin Jackson's career. He let them go through a marriage ceremony in the belief that a divorce had been pronounced and then maliciously shocked the world with a suit for divorce that stamped their union and made necessary a second marriage ceremony. It did not break Jackson as Robarts hoped, but it affected Rachel deeply and undermined her health. To Jackson, the fact that she did not enter the White House with him made his triumph taste very flat.

It was a dramatic story they told Healy of that December, 1828, after the brilliant victory over other presidential candidates when, proud and happy, he prepared with Rachel to leave for Washington. On the seventeenth she was taken suddenly ill. On the twenty-second she was dead. Jackson had her buried at the Hermitage, and instead of the banquet prepared to celebrate his triumph, the city of Nashville stopped all business while the bells tolled a whole hour. The new President's last act before leaving for the capital was to plant four willows around Rachel's grave.

January, 1829, in Washington, though it marked the apex of his glory, was a black month for him, and the darkness never quite lifted from his soul. He entered the White House on March 4, and after eight arduous years of presidency left it undaunted in spirit but broken in health. Healy, blessed with a sound body, shuddered when he heard that for years Jackson had never been free from pain one full day—an hour perhaps, or two.... No wonder death held no terror.

Visitors added innumerable tales to the growing legend of the General. "Old Hickory's" stubbornness—of which Healy had suffered on his first unfortunate arrival—furnished endless anecdotes: Davis told Healy that once, speaking of one of his horses, Jackson said it was "seventeen feet high."

"You mean seventeen hands, do you not?"

"What did I say?"

"Seventeen feet."

"Well, by the Almighty, seventeen feet it is!"

Never had a man more devoted friends. William Tyack, an old intimate, came when he heard the end was near. One can imagine him roaming disconsolately over the magnificent place, missing the General's company, wondering if his friend could get up, then going to his own room and writing in his diary the faithful record of the day. On May 28 he finds the ex-President "more comfortable than he has been," and the next day mentions that "Mr. Healy was enabled to make much progress in his work today and as usual the General received many visitors, more than thirty...." Friday, May 30, has a longer entry. "The General passed a bad night; no sleep; extremely feeble this morning. Mr. Healy, with much exertion on the part of the General, was enabled to finish the portrait on which he has labored with great care. It was presented to the General. After examining it for some minutes, he remarked to Mr. Healy: 'I am satisfied, Sir, that you stand at the head of your profession. If I may be allowed to judge of my own likeness, I can concur in the opinion of my family. This is the best that has been taken. I feel very much obliged to you, Sir, for the great labor and care that you have been pleased to bestow upon it.' The family were all highly gratified. I consider it the most perfect representation I have ever seen...." *

Sunday morning, June 8, Healy was awakened early by a long, low, pitiful wail—the cry of Negro servants, "a sort of cadenced cry," he wrote his wife, "in which I made out, 'Oh, Lord, oh, Lord, old Massa's dead,' and the cry caught up by the outside Negroes spread all over the plantation like a primitive dirge."

But it was only a fainting spell, and Dr. Esselman had Jackson transported from his armchair to the bed. Healy kept out of the way so as not to intrude upon the stricken household, but toward evening he knocked at the door for news. It was "young Jackson" who opened, tears in his eyes, and asked him to enter. "Come in, he's dying." George saw several persons around the bed; Major Lewis and the body servant were holding his head. The General rallied once more, looked around. "Why should you weep?" he asked. "I am in the hands of the Lord, who is about to relieve me. You should rejoice, not weep. We shall meet in Heaven—all, black and white." Those were his last words before he lapsed into unconsciousness, and when the breathing ceased, young Mrs. Jackson, who still held his hand, fainted.

---

* Diary of William Tyack, *Niles Register*, June 21, 1845.

George P. A. Healy
SELF PORTRAIT, c. 1875–1880
Newberry Library, Chicago

François Pierre Guillaume Guizot
FRENCH STATESMAN AND AUTHOR
1787–1874

Lord Edward Robert Bulwer-Lytton
ENGLISH DIPLOMATIST AND POET
1831–1891

John C. Calhoun
AMERICAN STATESMAN
1782–1850

Daniel Webster
AMERICAN STATESMAN
1782–1852

James G. Blaine
AMERICAN STATESMAN
1830–1893

4

William S. Archer
UNITED STATES SENATOR
1789–1855

William C. Preston
UNITED STATES SENATOR
1794–1860

Lord Ashburton
ENGLISH STATESMAN AND FINANCIER
1774–1848

Lord Richard Bickerton Pemell Lyons
ENGLISH DIPLOMATIST
1817–1887

Louis-Philippe
KING OF FRANCE
1773–1850

Louis A. Thiers
FRENCH STATESMAN AND HISTORIAN
1797–1877

Leon Gambetta
FRENCH STATESMAN
1838–1882

Charles I
KING OF ROUMANIA
1839–1914

8

Elizabeth
QUEEN OF ROUMANIA
1843–1916

Henry Clay
AMERICAN STATESMAN
1777–1852

Henry W. Longfellow
AMERICAN POET
1807–1882

Leander James McCormick
AMERICAN MANUFACTURER AND PHILANTHROPIST
1819–1900

Franz Liszt
HUNGARIAN PIANIST AND COMPOSER
1811–1886

Jenny Lind
SWEDISH SINGER
1820–1887

John McCloskey
ROMAN CATHOLIC PRELATE, FIRST AMERICAN CARDINAL
1810–1885

Mrs. William T. Sherman
ELLEN BOYLE EWING SHERMAN

Mrs. Andrew Stevenson
SALLIE COLES STEVENSON

Mrs. Stephen A. Douglas
ROSE ADELE CUTTS DOUGLAS

15

Nicholas Jean de Dieu Soult
DUKE OF DALMATIA, MARSHAL OF FRANCE
1769–1851

Chapter XVI

HENRY CLAY AT ASHLAND, 1845

OUTLINED against the bright blue sky stood the tall, spare figure of a man wearing a wide-brimmed hat, a man looking over his land. Every line of the body, the possessive pose of the head, proclaimed a master's survey of his domain—the blue grass at his feet, the farm and its many buildings, the woods farther off, and that stately attractive house with its numerous gables and chimney tops.

Down the dusty road George Healy paused to fill his eyes with the picture. So this was Ashland, and this the persuasive Mr. Henry Clay, whose portrait he had come to paint for Louis Philippe, King of France.

What a picture this would make! Those ash trees from which the place derived its name seemed peculiarly fitted to a large canvas; the brick house on an elevation, its two wings spreading low on each side, made a perfect background for the man. But, no, it was not the Kentucky farmer, it was the Washington statesman, the political leader, the orator, he must paint, and with a shrug of regret George Healy trudged on until, turning his head in that direction, Henry Clay saw a guest approaching.

With the outstretched hand of Southern hospitality, the owner of Ashland hastened forward, a light of recognition in his gray eyes, while the curiously wide, thin mouth broadened into a smile of welcome, and the rich voice that so often hypnotized Congress rang out cordially.

"Why, Mr. Healy! I did not know you had arrived. Why did

you not send word as soon as you reached Lexington? I would
have sent for you."

"Sir, I only landed this morning, and when they told me Ashland was a mile or so from the city I thought I'd walk—it's such
a wonderful day! I am most happy to be here."

"Kentucky weather, sir . . . a good omen. We have been expecting you, but I did not know the boat had docked. And so
you walked? Don't you know how proud we are of our horses?"

As he spoke two riders came trotting up, hailing Clay while
they stopped to alight near the house. Presentations over, Clay
called one of the Negroes who at the sound of hoofs had sprung
up from, it seemed to George, every direction. Their master sent
this one to fetch Mr. Healy's baggage at the hotel and detailed
another to show him to his room.

"There's a good north light in that room, Mr. Healy, in case
you wish to draw and paint there."

Soon the artist joined Clay and the other recent arrivals in the
superb library, where cool drinks and comfortable chairs induced
an atmosphere of social ease. Questions were asked about the
King and the rumored growing unrest in Paris, the mutual friends
Healy had seen in New York and Washington, but of his latest
mission not a word. No doubt, before he came down, they had
mentioned Healy's stay at the Hermitage and Jackson's death.
Yet the great rival's name was not brought up—only the portrait
the artist was now to paint.

"See where you prefer painting me, Mr. Healy," suggested his
host.

The library, a beautiful high-domed octagonal room in the
north wing, had too many intersecting and conflicting lights,
said the painter, explaining that, tempted as he might be by the
décor, he had to limit his canvas to the portrait.

"It is yourself and your fame His Majesty wishes to see represented in his Versailles gallery, sir."

Clay was pleased. The veil of sadness that had often shadowed

his features since the political defeat of 1844 that had climaxed
his presidential campaign lifted completely, and Healy saw only
the charming country gentleman, the diplomat and popular
leader who had for many years captivated the whole country. He
soon discovered, however, that Clay's interest in the land itself
was no pose; "Harry of the West" they still called him, a title the
artist understood when Clay took him over the estate, showing
his hemp fields, explaining how wild that country had been
only a few years back and what untold resources America still
offered to the pioneer.

"To stay free and independent, Mr. Healy," Clay repeated many
times, "we must remain close to the earth."

One day, during the two delightful months of Healy's prolonged visit, Clay chided his guest.

"You may know your way at court, young man," he remarked,
"but you'll never be a true courtier.... You haven't even asked to
see my cows, of which I am prouder than of my best speeches."

And as Healy looked at the cattle with evident ignorance of
their fine points, trying to remedy his omission by saying they
would look well in a picture, Clay watched him with his peculiar
wide smile and shook his head, murmuring:

"No courtier at all," an assurance which seemed to afford him
pleasure and greater liking for his compatriot.

But another time, when he questioned his visitor about the sincerity of Jackson's religious sentiment, the artist, filled with a vivid
memory of that touching last scene in the dying man's room,
exclaimed ardently:

"If ever a man was sincere in his faith, General Jackson was!"
Clay shot him a keen look and observed shortly:

"Ah! I see that it is with you as with all who approached that
man. He made you at once his partisan!"

It irked Clay more than anything that Jackson's partisans
after his death exhibited a hero-worship greater even than they
had shown in his lifetime. The General's idiosyncrasies became

examples of happy originality, and the hardships, the injustices he had suffered, turned him into a martyr and a saint. That Henry Clay, adored by so many, should have failed to secure the presidency Jackson had won without trying seemed to George's sitter one of those inexplicable turns of fate which he resented most bitterly. In regard to the question of religion, Healy did not inform him that rather wickedly Jackson had predicted Clay would either join the church or die drunk.

That summer in Kentucky and the long talks Healy held with his host as they followed his favorite serpentine walk shaded by superb trees, in a mood of friendly intimacy, caught the artist in Clay's hypnotic web of voice and words; it made him feel in strange accord with an unexpectedly sympathetic nature. Clay's human traits compensated for an indifference to art that otherwise would have seemed heathenish to the painter.

The great Congress leader let the young man speak, drew from him the story of his home life, showing his own strong family ties; if Healy quoted some of his children's sayings, the master of Ashland promptly matched this, showing off his grandchildren, whose visits constantly enlivened the farm, and when Clay mentioned the six daughters he had lost, his eyes filled with tears, and his voice broke. Ashland radiated a patriarchal atmosphere that appealed strongly to the artist's romantic and religious temperament, and while at times, watching Clay, Healy thought, "What an actor he would have made!" he corrected quickly this passing notion with compunction; how unfair to think of acting with a man so sincere!

Therefore the shock was great when some two years later, remembering this visit, Healy called on the Senator as he reached Washington; always a little too quick, he had followed the usher so closely that he overheard Clay exclaim wearily, looking at the name on the card, "What! Another! Well—show him in." It was too late to retreat, and while listening to an apparently delighted greeting—"You here, Mr. Healy! I thought you were with the

King," the artist found it difficult to adjust his feelings to this new Clay, and his response lacked its usual warmth.

But in 1845, on the farm, not hounded by political intruders, Henry Clay truly enjoyed his guests; the social and familial atmosphere of Ashland, graciously fostered by Mrs. Clay, kept in leash those violent outbursts against which the painter had been warned. The Kentuckian's friendly geniality turned the simplest gathering into a festive occasion, and he was constantly seeking some new form of entertainment for his guests.

There for the first time, at a dinner, the painter saw and heard a minstrel show. It was so new, so different from the revues in vogue, that Healy talked at length with the minstrels' leader, who asked the artist if he thought they might have success in England. Whether his enthusiastic assurance that the show would delight Englishmen decided him or not, Healy could not tell, but the following year, when he stopped in England, he found that the Negro minstrels were Queen Victoria's favorite entertainment and that the Kentucky band was overwhelmed with engagements.

The Hermitage's stream of visitors had been very different, with its undercurrent of death, from the bustling crowd constantly milling around Ashland. Amid gay voices with their soft Southern drawl and the deep-chested laughter of Negro servants, Clay's enveloping charm reached out to every arrival. Truly Dickens had defined him well—"a perfectly enchanting and irresistible man."

Among the visitors to Ashland came Healy's Paris friend, the painter Oliver Frazer, who now lived in Lexington and had recently finished a portrait of Mrs. Clay; a pupil of Matthew H. Jouett, Frazer had studied with Healy in Paris about ten years before, and the news of the latter's arrival delighted him.

"Make your home with me in town," he urged, "and use my studio to your heart's content; it will inspire me after you are gone!"

Healy looked forward to a few days in which they might take up the threads of their old comradeship. The two men exchanged reminiscences as the visiting artist worked on his Clay portrait and Frazer, with the statesman's consent, also made a pencil sketch. Restless and impatient by nature, Clay was a difficult model, yet he consented amiably enough to pose for two Healy portraits and the artist had the satisfaction of painting one on the Ashland grounds.

"You are a capital portrait painter, Mr. Healy," Clay told him one day. "You are the first to do justice to my mouth, and it is well pleased to express its gratitude."

Meanwhile, however, the statesman confided in a letter to his friend Charles Edwards Lester, the author and American consul at Genoa, that he had to pose for a portrait for the King of France, but having "submitted to that operation more than a hundred times," he felt great repugnance at doing so again. If this statement was exaggerated, it might be said that the annoyance existed not only on Clay's side; inwardly Healy fumed at the irregularity of sittings so often interrupted by new arrivals, and at his model's habit of taking a pinch of snuff or chewing a striped stick of peppermint candy just when he was trying to catch a particularly characteristic line of nose or mouth....

Occasionally, however, launched on some favorite subject, Clay forgot the passing of time, and then the portrait made progress. When Healy remarked that during one of his sittings Webster had referred to Clay as an astute treaty maker, the latter mentioned his one and only visit to Europe after the War of 1812 to draw up the Treaty of Ghent. In November, 1814, he had crossed the ocean to join John Quincy Adams, Russell, Gallatin, Bayard, and the British commissioners; the English wanted a London treaty, but Clay protested vigorously against meeting their defeated adversaries in their own capital, so they compromised on the neutral Flemish city. Both sides fought fiercely for every point, and Healy could well imagine Clay's persuasive manner covering an inflexible purpose that in the end won out. On December 14, 1814, the weary delegates affixed their signatures to the document while in New Orleans, unaware that war was over, General Jackson won his celebrated victory.

A subsequent commercial treaty called the commissioners to later conferences in London; during the interval Clay enjoyed two months of leisure, January and February, 1815, in the French capital, where he received many courtesies from the most polished diplomats in Europe.

"Madame de Staël received me delightfully in her salon in the rue du Bac," he told the painter.

"Was she as ugly as some critics say?" asked Healy curiously.

"She was so vivacious, so interesting and animated that you really could not notice her looks," he replied. "Hers was beauty of the mind."

This remarkable daughter of the Swiss banker who had become Louis XVI's minister hated Napoleon bitterly and professed a deep love for America—the true democracy. Clay met at her house the *gentilshommes négrophiles* who never lost an opportunity to bring up the slavery question; they expressed surprise at finding a Southerner in sympathy with their views.

"Slavery is an evil thing," Clay proclaimed, "but it can only be suppressed gradually." These gentlemen, he realized, would never understand conditions in the United States. He expounded his plan of organized colonies for freed American Negro slaves and tried in vain to make them see that were this done suddenly it would tear the whole fabric of the South, bringing a fatal disruption of the States. Fear of disunion ever ruled Clay's policy.

"Madame de Staël introduced me to Wellington," he continued, "and I found the Iron Duke far more affable than I had expected."

The artist gave a graphic description of Soult and Wellington acclaimed in the streets of London at the time of the Queen's coronation.

"To meet on friendly terms after the battle is much easier for
enemy soldiers than for politicians," remarked the Kentuckian;
he laughed at the painter's account of the Queen's visit to Wellington's beautiful estate, Walmer near Dover. She had intended to
remain a couple of days, and the Duke had turned his house
over to the Royal party, removing himself to the Ship Hotel at
Dover. The Queen's early dislike had apparently vanished, and
Wellington, providing lavish entertainment for his sovereign,
visited her daily. But Her Majesty contracted a cold that kept
her housed for three long weeks while amused Londoners wondered what expletives the crusty old general, addicted to his own
habits and comfort, allowed himself in the privacy of his hotel
room.

In spite of many delays, Clay's portrait advanced. Emotional,
quick to anger or to sympathy, the Kentuckian's face changed
expression so rapidly that Healy tried to put in the features more
than pencil and paint could reveal; some faces were dull—this
one confronted the artist with an excessive wealth of feeling.

The high forehead, the longish straggly hair whose blondness
had turned white, and the fiercely intelligent small eyes over a
long nose and wide, tight mouth gave Clay tremendous indi-
viduality. "A genial fox, but a fox," said Frothingham when he
saw the portrait; it was true that Clay relied more on his keen,
quick mind and his persuasive powers than on deep learning,
and until this last defeat, he had felt he could always outwit and
outtalk the most persistent of his enemies. And at this time of
political wrangles these were more numerous than ever.

Despite his quick temper and fighting spirit, he believed in
compromises; in his long political career he thus frequently
averted disaster, too prone perhaps to forget that a question postponed is far from settled. In their talks Healy discovered that,
lover of freedom though he was, Clay still retained the conservative spirit that could not accept radical measures; he seemed to
be forever straddling the forces that carried America forward

and those that would maintain an orderly, unchangeable form of life.

This attitude and his sensitivity to surrounding atmosphere made him somewhat of an opportunist. It explained the seemingly illogical and much-publicized letter on slavery that Clay had sent from Raleigh to the *National Intelligencer* in 1844, soft-pedaling antislavery and thus confusing the Northern Clay-ites without convincing the radical South. A Southerner with Northern trends, Clay opposed the immediate annexation of Texas, which, by adding a large slave territory to the Union, might wreck the balance of power between North and South. Against him Van Buren, a Northern man with Southern trends, led the Democrats, and while the Whigs nominated Clay with an overwhelming majority, Van Buren, unable to secure the nomination for himself, urged the candidacy of Polk, whose cry, "Texas or disunion," carried the state of New York and with it the election.

Healy caught many side lights of that hard-fought battle, filled with vituperations, slander, and whisperings; Clay's peculiar features lent themselves to caricatures, and there were lurid tales of his youth allegedly dominated by wine, women, and gambling. Once at a banquet, said the gossips, young Clay had climbed on the sixty-foot-long table, dancing the length of it, regardless of glass and china that littered the floor. Looking at his dignified host, Healy tried vainly to conjure up the picture of his lanky six feet, then young, limber, and graceful, performing a *pas seul* on the banquet table to the accompaniment of hilarious applause from disreputable companions—it didn't ring true. Later, it was proved inadmissible, even by his enemies.

On election day—that heartbreaking day for Clay—when the vociferous electors rushed en masse to announce the result in Washington, they discovered to their amazement that the news had preceded them flashed by the magnetic telegraph over a line just completed, the first public message in the world sent in this manner, to the lasting glory of its inventor, Samuel Finley Breese Morse, who thus relinquished his earlier fame as a painter. To Healy it brought back memories of his long past visit to Morse.

A lovable trait Healy discovered in his model was great generosity; at times it placed him in awkward straits; careless about money, Clay found himself seriously embarrassed in his finances after the campaign; too preoccupied to straighten his affairs and those of his son Thomas, he mortgaged his home for twenty thousand dollars. Faced with foreclosure, sad but resigned to the thought of losing his cherished Ashland, Clay went to his banker. The latter then announced with a happy grin that mortgage and debts had all been paid by a group of friends who wished to remain anonymous. It was their way of expressing their regard and their sorrow over his defeat. In the same spirit presents poured in from every part of the country—quantities of silver that delighted the younger members of the family and touched the parents; an old lady of ninety-three sent a counterpane made by her busy fingers. Under the warmth of these messages Clay's bitterness slowly melted. Yes, he was loved, even if he had made more enemies than any other political leader in Washington.

Healy thanked his stars that Clay chose to sit for his portrait at Ashland and not in the capital, where the artist's work had thrown him in close relation with the statesman's various *bêtes noires*—Calhoun, Tyler, Webster, who all, in or out of Congress, had tilted many a lance with Clay. In the country, daily contact with nature seemed to soften his mood as the rambling vines and roses softened the formal pillared entrance to the house at Ashland. The whole family responded to that special appeal of the soil, and Clay used to say with pride that his wife was a better farmer than he. In truth she took over the management many times when she could not accompany her husband to the capital, and Clay, who on leaving always handed her a good-sized check, knew that on his return she would hand it back to him with deep satisfaction. Their experiments in hemp fields, while not particularly profitable to them, set an example that brought prosperity to Kentucky.

It amused Healy extremely after his years of city life to see here farmers, small traders, politicians, artists, writers, and lawyers meeting in a common appreciation of Clay's agricultural efforts, all keenly aware of the value and tremendous future of American land.

At this time, Joel T. Hart, the sculptor, came to make a statue of Henry Clay ordered by a committee of women, indignant that their hero was not President. In this accidental association Healy and Hart laid the foundation of a friendship that developed abroad, for Hart preferred to work in Rome and took his materials there to complete the statue.

In the studio of Oliver Frazer at Lexington, Healy met Mrs. Matthew H. Jouett, widow of the artist who had brought to Kentucky the teachings of Gilbert Stuart. She consented to sit for the young man, and her portrait turned out to be one of the most delicate expressions of womanly kindness and dignity he ever painted.

As the time to leave approached, the artist visited Louisville, where, commissioned to paint several portraits, he promised an early return.

Word from Dubourjal in Boston informed him that Mr. John Quincy Adams declared himself ready to give the requested sittings.

So in the west, George Healy made his adieus. The day he left, Clay seemed very tired, his long face thinner than ever, his tall body as he stood in the twilight a mere shadow, and the artist's heart contracted at the thought that perhaps this was a final good-by.

In spite of the somber premonition, Healy saw Henry Clay several times again in Washington, but the statesman's health was failing, severely drained during the critical debates that shook Congress in 1848 and 1849.

Clay, when he began his noted speech early that year, was so weak that he had to be supported up the steps of the Capitol. Yet he spoke for three long hours, his voice gaining strength with the intensity of his feeling, and each day thereafter he continued to face his opponents, demanding for the territories acquired from Mexico no restriction or conditions in regard to slavery. As a sop to the irate Southerners, he agreed that slavery should not be abolished in the District of Columbia as long as it existed in the neighboring state of Maryland; and to pacify the Northerners, he insisted that traffic in slavery should be barred from the capital, but Congress was not to interfere with slave trade between slave states. The abolitionists fumed. Yet this compromise averted immediate secession. Ably supported by Stephen Douglas, Clay's proposals gained ground measure by measure. Zachary Taylor's unexpected death on July 9, 1850, made Millard Fillmore President, a partisan of the Kentuckian's policy.

But the struggle had lasted too long for Clay to savor his success; it had taken too much of his life's blood. After a vain attempt to recover his health in Cuba in 1851, he returned exhausted to Ashland, seeking his wife's care and the comfort of religion. He made a will leaving the use of Ashland to Mrs. Clay, various portions of his estate to his sons Thomas, John, and James with a trust fund for his feeble-minded son Theodore. There was a provision to free, after a number of years, the new children of his slaves with wages enough to transport them to those African colonies that, in Clay's mind, would solve the Negro problem. Back in Washington, Clay, in order to secure his successor among the Whig party, resigned his seat in the Senate, effective September 1, 1852. Death called him before that date. On June 28, they heard him murmur, "My mother—my dear wife!" and he spoke no more. At eleven o'clock the next morning he died. The funeral services in the Senate chamber brought an immense crowd, everyone deeply affected, most of all perhaps Daniel Webster, who was so soon to follow him.

Chapter XVII

JOHN QUINCY ADAMS IN BOSTON, 1845

IT was mid-August, 1845, when George Healy left Ashland for Boston.

"And now you are going to paint 'Old Man Eloquent,' " Clay remarked with a knowing smile that conveyed many conflicting memories. Then, apparently discarding all criticism, he added in more serious tones made impressive by his resonant voice, "Pray give him my sincere regard, sir. I saw much of him as his Secretary of State twenty years ago, and I claim that he is truly great— a patriot and a fine American."

Such a tribute from the sharp-tongued and embittered political leader struck Healy forcibly. Some two weeks later in Boston he repeated it to his model as he sketched the ex-President's half-length figure. Adams responded promptly.

"I can return the compliment—Mr. Clay is a fine man, difficult to get along with, but he gave me little trouble during my presidency." Then he added dryly, "He has certainly made up for it since!"

From Kentucky to New England was a wide jump—a gap unbridged. Captivated as he had been by the South, the artist's Yankee blood asserted itself in his native atmosphere. He felt more in his element facing John Quincy Adams than in the impressive surroundings of Jackson's Hermitage or of Clay's beautiful Ashland. This feeling would increase with every sitting though he had yet to fathom Adams's keen analytical mind and dry wit.

A fearless appreciation of himself and others fascinated Healy as the great American talked freely on an infinity of subjects. Even during that first sitting, they touched on art and travel, England, Berlin, Russia, home politics, and the violence of senatorial debates.

The artist thus caught glimpses of John Quincy Adams's early diplomatic career as secretary to his father, who had been urged by Washington himself to use this bright youth abroad in the service of their country. Then as Ambassador to Holland, young Adams stopped in England to deliver dispatches to John Jay. This was the time King George III asked, as the American was presented to him:

"Do all the Adamses belong to Massachusetts?"

"They do, sir," had replied Lord Granville.

Adams later represented his country in Berlin, and his next appointment took him to the far more important legation at St. Petersburg; a nephew, another Adams, accompanied him as secretary. If America knew little of Russia, the vast European nation knew still less of America, for when the new Minister presented himself at the city's gate, a St. Petersburg guard demanded by what right he sought to enter. The indignant nephew exclaimed:

"But this is the Ambassador from the United States."

"The United States?" and the guard's face expressed blank amazement as an officer hastened forward, full of apologies for the delay caused Mr. Adams. Czar Alexander showed the American great favor, and Mrs. Adams was soon made welcome at court.

In 1814, at St. Petersburg, Adams received orders to go to meet the British commissioners and United States delegates for a treaty to end the War of 1812—that same treaty Clay had described to Healy. Adams now told the artist of the dangerous journey his wife took through war-torn Europe to join him in Paris. With their little boy Charles, she had left the Russian capital on February 12, 1815, and was stopped at almost every step through Prussia. By the time they reached the French frontier, Napoleon was back from Elba, and the whole country seethed with hysterical joy or fury. Her German carriage attracted attention and at times caused violent demonstrations. One day she found herself caught in the midst of Napoleon's Imperial Guard. A courteous general approached the carriage, while murmurs grew loud around them. As soon as he discovered her identity, the officer turned to his men, saying:

"This is an American lady going to meet her husband in Paris!" at which they all shouted:

"*Vive les Américains! Vive Napoléon!*"

"Then you saw Napoleon enter Paris, sir?" asked Healy full of excited curiosity.

"Indeed, yes—and what a day!" Adams replied. "Louis XVIII had left the city the night before. From one end of the boulevards to the other the mounting shouts of '*Vive l'Empereur!*' drowned everything else. A pity Clay and Russell missed that; Clay had already left for London and Russell for Sweden; only Bayard and Gallatin were with me. It was March 21—Paris went wild! Two days later my wife and child arrived, and we spent some time at La Grange with Lafayette."

In his Boston studio in September, 1845, listening to a man who had seen much and had long shaped the course of United States policy, Healy felt himself part of that turbulent stream of American history. His alert mind opposed the widely contrasting personalities he had lately painted: Jackson, powerful and probably the best lawyer among them, his studiously acquired knowledge humanized by feeling and passionate eloquence; Calhoun, fiercely partisan, hard-working, ascetic, and austerely honest— on the order of Guizot; Clay, the most hypnotic and sensitive of all; now Adams, the most cultured—a man of stern integrity, inflexible independence, and wide understanding, capable also of deep enthusiasm.

What a strange unity of purpose bound them all, mused Healy; in the midst of their quarrels, friend or foe, they each represented a phase of America—Adams, who hated slavery and the Southern point of view; Calhoun, who accepted it and scorned the mercantile North; Clay, who placed his devouring ambition after his love of country; Webster, whose beacon was the Union, one and indivisible—they were all America, Healy's America, the democracy that must bring freedom to the world.

Charcoal in hand, Healy outlined the bald domed head whose whiteness, people said, turned red in anger and the face grown a little square with age framed in discreet sideburns, ears close to the head, a firm round chin resting on the high wings of a modish collar with white cravat.

Moving with his usual swiftness, the artist stepped up to his model to change his position, and Adams, watching him, let his straight mouth curve slightly in a smile that reached to his eyes as he said:

"You are quick in everything, Mr. Healy. Your painting, your movements; even your journey from Kentucky was very rapid."

"I was eager for these sittings, sir."

"But arriving only yesterday, how did you manage to find this studio? It smacks of magic!"

Healy laughed; the magic, he confessed, was only his friend Dubourjal's kindness. The latter had secured the studio and put it in order before his arrival. Adams looked around the painting room.

"I have been here before," he remarked. "This is where Page did the half length that is at Faneuil Hall."

"I saw it last year, sir."

Seizing his compass, the artist asked permission to measure the head. Since that incident at the Tuileries he had been careful never to surprise his sitters with his innocent instrument.

"Do you know, Mr. Healy," noted Adams, "that of all the

artists to whom I have sat, you are the first since Copley to use
the compass? Copley when he painted my father's full-length
portrait measured even the arms, legs, and body."

This detail interested Healy, who remarked that his first portrait study had been a copy of John Quincy Adams's youthful
head by Copley.

"That portrait, Mr. Healy, was painted in England, and Copley
sent it as a present to my mother in recognition of some service
I had rendered him."

"You have sat to many painters, sir...." George Healy hesitated a moment. "I hope you do not look upon us as Mr. Webster
does. He says we are like horseflies: 'Brush them off on one side
and they return on the other.'"

The old gentleman chuckled.

"It sounds like Webster! No, sir; there are, I admit, some dull
men in your profession, but it is my good fortune to count several
painters among my most agreeable acquaintances."

They mentioned artists in America and abroad; they spoke of
the Royal Academy and of American-born Leslie, the friend of
Washington Allston, Charles King, Washington Irving, and
Coleridge, who in his early London days had shared quarters
with Morse on Fitzroy Square—that delightful spot associated
in Healy's mind with happy memories of his courtship.

"You must see the likeness Mr. Leslie took of Mrs. Adams,"
said his sitter, adding some remark about his marriage abroad
with a London-born American young lady.

"I was married in London!" exclaimed Healy. "My wife,
Louisa Phipps, is English."

"Louisa? That is my wife's name also." And the two men,
generations apart, looked at each other with reticent understanding while Adams continued somewhat sententiously but
with evident sincerity, "A happy marriage is the greatest help
to a man's career and a gift of God."

From that moment the painter's awed admiration for the ex-

President became tinged with a respectfully affectionate regard. When the clock of the Old South struck two, John Quincy Adams sprang up like a young man, and Healy thanked him profusely for having made his first sitting so interesting.

"I consider it an honor, sir, to sit for you at the request of King Louis Philippe," graciously answered the ex-President.

Every sitting brought out some new bit of wisdom and memories that reached far back; Adams's cutting judgment added salt to the conversation. Healy's ardent Americanism pleased the New Englander but also amused him; he did not share the painter's enthusiasm for some of his contemporaries. Healy's intense admiration for Webster particularly aroused his bile— the "godlike Daniel" irked Mr. Adams, who indulged in caustic remarks.

"Yes, a gigantic intellect," he admitted, "but a ravenous ambition," and noting the painter's pained surprise, forbore to add what he had written in his diary—"a rotten heart."

They spoke of writers and actors. Adams always felt a keen interest in acting; he had discussed Shakespeare with Mr. Hackett; he knew Kemble and Keane and Mrs. Siddons; had lunched with Fannie Kemble before she became Mrs. Butler.

Occasionally the old gentleman nodded, and Healy tried to attribute this to thought rather than fatigue, for he was very unwilling to shorten the sittings. In fact, the minute Adams raised his blue eyes, their penetrating glance in spite of seventy-eight years of active life showed no sign of weariness, but, remembering Copley's early portrait of the young man glowing with health, Healy recognized that age, which could not dull Adams's spirit, had sharpened the nose, straightened the shapely mouth, and whitened the fair skin, so different from Clay's deep tan and Webster's dark complexion.

One day Healy presented to Mr. Adams his friend Dubourjal, who marveled at the American's flawlessly fluent French.

"I was in school at Passy with Franklin's grandson Benjamin

Bache, Monsieur Dubourjal," said Adams in his peculiar high-keyed voice, "and at that time French seemed easier than English."

Healy mentioned Lafayette, who had been Adams's guest at the White House on his last visit before embarking on the *Brandywine,* the frigate christened to commemorate a battle where Lafayette received his first wound. He spoke of the hero's funeral in Paris in 1834, and Adams said that on the last day of that year he had delivered Lafayette's eulogy in Washington before a crowded and deeply moved House and Senate.

"During the Terror," Adams added, "I was able to help Madame de Lafayette's escape from France." And as the two men looked up inquiringly, he explained: "Her money had been confiscated; fortunately our American dollars came to her rescue, and with her two daughters she joined her husband in his Austrian prison; their son, you know, was in America at that time."

According to other memoirs Adams was not alone in helping the Marquise to escape. Both Healy and Dubourjal dwelt with emotion on the hardships of prison years at Olmütz. It was during Lafayette's last visit to the United States that Adams became President.

"Before that," he told them, "as Secretary of State I sat next to Lafayette at a banquet in Alexandria when news came of Louis XVIII's death, and the mayor hesitated about giving the sad tidings to the nation's guest. I took the task upon myself as I knew there was no love lost between the King and the General." Here Adams chuckled. "Lafayette was obliged to put his hand before his mouth to conceal an unseemly smile."

While speaking of historical events, Dubourjal expatiated on his friend Healy's two large pictures for Versailles, "Franklin at the Court of Louis XVI" and "Webster Replying to Hayne," and Healy explained that his first impression of Daniel Webster had been at the Bunker Hill ceremonies of 1825.

"I, sir, heard the cannon of that battle fifty years before," remarked Adams. "I was eight and my mother held my hand as we listened to the crack of muskets and watched the puffs of smoke."

About Revolutionary heroes, Healy's sitter possessed an endless fund of information. He spoke of Joseph Warren, whose portrait Healy had copied for Louis Philippe's gallery.

"Dr. Warren with my father belonged to the first three provisional Congresses," Adams said. "Having no military qualifications, he refused to lead a regiment at Bunker Hill but fought on the battlefield—and there he fell, his face practically shot away. Later Paul Revere recognized his dental work and was able to identify the corpse."

"Gruesome!" murmured Healy.

"But quite scientific," answered Adams, always attracted by science as shown by his tenacious fight to establish the Smithsonian Institution. On that subject Adams waxed quite eloquent, holding the artist spellbound.

At that moment the clock struck three, startling them all.

"Mr. Adams," said Healy, "I so enjoyed your conversation and description of the Lafayette dinner that it has made me miss mine."

At which the old gentleman answered, "And I must run or I shall lose mine."

Another time, noticing in the studio the busts of Franklin and Voltaire, Adams addressed the painter:

"These two men, sir, are truly representative of their respective countries. In Voltaire there is something very keen, satirical, and energetic, and devilishly intellectual, too—it seems to foreshadow the Revolution. By his side, Franklin's head appears a little heavy, but it is a good, strong English head.... There is something very fine, great, and good in contrast with the cruel mocker."

Between times Healy had begun several other portraits and saw frequently his old friend, Mrs. Otis, very busy that year urging the Massachusetts legislature to make of Washington's birthday a legal holiday. Her efforts were crowned with success, and little by little the other states followed suit; years afterward every February 22, the troops marching by her house in Boston would stop and salute. She asked about Healy's growing children; she urged him to settle in Boston, where his fame surpassed their greatest hopes. She praised his portrait of Mary Welch, painted the year before, and was glad to hear that Mary's father-in-law, Francis Welch, also intended giving him sittings. Healy was then painting James T. Field, George Ticknor Curtis, and others. He also spoke of the Everetts whom he had lately seen in Washington.

In Cambridge he visited the Longfellows in their lovely home, Craigie House, and the Danas a few doors away. He saw Edward Everett, just back from England, where Healy's portrait of Charlotte Everett had been exhibited at the Royal Academy.

Indefatigably the artist multiplied his evening calls, not only for pleasure, but also to obtain from people who were, or should have been, present at the Webster-Hayne debate, a promise of sittings for his big picture.

In the press of work the artist sometimes forgot his meals. Horrified, Dubourjal would try to drag him away from the studio or, in despair, bring him some fruit and crackers. One evening he asked George:

"Are you not completely exhausted?"

"Why, on the contrary," George exulted, "work acts like some generous wine; it gives me a sense of pleasing excitement!"

Dubourjal looked at his friend solemnly.

"Those are the symptoms of madness brought on by starvation," he prophesied, and seemed indignant when Healy burst out laughing.

On September 23, John Quincy Adams brought his friend Dr. Francis Parkman, father of the noted author, to the studio for what the artist had announced as the last sitting. Conversation never flagged and the hours flew by. Somewhat awed by a minister whom he instinctively associated with the well-remembered puritanical side of Boston, Healy was soon reassured by Dr. Parkman's keen sense of humor and the definitely liberal views of this North Church Unitarian pastor.

Parkman mentioned with pride his son Francis.

"Is his health improved?" asked John Quincy Adams.

A shadow fell over his friend's face.

"Not as much as I would like. He is too hard on himself, too determined to conquer his body. That trip of last summer to collect historical data was very exacting, but he wanted to study the frontier."

"Is he going to abandon the law for history?" questioned Adams.

Healy looked up. "Oh," he asked eagerly, "is that sketch of frontier life that appeared in the *Knickerbocker* magazine by your son?"

"Why, yes," replied Parkman, surprised, "but it isn't under his name."

"But it is on frontier life," replied Healy, pleased at his correct guess. "It struck me as so vivid. I can see why. On the spot one pictures the events of the past—the way Versailles brings before my eyes Franklin at the French Court."

Adams asked Healy if his visits to the Senate were for the purpose of evoking a past atmosphere.

"Yes," replied the artist, "I get the feeling of Mr. Webster standing there and see the audience moved by his words...."

"How far along are you?" asked Dr. Parkman.

"Only at the stage of separate portraits," explained Healy. "I expect to finish the work in France."

"Why?" questioned the clergyman as Adams interposed:

"Paris offers facilities for painters that you can't find in America. The studios, the material—"

"Someday we'll have all this here," asserted Healy.

Speaking of painters, Parkman mentioned West, of Kentucky, author of Byron's last portrait.

"I met him in London in 1837," remarked the artist.

"I was over there that year," Parkman told him, "and made the return trip with him."

The name of Beau Brummell came up, and Adams told his listeners that the young dandy with a friend of his called on him in Berlin.

"Was he very handsome?" asked Healy.

"Was he really intelligent?" asked Dr. Parker at the same time.

"Well... he was a man of wit and spirit, handsome, insolent often, but not deep. His success, I think, came from the gift of making himself a delightful companion. I doubt if he was happy —such lives are too empty. His companion, I know, committed suicide and, after having rivaled the Prince of Wales in the fashionable world, Brummell died miserably in a Boulogne inn."

"Oh?" Healy looked surprised. "I understood he moved from Boulogne and became consul at Caën in Normandy; then lost his position. I was told he spent the last three years of his life in the charitable asylum of Saint-Sauveur, and died there in 1840."

Healy put down his brushes. Placing the picture in a frame, he turned to show it to Mr. Adams and Dr. Parkman.

"I hope, sir, that you will not see in this a tiger! Mr. Frothingham says that I have made of Jackson a lion, of Clay a fox, and that I would probably make of you a tiger."

The two men laughed, looking carefully at the portrait.

"Well, if it is a tiger, Mr. Healy," Adams answered with a smile, "I must be one, for you are essentially true to nature; the other day as I looked at your portraits of Jackson and Clay, I said that it seemed more like seeing the real men than their counterfeits."

Adams's family agreed so heartily with his praise that they ordered a portrait for themselves, and as he had done for Jackson, Healy let them have this first work, assured of new sittings from Mr. Adams for the Versailles painting. Thus it was that another portrait of John Quincy Adams, dated Washington,

December 10, 1845, was presented the following year to His Majesty. It hung at Versailles through the Revolution of 1848, the Second French Republic, the Second Empire and the Third Republic. It weathered many storms.*

* In gratitude for Miss Anne Morgan's magnificent work of rehabilitation after World War I, the French government gave this and other Healy pictures to the museum at Blérancourt, where it still hung at the opening of German hostilities in 1939.

Chapter XVIII

AN ENGLISH WIFE IN AMERICA

WHILE busily painting in Boston, Healy received from the Hone Club of New York a flattering invitation to paint a portrait of "Squire" Webster for them.

"What is the Hone Club?" Healy asked Webster one day while visiting the aged statesman at his Boston home.

"A very select, witty, and interesting group of men of letters," the latter answered. "You will enjoy them, Mr. Healy. They are learned but not pedantic; they enjoy sports and good cheer and wield their influence in the right direction. Judge Story's son-in-law, George Curtis, is one of them. As you know, he divides his time between Boston, Washington, and New York."

Healy had read some of George Ticknor Curtis's commentaries on the Constitution...it was pleasant to hear of the New Englander in a lighter mood!

On November 12, Philip Hone, R. M. Blatchford, and George Curtis arrived in Boston and visited Healy's studio. That same evening they all dined at the Paiges': Mr. and Mrs. Webster, Fletcher Webster and his wife with the latter's sister Miss Joy; Samuel Appleton and his wife Julia Webster.

From his diary, one gathers that Philip Hone felt slightly aggrieved because the artist could not start at once on the Webster portrait they wanted. About Healy he writes: "I am afraid that he is so much in vogue that the price and time required may be beyond our patience and means...." Yet, in April when he received the picture, Hone's mood had changed to one of keen appreciation: "This counterfeit presentment of our honorary member is a great picture, the best by far that has been done of him," and adds facetiously that "Louis Philippe, if he came over, would see as good a picture as any in his American Gallery at Versailles!"

As the Webster-Ashburton Treaty seemed near conclusion, the demand for portraits of those two men became rampant. Webster complained, telling the painter that artists were like horseflies: "brush them off on one side—they return on the other!"

One morning Webster, his son Fletcher, and Healy rode out to Marshfield. There, under one of the great elms, the artist made a vivid sketch of the squire in hunting coat and slouch hat, holding a gun. A brace of birds lately shot lay on a bench by the tree; both father and son were delighted with that unusual and informal picture. The "squire," like Healy, was an early riser and many a time thereafter the two men enjoyed uninterrupted, long, and lively pre-dawn talks.

It was Webster who, at times, gave the artist advice that proved extremely wise. Healy, very eager to work on his "Webster Replying to Hayne," asked him if he would consent to some more sittings for that picture which the King wanted.

"Mr. Healy," answered the statesman, "much as I would enjoy having you stay here, I believe that you should go straight back to France and see for yourself what the conditions are today. To me, they look ominous."

From a man as astute as Webster the remarks were not reassuring. Healy took them to heart and in his letter to Louisa informed her that he was hurrying his work as much as possible and would be back with her before long.

As Healy's ship stopped in an English port, he landed, taking several cases of portraits to the Royal Academy. There he left them and took the very next boat for France, surprising the family in Versailles. The joy and confusion attending the reunion made connected ideas or plans impossible.

The new cases were added to those whose uncrating had been

stopped when Louis Philippe had ordered him back to America two years before to paint Jackson.

There were still a lot of portraits to be painted in America so George used all the sophistry he was capable of to persuade Mrs. Phipps that while he and Louisa took a much-needed second honeymoon she, with the help of Dubourjal, could still enjoy the quiet of Versailles and its beautiful park with Louisa's children, and they would bring back the rest of the orders as well as recent news from New York of her other daughter, son-in-law, and little granddaughter Emily.

While the women and children were in the park, Healy tackled Dubourjal to ask what was happening about the King.

"Why? Nothing that I know of," exclaimed Dubourjal.

"American newspapers speak of unrest."

"Oh, unrest! You know Paris is always effervescent. It may mean nothing. The anger seems directed more toward Guizot than toward the King. But don't worry. I shall watch here in your absence."

And surely, thought Healy, Mr. Webster will also keep us informed, as he is following the political complications of Europe as well as those in America.

Healy at last would have his wife with him, and he felt sure that under those circumstances she would lose her fears concerning the unpleasant ocean crossing.

Hard as it seemed to Louisa, even with her mother of whose tender care she had not the slightest doubt in charge of the children, the idea of being at last with George filled her heart, overcoming her last misgivings.

So they sailed. A bad sailor Louisa proved herself at once, and would at every one of the many crossings that from now on were to direct her course.

To divert her thoughts from the separation that deprived him also of his children, George spoke mostly of the things they would do on arriving after their visit to the Hanleys. In New York they would not remain long, although if the Wards and Thorns happened to be there, he must see them, and it would give him a chance to show her his portraits of all the beautiful Thorn girls.

Otherwise, the easiest thing for them and the best would be to take a little apartment in Boston.

"You will never be lonely there, and if I go to Marshfield, you probably can come, too."

She beamed. "I'd like that," she said. And George recalled how she had regretted not seeing the Websters during their visit to France the first year of her married life.

The thought of Marshfield made George realize how imperceptibly the pattern of his life had changed, attuning itself to that march of events of the nineteenth century to which he belonged. Perhaps Webster with his keen intellect and penetration of great questions could give him and Louisa a more living sense of progress and change, not only in America or France, but all through Europe—in fact, all through the world.

April again! And this time Louisa was accompanying George to the United States. Mrs. Phipps remained at Versailles with their four children, as they planned a full year's absence during which the artist hoped to complete all the portraits needed for his big American picture. The King had consented to the postponement of his "Franklin at the Court of Louis XVI," since the two pictures would be placed at the same time in the Palace Gallery.

Even on the great liner *Europa,* for Louisa who dreaded any short trip across water, this ocean crossing was a nightmare and a prolonged torture. . . . But they finally reached New York where her sister and brother-in-law James Hanley met them with the little niece Emily whom they had never seen. It was their first reunion since George and Louisa's marriage in London!

A stack of letters already awaited them: greetings, invitations, requests for portraits—so many cities called them! In New York they saw the Thorns, the Wards, and other American friends from

Paris, among whom were several artists. With sadness they learned of Audubon's ill-health: his sight had failed and his mind wandered at times as he tramped along the Hudson in quest of the birds that had filled his artistic life and which he could no longer see.

In Philadelphia, George and Louisa enjoyed the Sullys' hospitality and George was enthusiastic over the unfinished portrait of the Queen which Sully had painted at the time of the Coronation and made a sketch for his own studio.... The Binghams, the Biddles, and other friends or acquaintances stopped in to see them also—the Sullys always glad to open their home to friends.

In Baltimore, Louisa and Agnes met for the first time: George had looked forward to bringing together his beloved wife and his cherished sister—"two wonderfully attractive young women," he thought as he watched their greeting. But somehow the warmth he expected seemed lacking. Bound by a common admiration for the brother and husband, each one resented sharing his affection.

Washington fascinated Louisa. Warned about the big vacant spaces in this beautifully planned city, she noticed particularly the buildings: she found the White House beautiful, the Adams, Carroll, and Webster homes inviting. Washington's social season was not quite over and the young wife found herself asked to share informal meetings at the homes of George's friends who quickly became her friends, too.

The Francis Markoe, Jrs., had just lost an infant son: their sorrow found warm sympathy from the Healys. Markoe's work in the State Department had not made him forsake painting, and the two men often launched into long discussions about exhibitions, new galleries, needed official encouragement of art—and in this Mr. William W. Corcoran was later to prove his sincerity by the munificent gift of an art gallery.

A wave of heat such as Louisa had never known made the Healys turn northward. They stopped again in Baltimore, Philadelphia, New York, and Providence. When at last they reached

Boston, as George had expected, Mrs. Otis promised him to watch over Louisa and do all she could to make her love the city she hoped would become their permanent home.

The Appletons, Henshaws, Tuckers, Frothinghams, Everetts, Cabots, Lowells, and Mr. Prescott immediately included the English wife in their enthusiastic greetings.

At Mrs. Otis's Louisa saw the youthful portrait of the lady and was thrilled at the thought that before he was twenty George had shown so much life and originality in his painting. She easily understood how it had lured new sitters and how, even then, he had managed, while still helping his family, to go abroad and study. Her pride in him shone through her eyes as she looked at him so lovingly and admiringly that Mrs. Otis had to laugh.

Then George took Louisa to the Webster house, often closed these days, for the great man needed rest and preferred preparing his speeches or his writings in the solitude of Marshfield. Today, he happened to be in Boston, and received his painter warmly while he made himself as charming as he could—and that was very charming indeed—to the young wife. Webster always felt that he understood the British, as he proved effectively in his dealings with Lord Ashburton. Louisa, like most women privileged to meet the orator, fell completely under his spell. He was, she thought, really as fine as his portrait!

When the young couple left, Webster told George that he would like him to come back in the evening to meet a remarkable man, an inventor named Goodyear, whose discoveries and manufacturing genius might have tremendous influence on industry. He did not invite Mrs. Healy, he said, because women did not care generally for purely technical problems, but her husband would tell her that, if nothing else, this man would be a wonderful subject for a portrait!

Later in the evening, when George returned from this second visit, Louisa wanted to know if it had been worth while to go again....

"Darling, it's extraordinary—and the man will make a superb model! Oh, yes, I shall paint him; just think, he pretends that he will make a book whose pages—as thin as paper—will be of rubber!"

Louisa was rather intrigued, but laughed at it, as did most people at the time....

George Healy had brought from Paris some of his artist friends' pictures, hoping to sell them. He found Boston somewhat dubious about French subjects.

"Mr. Healy," one said, "I would like to buy your friend's work, but can you imagine this nude on our parlor wall? Or if I placed it in our bedroom, what would my wife say?"

When Franklin Pierce ordered a portrait of his friend Hawthorne, Louisa was surprised to see her husband come home exhausted, after the first sitting.

"Are you very tired, dearest?" she asked.

"Not so tired as discouraged. How can I paint a portrait when my model is so shy that he looks down, blushes; it's awful! The only moment he seems at all natural is when he talks about books...."

"And he writes such fine ones!" Louisa was surprised. She reflected a moment, then asked: "Would it help if I came in and read?"

Immediately her husband brightened.

"Splendid idea! And you read so well! Dearest, are you too tired or can we try that for tomorrow's sitting?"

"I'd love to do it. And we have some nice books here, new ones that I brought from England!"

Apparently relieved at the thought that he would not have to converse, Hawthorne agreed willingly. And to the much-admired author of *Twice-Told Tales* Louisa Healy read aloud, choosing Bulwer Lytton's recent historical story, *Last of the Barons*. Louisa charmed Hawthorne, who relaxed while Healy painted contentedly. Shyness disappeared. Mrs. Hawthorne came to watch the progress of her husband's portrait; she, too, liked to paint, and felt herself quite a judge of art. After a while she sometimes brought one of their two children. They all became friends and from them Louisa heard a good deal of all the new movements, philosophical or literary, and of the experiment at Brook Farm, which made her think of the Saint-Simoniens in Paris!

In the privacy of their chamber Louisa and George tried to figure out how this shy, nervous man had ever managed to propose to the attractive but rather formidable Sophia Peabody. There was no doubt of the love between them, and in the growing intimacy of sittings, in visits exchanged afterward, the Hawthornes spoke of their early married days in Concord. The young writer had planned his marriage at Brook Farm, but in the little colony he soon felt the chasm between intention and accomplishment. He gave up the Transcendental dream.

More, perhaps, than any other, Nathaniel Hawthorne presented an amazing mass of contradictions: in politics he was a Democrat among Whigs; a writer and sensitive scribe of human hearts, he shunned his fellow men; a scion of conservative English ancestry, he disliked and distrusted the English.

Franklin Pierce was highly pleased with his friend's portrait; he, himself, proved an excellent model, and his portrait was to attract particular notice from later visitors to the White House.

As the weeks went by, Louisa Healy's suspicion of a new pregnancy became a certainty—a fact that rendered comfortable quarters necessary, and not too much traveling. Yet they had to return to Washington. Mary Ann Hanley begged her sister to stay with her in New York, but the artist's wife had not faced an ocean crossing and parting from her children to be separated from her husband in America. So it was Mrs. Hanley who joined Louisa and George in Washington after the new year in time for the expected addition to the family.

In Washington, January 30, 1848, the baby girl Edith was born. "My three capital daughters!" gleefully boasted the artist—for

Agnes had come into the world in London, Mary in Paris, and now Edith in Washington!

His Washington portraits completed, Healy turned to Boston, where most of his other models awaited him. A house in Cambridge was rented, and as soon as Louisa felt equal to the journey, they moved north.

Cambridge proved as pleasant as they had hoped—an ideal spot in which to work and rest until time for their return to France. They established a pleasant intimacy with a most agreeable group revolving around Longfellow at Craigie House.

Never had the Healys felt so sanguine over the future, close and secure in their love, strong in their faith. The future appeared to them in golden hues....

"Would you like to live here always, my darling?" Healy asked his wife one day. She toyed with the idea. It would be nice for the children, better than being cooped up in a Paris apartment.... Then she smiled.

"It would be rather foolish, dearest, to cut yourself off from the King's favor and your prospects over there...."

His heart pounded; she had said "over there." Yes, eventually they would live in America.

"You look so tired," continued his wife, "perhaps we had better go back now."

"But the work is almost done, dear," he protested. "Only a few months more.... I hope the King will be pleased."

"Of course he will—how could he help it!"

Then the blow fell. One morning, Louisa was startled to see her husband coming in at an hour he always spent at the studio. He carried a newspaper and looked white.

"What's wrong? What is it, George?" she kept repeating as his eyes, very sad, turned to her; but he was looking beyond her, at something far away, unbelievable; then slowly he told her:

"The King has fallen!"

She gazed at him, uncomprehending. Fallen? She thought at once of the Duke of Orléans killed in an accident ... But George was talking.

"A revolution in France. The news came from Minister Rush last night. It was telegraphed to all the big newspapers. A republic has been declared. Here—read it. The King escaped to England: he's in exile; they give some details. Poor King, poor Louis Philippe...."

And in Europe, despite some needless abuse heaped upon the dethroned monarch who would not long survive this catastrophe, others repeated in wonder, "poor Louis Philippe...."

"Oh! his poor wife!" whispered Louisa as she took the paper from her husband's hand and led him to the sofa, sitting very close to him. As she read, exclamations escaped her lips while he remained silent, absorbed, plunged into confused thought. When she had finished reading, they looked at each other without words, sharing their sorrow for a good man in danger, a king who loved his people and thought himself loved by them—only to find himself suddenly overthrown. All at once, frightened, Louisa exclaimed:

"Mama! the children!"

"They are safe. Nothing happened in Versailles: but we'll write to the Minister at once."

"Your work! What will happen ...?"

"I don't know, my dear. I don't know."

For days the talk was of this new French revolution. Few details were known as yet, and when Minister Rush's letter came saying that he had gone to the new Provisional Government at the Hôtel de Ville to be recognized, as representative of the United States to the new republic, there was indignation at this diplomatic breach of etiquette, even from those who felt completely in sympathy with French liberal ideals.

In his letter to President Polk, Rush justified his move by saying:

"In recognizing the new state of things as far as I could without your instructions and in doing it promptly and solemnly I had a deep conviction that I was stepping forth in aid of a great cause of order in France and beyond France and that I was acting in the spirit of my government and country, the interpreter of whose voice it fell upon me suddenly to become. If I erred, I must hope that the motives which swayed me will be my shield. The Provisional Government needed all the moral support obtainable after a revolutionary hurricane that shook society to its base and left everything at first portentous and trembling. In such an exigency hours, moments were important, and the United States are felt as a power in the world."

Nevertheless, though comforted by Polk's personal approval, Minister Rush had to leave France.

"If only Wheaton were over there"... thought Healy. But Wheaton had died suddenly and, now again in Washington with his friend Dubourjal, where both men were painting Polk, George gave the President this sad news, repeating how bitterly he felt and, laying down his brushes, said he could not go on with the portrait. The President, said Dubourjal later, seemed very upset by the tragic news as the two men left. Polk had promised to name Wheaton to Paris or Rome if "the Party" agreed. Did he try, or did he simply fail to present Wheaton's name for the post desired, to which this career diplomat was eminently fitted?... The harm was done. This explains why the upper body in Polk's portrait by Healy is so very recognizable, while the hands and lower body are definitely not G. P. A. Healy's easily distinguishable painting.

In Paris the official critic of the Paris Salon must have heard what happened for, in his Catalog, he wrote in his own hand on the page opposite the list of paintings, that though Healy had not that year sent in an exhibit, he wished to mention the American artist for, he added, he considered "a fine action as great as a fine picture," and he, Montaiglon felt that "Healy who lived by his work, in renouncing an important commission, had done a noble deed."

In June, 1848, the Healys returned to Versailles where the grandmother and four older children impatiently awaited them. They sailed on the *Europa;* the crossing Mrs. Healy found no easier than the first one. In the throes of seasickness, when a well-meaning priest came up to her day after day telling her how ardently he prayed the Lord to spare her such discomfort, she exploded finally, and startled the poor man by exclaiming:

"For Heaven's sake stop your praying, and maybe I'll get better!"

Her fellow traveler sorrowfully concluded that she lacked Christian fortitude.

It was a changed Paris the Healys found on their return. No king at the Tuileries, and at the Elysée, for this Second Republic of France, a Prince President, eager to recover the glory attached to the name of Napoleon—a peculiar condition, ominous in the eyes of true republicans.

Dubourjal the faithful met his friends at the station and accompanied them to Versailles where he gave them many details of the sudden revolution. He felt grateful that his modest home had served as a refuge for Guizot, Louis Philippe's hounded Minister who had managed to slip unnoticed from Dubourjal's apartment into Belgium and thence to England. There, exiled like his King, he was writing instead of making history.

"Imagine!" exclaimed Dubourjal, who seemed to be living again those dramatic hours. "Can you see the King in his palace listening to the mounting sounds of the mob—an angry mob, ready for violence. . . . It must have reminded him of his youth, the terrible massacres of '89. . . . How could he understand . . . ?" And the Frenchman described how His Majesty had exclaimed:

"My horse! Order my horse!"

"Sire, do not attempt it. . . ."

"My horse! I shall speak to my people!"

Louis Philippe's appearance on horseback, unguarded among the populace, failed to calm heated spirits. His courage, his gallant presence no longer aroused, as in 1832, a shout of *"Bravo le Roi!"* Only lowering looks met his eye, and Louis Philippe sadly returned to the Tuileries. One by one the ministers and the generals urged his abdication. Very well—he would abdicate in favor of the little boy, son of the Duke of Orléans. With a heavy heart but a steady hand the King wrote: "I abdicate this crown which I held from the Nation's will and accepted only that peace might reign in France. Since I cannot accomplish this, I leave the task to my grandson, the Comte de Paris. May he succeed better than I. LOUIS PHILIPPE."

A dignified abdication, but as the King left the Tuileries with the Queen, a son and a daughter-in-law, the shouts and threats mounted in furious waves from the swirling crowd pressing against the tall iron grating of the Tuileries Gardens. The royal group hastened back into the palace and slipped away through a secret passage built by the first Napoleon. . . .

"Shocking!" whispered Mrs. Healy.

"But the people loved him," insisted Healy. "I cannot understand . . ."

"American republicans do not have to fight so hard for freedom," said Dubourjal. "Our people felt they were losing what the King first brought them with Lafayette. . . ."

Only the noble leadership of Lamartine saved France at that moment from the renewed terror of the Red Flag. The poet's eloquence had reached the hearts of all Frenchmen when he exclaimed: "The Red Flag floats over this Square, but the Tricolor will float over the world!"

To Healy, just back from America, the thought of a French republic seemed right. It hurt him, however, that it should have risen with cruel injustice against the democratic monarch who sincerely wished the good of the nation. And at Claremont in

England, while his people shouted gleefully their regained *"Liberté, Egalité, Fraternité,"* the exiled King ate out his heart.

From English as well as from French friends of the deposed monarch, the Healys heard some touching and some amusing echoes of that exile. Eugène Scribe, the noted playwright who had many friends in England, crossed the Channel quite frequently and, like many other French visitors to England, did not fail to inquire about the exiled monarch. One day the exiled Queen, very troubled, told M. Scribe that she wished he would wait a little and she would see if the King could receive him.

"He is so silent, so unhappy. Your visit would do him good."

Of course Scribe was delighted, and when ushered into the King's room, he went forward eagerly. The monarch immediately greeted him with the words:

"Oh, Monsieur Scribe! You are just the person I want to see! But don't laugh. I am trying to write a play."

"Parfait!"

"Wait until you hear it."

"Well, you know that authors are the harshest critics. . . ."

"That's just what I want." And almost surreptitiously the King drew from his pocket a sheaf of papers, saying, "Let me read you the beginning."

And as he listened, Scribe at first seemed a little dubious; then his face cleared. *"Majesté!* You know what you ought to do with this? It's an opera."

"No, no, no. I want it as a play. . . ."

"No, no, no. Don't you see? Here a little music."

"But I don't know music."

"Doesn't matter; you won't be writing the music."

Now both of them got excited, and the listening Queen at the door smiled to herself. At last, at last, the King was interested in something. Gently she opened the door and not even noticing that she hadn't been there, Louise Philippe turned to her at once.

"Do you really think I could arrange it that way?"

And the discussion between the two men went on while a very good lunch was served.

When Scribe returned the next day, it was the Queen in person who opened the door to him and took both his hands, saying, *"Merci!* For the first time the King laughed last evening and he's still working on the play."

When the Healys heard this account, they were so deeply touched that even this talkative pair had no words.

A year later, on his deathbed, Louis Philippe would ask: "Will not one voice be raised to say, 'There was good in this man'?"

Chapter XIX

"WEBSTER REPLYING TO HAYNE"

WRANGLES between the French and American governments delayed the arrival in Paris of William Cabel Rives who had been named to succeed Rush. Healy heard echoes of this in Washington where he had returned to complete unfilled orders. It was at this time, in 1850, that he painted another portrait of Longfellow for Mrs. Otis. On his return to France, aware that without the patronage of Louis Philippe Versailles had little to offer him, the artist moved his family back to Paris, 68 rue de l'Arcade. Arthur was entered in a boys' school. But that year proved a tragic one for the Healys. Little George died of scarlet fever and then, in November, Arthur, the beloved gifted eldest child, fell down stone steps during play hour at school; at first he seemed only dazed, complained of a headache, but soon his mind wandered, and when the distraught parents arrived he no longer knew them, calling for his mother who, brokenhearted, never left his side. With him were buried the hopes of a great talent. His loss would be mourned for a lifetime.

A letter from Guizot, newly returned to Paris, touched Healy greatly, and his work became so absorbing that he could not allow sorrow to interrupt; like Montaigne in the sixteenth century, who said that no sorrow could be so great that an hour's good reading would not assuage, Healy found in his brushes some of that healing balm.

From the city of Charleston that winter came the order for a portrait of John Calhoun, who had died in Washington the preceding spring. This commission was particularly pleasing to Healy, not only because of Calhoun's personal attractiveness, but because the artist represented the highest type of American—sincere in his objections, but always willing to find a passable bridge. For Healy it also brought back vividly every moment of the years spent on his "Webster Replying to Hayne," now nearing the completion of the 135 portraits; and he expressed to Webster the hope that Bostonians would fulfill the great wish of his heart and place the picture in Faneuil Hall.

Webster's fatigue in the midst of political dissension between the South and the North, and trips to Washington where the great Daniel thundered in favor of Union: "Liberty and Union, one and inseparable, now and forever," forced the great man to remain away from his beloved Marshfield. Time was passing, and George must take his huge canvas and innumerable portraits to his Paris studio where he could work at top speed. To some people it seemed strange that he should go to the trouble and expense of transporting his big picture to Paris, but any painter could understand how impossible it would be in a new country to obtain the facilities offered by an old and artistic land.

In Paris again, George did work on his big picture. Remembering his famous subject as he had seen him in Marshfield, Webster seemed larger than his five feet ten, perhaps because of his superb carriage and heroic features. The dark, vivid complexion, the deep-set eyes and glorious brow harmonized with his dignified bearing. No one could fail to be impressed on meeting the orator and statesman.

To many it was a surprise that the two principals in the Debate had remained warm personal friends. On the evening of the celebrated Debate in 1830, both were guests at a reception in the White House. Webster greeted Hayne pleasantly:

"How are you tonight?"

With a twinkle in his handsome eyes, the Carolinian answered: "None the better for you, sir!"

In April, 1851, Healy wrote to Daniel Webster:

"I am happy to inform you that my great work will be finished in time to be publicly seen in Boston about the first of September next. It has occurred to me that if the Mayor and the Corporation of that great city could be induced to favor me as they did Mr. Weir some years since by lending me Faneuil Hall, it would be well that the public should first see it where it is intended finally to be placed."

Previously, when Healy had described the uncertainties of politics in France he had reminded Webster that his premonition had really hastened the artist's return to France.

In reply, Webster wrote to him that it might be wise for him to come back now—which he did. By fall an article in the Boston *Daily Advertiser* announced the arrival in Boston of the much-heralded picture. The writer spoke of it as follows:

Webster Replying To Hayne

Mr. Healy has been kind enough to permit me to see this picture before it is exposed to the public view, and the delight it has given me I wish to communicate to others. They will soon share it. I found an historical picture, I think, unmatched in the country. I was surprised and invigorated by the manliness, simplicity, and good taste of the treatment. I need not describe the picture. Mr. Webster is standing in the natural focus of interest, with the Senators about him, and a gallery of ladies above. No one need fear anything French, grotesque, or vehement in his action. It is no Ajax defying the lightning. He is all concentrated thought only and easy power. . . .

Mr. Healy might easily, from his full preparatory studies, have given us careful miniatures of well-known gentlemen, a hundred exact portraits set in a lifeless space. He has preferred to give us a picture—something better than a canvas or portraits—a picture of a great man in the highest use of his faculties; and we share in the life and reality of the scene. In this sense, this is a far better picture than any of Trumbull's, or indeed any kindred picture in America. It is alive. We feel the muscular vigor of those acting in it, and become breathless as they are, waiting for the next word of power.... The picture will soon be submitted to the public eye, and an engraving of it by the best artist will follow, I hope, before many months.—T. G. A.

The painting was duly placed in Faneuil Hall in the fall of 1851 and Mr. Webster, leaning on Healy's arm, feeble though he was, saw it in place. Both model and artist felt a deep satisfaction. To Healy, this placing of his picture in the presence of the man who inspired it was a happy culmination to seven years of work.

A lady who witnessed Webster's last visit wrote:

"Mr. Webster was very feeble and was led in by the artist. Ascending the platform which commanded a view of the picture, Webster looked at it for some minutes, making pleasant observations to his friends respecting different picturesque positions of the listening and pondering senators below. Mr. Healy has greatly relieved this difficulty by the skillful disposition of his shadows. He has given us a fine scale of color without obtrusion. From the highest lights to the deepest shadows we have a richness of harmony which imparts to the painting a lasting quality."

Years later, the Boston *Daily Advertiser,* Saturday morning, August 31, 1912, was to comment:

This is not a picture to be glanced at and passed by with a comment on its striking technique, but one is inclined to look upon it with increasing interest in the subject and the manner of its rendering. In proportion to the aesthetic culture of the people so will this production of mental power and aesthetic culture be appreciated.

Again heeding Webster's advice, Healy started back for Paris— but it was a different Paris.

Healy found the city a veritable caldron of political upheavals. One early morning at the beginning of December, on his way to early Mass, the artist suddenly noticed upon the light blanket of snow a trail of blood—a startling sight.

At the Elysée Palace the night before there had been dancing as usual on Monday evenings. A congenial company surrounded the Prince President. If a few officers left early, no one commented on the fact, nor did many notice that the President and Count de Morny, his half-brother, retired to a private salon. There, after the guests had dispersed, three men joined them: Saint-Arnaud, head of the Army; De Maupas, head of the police, and Persigny, faithful shadow of Prince Louis Napoleon. They remained in conference until a late hour, after which General de Saint-Arnaud issued special orders to his troops, and the Chief of Police secretly called the heads of every precinct.

Suddenly across the sleeping city the sound of marching men resounded. Wakeful Parisians or late pedestrians might have heard the noise of scuffles in various quarters, of shouts and guns, but there was no uproar loud enough to bring out the populace. By morning the coup d'état of Prince Napoleon had taken place, and men hastily pasting placards throughout the city apprised the citizens of a melodramatic change in government. The President's proclamation announced the dissolution of a rebellious Assembly. News spread rapidly among passing workmen, shopkeepers, and café waiters. It was said that all opposition leaders had been arrested in the dead of night and locked in the Mazas prison. Only a few escaped and remained in hiding until some resourceful friends could manage to spirit them out of Paris; among these, the poet Victor Hugo sought refuge at first in Belgium and from there sent pamphlets and launched insults against the new tyrant. His long exile in the Islands of Jersey and Guernsey made of him a popular hero and allowed him the seclusion necessary to write without interruption some of his greatest works.

The city under martial law and an accomplished coup d'état furnished excitement to the ever-effervescent Parisians. When Prince Louis Napoleon rode out in grand uniform that day, some troops guarding the streets shouted obligingly, *"Vive l'Empereur"* —a cry gleefully taken up by a good portion of the population. And throughout France the cry was repeated until a plebiscite established the Empire as the will of the people. Ever mindful of its democratic claims, the government had new coins struck that bore the naïve legend: *République Française—Napoléon III Empereur ...*"

George Healy's Americanism balked at this emperor worship, for it was now certain that the Prince President would soon be acclaimed Emperor—and it was whispered that the very beautiful Mlle. de Montijo, the envy of all women, would undoubtedly become Empress, to the intense indignation of Prince Napoleon's family. When Mlle. de Montijo had visited Healy's studio the artist in him reveled at the grace, poise, and ineffable blond beauty of this French-Spanish young girl.

In spite of polite words and occasional invitations to the Palace, the Healys knew that no artist favored by Louis Philippe would be *persona grata* with Napoleon III. However, in spite of the loss of royal patronage, orders for many portraits brought a harvest needed for the rapidly increasing family. It meant several months in America, and Louisa agreed to accompany her husband while Mrs. Phipps mothered the children during her absence.

In May, 1852, George and Louisa Healy arrived in Boston where the artist set at once to paint another portrait of Hawthorne in an easy, happy atmosphere very different from the first tense sittings of a few years ago. Several portraits were started: of Prescott whom Healy had painted in 1843, of Longfellow and others, some finished when, two weeks later, the Healys went on to Providence, New York, Philadelphia, and Washington. George reveled in the excitement of this rush of work, while Louisa wondered if this amazing husband of hers would ever settle down to a sane, moderate tempo. Yet she would not have him otherwise; this breathtaking enthusiasm of his still thrilled her as it had during their courtship, and it no longer frightened her. In her quiet, wifely wisdom she knew who really ruled the home!

In October they were at Baltimore for an unexpected event. On the twenty-eighth, Agnes Healy married Dr. Dyson of Charles

County, Maryland.* Her brother George gave her away, and
Louisa felt a truer sisterly affection for her now that Agnes had a
man of her own, who would absorb some of the admiration she
had lavished on her brother for years. The happy marriage was to
last only eight years, for Dr. Dyson died in 1860 after a painful
illness.

Washington, Richmond, Philadelphia, Providence, and again
Boston saw the Healys in full activity. In May, 1853, they stopped
at the Thorn home in New York, before sailing back to France.
Mrs. Phipps had the children once more in Versailles, 1 rue Neuve,
as the country seemed preferable, especially since, on November 18, little Emily was born. George hurried back to America
to finish the promised portraits and bring back those destined
to the Exposition. He returned in good time, and having retained
his Paris studio, set to work at once. Louisa would be free to remain with her mother and the children in the country or join
her husband in Paris whenever she wanted.

---

* Baltimore *Sun,* November 3, 1852—"Married on the 20th ultimo by Rev. J. P.
Donelan, Robert Dyson, M.D., of Charles County, Md., and Miss Agnes E. A. Healy of
Misses Kilbourn and Healy's Academy of this city. (We are gratified to learn that this
admirable Institute will be continued by the highly talented and very competent Miss
D. T. Kilbourn, assisted by young ladies educated at the Academy)."

Chapter XX

CULTURAL PIONEER

IN George Healy's Paris studio a newcomer occupied the model's chair—a very good-looking and inspiring model, thought the artist. Mutual friends, Dr. and Mrs. Brainard, had brought them together, and William Butler Ogden had there and then ordered his portrait. This was the first sitting.

"You are both pioneers," Mrs. Brainard had said, "and should really have much to discuss." The pioneering, she explained, while in very different lines would make them congenial. "Mr. Healy has made of art a requirement for us, where it used to be only a luxury. And Mr. Ogden has opened new horizons, new means of transport. We call him 'the railroad king'!" And Mr. Ogden had laughed.

Now that they were alone, he asked the painter: "Tell me, Mr. Healy, how is it that you kept your residence over here under this regime?"

"For many reasons, sir. First of all, a rather large family to transplant; traveling is a costly luxury."

The artist changed his stance to get a full-face effect without the stiffness of too straight a look, and continued: "Then my work. These two very large historical pictures necessitate space and good light, and large studios are somewhat of a luxury. Orders from Louis Philippe used to smooth the path. Then we could live in Versailles and I worked where the pictures would hang."

"That's just it. I was wondering why, since the late King's wishes would hardly be considered by the Bonapartist regime, you did not take that fine work where everyone is ready to receive you and yours with open arms."

Flattered, Healy added: "There is also the question of material: besides a large studio, good brushes, good paints, the canvases, the right light.... It would take time to find all this combined with the necessity of proper quarters for young children."

"You would find all this in my bailiwick," Ogden laughed, "and we need men like you to furnish the culture still lacking in a new country...."

Healy found his sitter most interesting, besides being one of the handsomest men he had painted of late. At each new sitting, the understanding grew between them. Mr. Ogden kept harping on the need for Americans of Healy's stamp to come over and bring that culture he had received so early and enriched by his contacts with the best of old countries. The artist repeated much of this to Louisa who, intrigued, came to the studio to meet the "railroad king" of whom the Brainards had spoken so affectionately and admiringly.

It was a new friendship and a very interesting one, and one day William B. Ogden startled his painter by saying:

"Mr. Healy, if you will honor me with your presence as my guest in my Chicago home for a year, I can guarantee that at the end of that time you will bring your family over and make a greatly needed addition to our community."

What a tempting invitation! Even Louisa, when George told her, considered seriously this wonderful opportunity. Perhaps this would be the chance for them to establish their home in America.

Again in his studio, Healy was thinking over Mr. Ogden's proposition, sorting the pictures against the wall, straightening chairs and easel, when a knock called him to the door.

There, holding a large flat package, was the man he had met at Mr. Webster's and thought of so often since.

"Why! Mr. Goodyear! How wonderful to see you!"

"Mr. Healy, I told you I would come and bring the gutta-percha panels you thought impossible. Here they are—and here I am. Will you paint my portrait?"

Delighted, Healy immediately placed a chair in the best light to bring out Goodyear's strong face, fine features, and piercing eyes, and here the artist enjoyed one of the exciting experiences of his career as he realized the smoothness of those panels. Palette in hand, he began a quick and bold outline of the face and figure before him. After working in silence for a while Healy suggested a rest, and Goodyear at last burst out with all the questions he had refrained from asking while he sat. Both men felt elated, sure that this would mean a new success. On the morrow they would continue.

"Where can I reach you, Mr. Goodyear?"

"At my shop—40 rue Vivienne...."

"Oh, of course!"

"If I am not in, give the message to my partner, Mr. Morey; he's almost as interested in this as we are...."

When he left, Goodyear was already very recognizable on the still-unbelievable gutta-percha! And Healy felt that this would be one of his best, most satisfying portraits. But, active always, he started arranging chair and easel for the next sitter....

A newsboy tapped at the door, handing the artist his paper. As Healy carelessly looked through it, he was startled by the name Goodyear, and almost jumped out of his chair when he read that Mr. Goodyear's partner, having been arrested last night "for debt," was shot by a guard who, seeing him at a window, thought Mr. Morey was trying to escape....

George felt himself grow cold. Mr. Goodyear certainly knew nothing of this—he had seemed so proud, pleased, and happy just about an hour ago!

The artist immediately went out to get a London *Times* for more details. The paper explained that costs for bringing over the Goodyear invention had been so high that Mr. Morey, Goodyear's partner, was unable to pay in England the sum demanded—

175,000 francs. As he landed in France, he was arrested and taken to the Clichy prison. Mrs. Morey, notified, hurried over and the Court assured her that her husband would be released in the morning. They regretted the inevitable night behind bars, but she need not worry. The arrest was a mistake and she was given the Court order for his release in the morning. That night a new guard, seeing Mr. Morey at a window, shot him—dead! Mrs. Morey, now a widow, instead of the expected glory, returned with her husband's body to the United States.

For a while, naturally, the Goodyear sittings were interrupted. But the manufacturer asked Healy to paint then the group picture of his children which they had also planned, and this was done quite successfully. The Goodyear portrait itself was excellent and obtained very favorable comments. Edmond About in his book on the Art Exhibit asks facetiously: "Are rubber pictures very elastic? If so, it would be a good plan to stretch those of M. Meissonier and to shrink those of M. Horace Vernet...." The former artist was well-known, of course, for his tiny pictures; the latter, notorious for his huge canvases.

Healy was able to transfer onto his rubber the forceful personality of Goodyear. This was done and finished before the formal May opening of the Exposition.

May, usually so lovely, was that year cloudy, rainy, and chilly, yet occasional bursts of sunshine over the glass roof of the white, glistening Exposition Palace produced dazzling effects. When noon chimed, a detachment of the *Cent Gardes* in their rather theatrical costumes of steel and sky-blue marched in and formed an avenue to the throne. Imperial pomp in these circumstances pleased both the populace and the titled foreigners.

Amid the throng of visitors, Healy met many more Americans, some of whom had heard about him lately from W. B. Ogden. The artist kept mulling over the amazing offer of his new friend. It was extremely tempting. There had been some opposition from Mrs. Phipps and a slight doubt in Louisa's own mind. As usual for his great decisions, Healy discussed every phase of the matter with his friend Dubourjal. As he had always done, Dubourjal promised that he would stay within call of Louisa and her mother, and keep George informed of conditions. Personally, he felt alone without his friend, but such an opportunity must not be neglected: he must find out if Mr. Ogden's prediction could mean as much as they all believed now. Thus it was that in the fall George again was aboard a big liner on his way to America, and because of the Exhibition, in the crowd of passengers, there were many friends and patrons determined to continue their Healy collection. Among American passengers, Healy saw the youngest Thorn girl, Ida, perhaps the most beautiful of that bevy of pretty young women, whose portrait he had painted lately. He also caught a glimpse of the lush English beauty, Miss Sneyde, who, he heard, had just been scratched off the list of ladies-in-waiting to the blond Eugénie . . . She knew too well the Emperor's strong predilection for English fair but warm figures. Yet she kept one of the prettiest Thorn daughters, the Baronne de Pierre, among her galaxy of beauties. All these portraits Healy had painted gave him unexpected prestige during the trip. Then other passengers, having read of the art medals he had received at the Exposition and now learning that he was on his way to visit Mr. W. B. Ogden, suddenly flooded him with so many new orders for portraits that he wondered whether he could even take the time necessary to bring over his family. . . . Of course they were now in condition to travel together without him, but . . . Oh well, that could all be decided after his visit in the hospitable Ogden and Sheldon home in Chicago.

Always alert for new landscape, new vistas, new ground, the artist gasped at the immensity of that lake they all spoke about so familiarly. Mr. and Mrs. Sheldon were as cordial to him as their bachelor brother and brother-in-law. He was made one of the family, met their neighbors, wondered at all the big roomy, rich-looking houses built upon what seemed pretty rickety ground.

George wrote enthusiastically to Louisa about this new city of Chicago where people were kind, interested in all sorts of things, and quite convinced that this city sprawling along the shore of a lake as large as a sea would soon be one of America's great, thriving cities!

If people make a place, then Chicago offered infinite variety and interest, for people arrived daily from every part of the continent —real people, imbued with the pioneer spirit, brave and bold and progressive; they erected homes, surrounded them with gardens, cultivated farms on the outskirts, built gigantic business plants.

Mrs. Leander McCormick wrote to a Southern friend: "The primitive life in this western town is extremely interesting and the people as well—many of whom are New Englanders whose provincial ways and customs are quite amusing when contrasted with those of Virginia."

A sprawling city of the plains, Chicago stretched along the shores of Lake Michigan, its better residences surrounded by trees and well-kept flowering gardens or "yards," as they were modestly called.

As guest of its first mayor and most influential citizen, Healy received at once marked attention which soon turned into personal friendships. The artist fell in love with the new city in all its uneven progress, its primitiveness and boastful Americanism! The boasts, he found, almost always became reality. Of the discomforts —the unpaved streets, the wooden sidewalks on stilts where one could hear and sometimes see scuttling rats, George wrote passingly, so as not to frighten the female members of the family, while he stressed the delight of a simple and well-mannered society that seemed inclined to order portraits enough for him to establish their American home!

In Paris, childish voices could be heard practicing queer Indian names: Tchikogo...was it as weird as it sounded?...Stories of Captain Mayne Reid and Fenimore Cooper took the place of Dickens and other English books their mother read to them....

Imaginations started working: would Redskins stalk them?...
What dangers they might face! Their dear Dubourjal almost wept
at the thought...

While Healy worked feverishly in Chicago, across the ocean on
December 29, 1855, a son was born to him whom Mrs. Healy
named George though it reawakened the burning sorrow of that
first little George they had lost so soon after the death of young
Arthur...but there must be one child bearing the father's name
which he, in turn, might also carry to fame....

The father kept up his letters to Louisa, but complained that
hers were a little slow coming—and, he told her, "the days are
black when I do not have news of you!" He encouraged her to get
whatever would hasten the journey and make it easier, and assured her that they could meet obligations, for a new important
order had just come. Congress had voted:

"To ENABLE the Committee on the Library to contract with Mr.
Healy for a series of portraits of the Presidents of the United States
for the Executive Mansion, provided the cost of same shall not
exceed one thousand dollars for each..."

So, as soon as health permitted, the Healy caravan started from
Paris, Dubourjal accompanying them to the boat....

It was headed by Grandmother Phipps aged eighty-four; following her came Louisa with her babe in arms, a nurse, and the five
little girls: Agnes, Mary, Edith, Maria, and Emily. To them all the
sea voyage was torture, for they were all as seasick as could be!

At last, in 1856, they reached Chicago, safe and sound in spite of
the slow, trying journey...

"How lovely!" exclaimed Louisa Healy at sight of the Ontario
Street house her husband had taken near his friends, the Ogdens
and the Sheldons. The house was surrounded by trees; flowers
bloomed along a grass plot and a wide porch with inviting steps
led to the front door.

"How strange!" murmured Mrs. Phipps, studying the frame
building, so flimsy-looking to Europeans accustomed to stone and

brick. Both women were terrified when they saw the big furnace, but central heat during the bitter winter months calmed their spirits and kept their bodies warm....

In congenial surroundings of simplicity and culture, elders and youngsters soon learned to think of Chicago as an unexpectedly free and agreeable paradise.

In Chicago, as she had in Boston, Louisa made many friends and found their entertainments as charming as "Papa" had described. The list of visitors to Healy's studio on Lake Street might give an almost complete roster of Chicago's "best people" of those early years. There so many sitters came that the hours of work stretched almost beyond endurance. And besides his own painting, the artist was trying to encourage fellow artists and to arouse civic pride in the artistic future of Chicago. His plans for an art center found quick response among the elite.

From Chicago Healy radiated to Washington, Baltimore, Philadelphia, New York, Boston—wherever he was called to paint portraits. He visited, when he could, his sister and brothers who had elected residence in the South. The prestige of his life abroad and of the King's patronage undoubtedly helped his fame, but his own talent and personality established it firmly.

Chicago life after a time became so strenuous that the Healys decided to live in the country. They bought a home in Cottage Hill (now Elmhurst) where Healy's good friend Thomas B. Bryan owned a beautiful estate. Another baby girl had come into the family circle, Kathleen, their last child. The father was inordinately proud of his many children. He thoroughly enjoyed startling people with the remark:

"I have six daughters and each one has a brother!"

And almost invariably the expected answer would follow:

"Oh! Mr. Healy—twelve children! How wonderful!"

But Mrs. Healy was quite content with her six girls and one boy.... She was growing acclimated to American life and liked it. The family no longer thought of travel; they were settled;

there seemed no good reason for moving away from a place that provided work for the father and healthy comfort for the children.

But Chicago, in true American fashion, built too fast. There came a panic in 1857—money tightened and portraits were countermanded or remained unpaid. The artist multiplied his efforts.

As the children grew, they needed schooling, so the Healys moved back to the city. On Wabash Avenue, between Congress and Van Buren streets, they bought a large frame house surrounded by lovely trees. Many happy reunions took place in the new home and the Healy house acquired a pleasant reputation as a center of cultured gatherings.

While trying to erect an art center in Chicago, George Healy lost contact with artistic battles then raging in Paris. He who had always been in the vanguard found himself cut off by distance from the new rebellious generation abroad, and when later he returned to France, the "Salon des Refusés" had become a thing of the past and the Impressionists formed a new power, relegating all seniors, whether great or small, to the obloquy of "old fogies." Meanwhile, alert and alive, Healy painted with incredible vigor. Thanks to his efforts and to those of his comrades in 1859, an art exposition was organized in Chicago, becoming thereafter a yearly event to which the former Mayor lent his hearty support.

Cultured and infinitely charming, William B. Ogden stood out as a romantic figure among those remarkable pioneers. His sense of honor was proverbial; when the panic of 1857 embarrassed his affairs, he received from a Scotch nobleman the following letter: "I hear you are in trouble. I have placed to your credit in New York one hundred thousand pounds. If you get through I know you will return it, and if you don't Jeanie and I will never miss it."

Needless to say the railway king of the West returned the loan.

Besides the Ogdens, Sheldons, and McCaggs, who all sat for their portraits, many prominent Chicagoans ordered paintings from Healy: Dr. and Mrs. Brainard, Dr. N. S. Davis, "long John" Wentworth, the Kinzies, the Drummonds, Ramsays, Blairs, Blatchfords,

McCormicks, and Rutters—in fact the list would comprise practically all the well-known names of early Chicago.

Stephen Douglas, popular, politically active, charmed Healy as he sat to him. Small, broad-shouldered, with a rather large head and sparkling eyes, magnetic, brilliantly intellectual, the "Little Giant," as his friends called him, was presidential timber. A Southern Democrat, he had married a North Carolinian who would inherit slaves; this could easily ruin his chances of election, but in 1850 Douglas worked actively for the Clay compromise that claimed no restrictions in regard to slavery for the territories acquired from Mexico. This only postponed the clash that must inevitably come sooner or later, and even Douglas realized it: talk about secession was dangerous, he told Healy—terribly dangerous. . . .

Chapter XXI

AN ARTIST'S FAITH

IN THE midst of a political upheaval that was to rock the
country, Healy, working harder than ever to meet heavy financial
obligations, was undergoing at the same time a religious re-
awakening.

This had been developing since the last visits to his native city,
Boston always affected him powerfully, and several of his models
happened to be men of deep religious fervor; indeed the whole
region seemed affected by a renewal of its early traditions, with an
added appeal to liberalism. Healy had painted his father's friend
"Father Taylor," the sailors' comforter, redeemer of souls; he had
listened to his learned sitter, Edward Tyrrel Channing, the great
Unitarian preacher; he had felt immediate friendship for the new
convert to Catholicism, Father Hecker, who was later to found
the Paulist Order in the United States.

As Bishop Fitzpatrick sat for his portrait, the two men conversed
in French. Healy's casual ways in regard to the Church amazed
the Bishop, who immediately tackled the artist. How could Healy,
Catholic-born, reconcile his conscience in letting his children be
brought up Protestants? ... Well, his own mother had been a
Protestant, and a fine Christian. ... No doubt, admitted the Bishop,
but did not the artist feel the greater closeness of the Church of
Rome to Christ? Was not his special gift God-given, and did he
not thrill at the divine beauty of Catholic faith, Catholic services,
Catholic history? ... They spoke of Saint-Sulpice, where Fitzpatrick had studied for the priesthood, and of other Paris churches

where he had first officiated. The Bishop was eloquent, the artist susceptible. At home, he tried in turn to convert Louisa, but his wife listened patiently, regretting that these discussions, which had troubled her before marriage, should begin again....

Then a strange note filtered into the tangle of thought and emotion. Healy painted a very charming young widow, Mrs. Goddard, daughter of Samuel F. Vinton, Congressman from Ohio, leader of the Whig party for many years. She was an ardent Catholic and, strangely enough, in days when the Roman Church still aroused violent prejudice even to the point of persecution, she was also a prominent leader in Washington society and an arbiter of good taste and manners. How deeply this well-read, lovely, and spiritually-minded young woman with French antecedents influenced George Healy it would be difficult to say, but one of his daughters blurted out laughingly one day that the only woman of whom her mother had ever been jealous was their great friend Mrs. Dahlgren, the former Mrs. Goddard.... Some of Healy's letters to her still exist. From St. Louis, on May 14, 1859, he writes his acceptance "with joy of the relationship you propose. Yes, let us be for the rest of our stay here below sister and brother," and the following sentence emphasizes Mrs. Goddard's ardent proselyting, for he adds: "Think of how much under God I shall owe you when all my family are united in our Holy Faith!" Mrs. Goddard's daughter, Romaine, attended the Convent of the Visitation—Mount de Chantal, at Wheeling, West Virginia, so Agnes and Mary Healy were sent there, and from that date Romaine and the Healy girls became intimate friends. Thus began the family conversion.

To please her husband, Louisa might then have joined them in this step had not the priest who undertook her instruction told her she would have to be married again. "What!" exclaimed the indignant wife. "I have had nine children and you dare to suggest that I am not married! This is too much. I will not join your church."

Her decision greatly distressed her husband, but the following January he rejoiced; his wife would join him in Holy Communion.

Not only did these letters indicate a suddenly exalted militant Catholicism, but they revealed many details of the Healys' life. To the artist, Mrs. Goddard proved an ever-sympathetic "confidante"; he informed her of his monetary difficulties and of his various transactions to get out of debt. In January he told her why the family could not move to Washington as planned:

Mr. Thomas B. Bryan offered me 80 acres 4 miles north of Chicago river where it runs through the city half a mile from the Lake at $400. per acre. He proposed to take my Cottage Hill property at $10,000; thirty of those heads from the life, including Jackson, Clay, Calhoun, Webster, etc., with the original study of "Webster Replying to Hayne" on a canvas 8 by 5 feet, together with the picture now in the Rotunda of "Franklin at the Court of Louis XVI" for $10,000. This leaves me $12,000 to pay in cash, to pay which he gives me three years, and during those three years I am to occupy Cottage Hill free of rent; thus you see our Washington plan is yet some way in the future. The papers were signed on the 28th; the following morning, the birthday of our only boy, I had the happiness to go to Holy Communion with Mrs. Healy.

And on July 5, 1860, he wrote: "Your good heart would have been touched if you could have seen us all go to Holy Communion on the morning of Wednesday last. My beloved wife was especially moved thus to go to the table of our dear Lord on the birthday of our little Kathleen who was then two years old...."

Healy's religion, however, was never obtrusive.

"Why! Mr. Healy, had I known you were a Catholic, I would not have sat to you for my portrait!" a woman once exclaimed with horror, and to this the fervent devout man with a twinkle gave a very unorthodox answer:

"And I, Madam, if Satan himself were the best painter and I wanted my portrait, I would not hesitate to sit to him...." Needless to say, the anti-Catholic lady had by that time become a stanch Healy friend, willing even to forgive him his religion.

Self-taught and individual in religion as in art, Healy con-
formed to rituals only insofar as they reached his inner aspirations.
The mystery of Mass did, and inspired him always; rare were the
times he missed early Mass—an unfailing source of strength for
his day. But he never flaunted his beliefs nor discussed religion
except with those who earnestly sought help or reassurance of
their own convictions.

Miss Eliza Starr, a young Chicago teacher whose great desire
in life was to paint, sought the artist's advice; George Healy looked
at her work and in trying to help her became interested in her and
her invalid mother who lived in a small house belonging to the
parish and known as St. Joseph's Cottage. The published diary of
Eliza Starr gives some instances. At one time she mentions:

"Mr. and Mrs. Healy have given me my carpets for parlor, bedroom, hall and studio...." A little further: "Mrs. Healy came and
told very droll stories..." and another time: "Mother enjoyed
Mr. Healy very much and said that although he was so witty, his
wit did not kill, but rather called out the wit of others. I said:
'This comes from his genuine kindness of heart.' "

And some time later she writes to a friend: "Ah! did you see the
picture of the dear Archbishop? Was there ever anything more
living, breathing, speaking? I am to copy it in miniature and have
it in my own room! If I do not grow good upon this I shall be a
very obstinate resister of grace...."

At Cottage Hill, in June, 1860, the Healys received the visit of
Dr. Thomas Evans lately arrived from Paris. For hours the family
avidly absorbed news of their friends abroad; but Agnes confessed
that night that she thought Dr. Evans looked older and it made
her feel sad to hear him say that he did not want to be reminded
that he had to die.... From her spiritual heights Agnes added in
a shocked tone: "This world has every charm for him."

In September, Healy was off again, painting portraits in Virginia, seeing old friends, and visiting at Audley near Belleville,
Clark County, the Lewises, whose home was filled with Washing-

ton legacies, furniture, plate, etc. He found Mrs. Lewis difficult to paint; nevertheless, he made a successful portrait.

Then Philadelphia saw him for a little while, and in October he was at the Thorns' New York home at 8 West Sixteenth Street—that massive, square, flat-roofed mansion with its imposing front porch, the entrance flanked by two huge stone dogs. In the yard a spraying fountain glittered in the sun and a great stone urn filled with flowers held overhanging vines that trailed almost to the ground. In this house Healy always found "his" room ready whenever he passed through the city. Colonel Thorn's pleasant laughter no longer resounded in the halls and most of the beautiful daughters were away, but the artist enjoyed being surrounded by the many portraits he had painted for them. . . .

In Boston, where he had gone to make a copy of Stuart's portrait of John Adams, he also saw many old friends. Edward Prince of Wales was then in the United States and Mrs. Harrison Gray Otis organized her famous $10,000 ball for the occasion. "A friend made me go to the ball Thursday night," wrote Healy to Mrs. Goddard. "I saw the Prince dance; he is like his mother and perfectly well behaved. I think he must have been pleased with his visit in our country."

There a letter reached the artist that postponed his projected visit to New Orleans and this enabled him to return home for Christmas. He found Chicago seething with political activity; the Lincoln-Douglas debates were long past, but the tall, gaunt figure of the presidential choice was taking heroic proportions, despite Douglas's long-standing popularity. Months before Healy had expressed the hope that Mrs. Goddard's father, Representative Vinton, would rally to the Lincoln camp: "I am sure your father will work bravely for the man from my state, who is now sure to be the next President."

Already Lincoln was his hero and the more he read about his candidate, the more enthusiastic he became. His great friend

Thomas B. Bryan's enthusiasm added fuel to the fire and one day
Bryan said:

"Mr. Healy, you must paint his portrait. I know you will render
justice to his greatness..."

Healy demurred: "Of course there is nothing I would like more
but it seems asking a great deal from an overburdened candidate,
to request sittings."

"Nothing like trying!" laughed the genial Bryan and thereupon
dashed a note which he then told the artist to read:

"This will be handed to you by Geo. P. A. Healy, esq., the
eminent Artist, whom Congress has commissioned to paint a
series of Presidential portraits to grace the White House, which,
although I am a Virginian, I am *heartily* glad you are soon to
occupy... As Mr. Healy is now en route to the South, I have commissioned him to stop at Springfield and solicit of you the kindness to give him two or three sittings, that he may add to my
National Gallery the portrait of the President-elect..."

When Healy presented his letter of introduction in Springfield, Lincoln immediately consented and the artist set to work.
The first sitting delighted the new President by its swiftness.

"Do you always paint as fast as this, Mr. Healy?"

"Only, Sir, when the sitter is interesting enough..."

And by that time both men were ready to "swap" their favorite
stories. They made an appointment for the second sitting and the
third sitting, the President adding:

"You understand, Mr. Healy, that I may have to change these
appointments."

"Of course, Mr. President. I feel extremely honored and happy
over this one."

Elated, Healy returned home and told Louisa about this first
sitting and how much their new President had impressed him.
Louisa, who by now was an excellent critic of her husband's
work, exclaimed:

"Why! That plain face is really beautiful!"

"That is because the soul shows through his eyes."

And the artist continued filling in the background, strengthening the lines of the face.

Thomas B. Bryan was elated over this new success of his friend Healy, for the next two sittings took place as planned and the portrait was announced in the Chicago Tribune November 17, 1860 inviting Chicagoans to go and see the portrait of their next President at the studio of the celebrated artist G. P. A. Healy—133 Lake Street.

After a happy Christmas with his family at Cottage Hill, Healy left for Washington. He spent a few days with Mr. Vinton and Mrs. Goddard, who gave him letters for the Governor and the Bishop of Cuba—a fine head to paint and a new country to visit! Taking along his new portrait of the Cuban Minister in Washington, Healy sailed from New York, but in Cuba news of illness in the Governor's family shortened Healy's Cuban stay to a week of picturesque excursions. By the end of January the artist once more was in New Orleans, where many orders awaited him.

A full-length portrait of Mrs. Semmes at the harp, painted the preceding winter, had received considerable notice at the New York Exposition. This year again the Semmes and Knox families wanted portraits—one of Mrs. Semmes with her baby boy.

To his chagrin Healy found Mr. Semmes, Attorney General of Louisiana, in favor of Secession. In spite of last December's declaration of Secession, the Yankee could not believe this to be more than a rift such as had shaken the Union under Andrew Jackson, and later under Polk at the time of the Mexican War. In the past, after bitter and heated debates, a compromise was usually effected that satisfied Congress and quieted angry spirits....

In those early months of 1861 Healy painted more portraits than during any of his former visits to Louisville, New Orleans, and Charleston: the Hunts, Sidells, Mathers, Wallises, the Mannings, the Willingtons, Dr. Gibbes, and many others. In New Orleans

Mr. Mather ordered Mrs. Mather's portrait without her knowledge; the artist painted from memory after frequent calls at her home. When Mrs. Mather and her daughter Mrs. Wallis entered his studio one afternoon, the surprise was complete! *"Ma foi! C'est moi!"* exclaimed Mrs. Mather delightedly. She was an outspoken social leader who took the Northern artist under her wing, and cautioned him against the wiles of girls who plastered themselves with cosmetics. . . . *"Elles sont si fardées!"* she would whisper to him with contempt. Perhaps it was this that gave Healy the bold assurance needed to ask his feminine models to wash the paint off their faces before he started work. . . .

As time went on, Healy noticed a stiffening of opinion among his Southern friends and deeply regretted their increasingly belligerent mood.

"When I first came here this winter, I found the feeling very strong against going back into the Union," he wrote on February 26. "Now I learn from high sources that the South begins to fear that without war their grand plan * may fall through, so they are extremely anxious that Mr. Lincoln should take the forts or do something to give them a pretext to fight."

At the Mathers' he heard the same thing: the South was ready; General Beauregard expected to leave for Charleston shortly. Healy remarked what a fine subject for a portrait the General would make, so Mrs. Mather arranged a meeting between the artist and the popular Beauregard, telling her old Negro butler: "Abraham, Mr. Healy is coming to breakfast tomorrow; we must have a good breakfast. . . ." Her strategy worked. Beauregard promised to make time for sittings and Healy at once began a half-length portrait of the man to whom Jefferson Davis had given command of the Carolinas' defense.

"I shall not have time here for more than one or two sittings, Mr. Healy," Beauregard said, "but if you happen to be in Charles-

* The "grand plan" was to establish direct commercial agreements with other nations, regardless of Union accords.

ton we may manage better there." And on Easter Sunday, March 31, Healy was in Charleston, expecting to finish the General's portrait. He had been at Millford, Governor John L. Manning's estate, painting the Governor and several members of his family, his wife, his sister, and also some of their friends. The Governor intended showing these works at the South Carolina convention, hoping that the artist would be commissioned to paint a series of great Carolinians for the new capitol ... "a finer building than the one in Washington, sir," the Governor had assured him. This project awakened dreams of a long residence with his family in this lovely town of blue skies, blue water, soft roses, and brilliant flowers....

Healy wrote Mrs. Goddard, speaking of the Beauregard portrait: "I am going to make a study of Fort Sumter tomorrow to introduce into the background. I believe this will be one of my best portraits. I hope to complete it by the end of the week...." He did complete it,* and incredibly people talked of war.

Friday morning, April 12, 1861, Healy, always an early riser, came out of the Willington house into the morning sunshine and walked toward the harbor. The evening before, he had vaguely heard rumors that General Beauregard was to demand the surrender of Major Anderson at Fort Sumter. Would the Union officer refuse? Major Robert Anderson had been Inspector General of Illinois in the Black War of 1832; in his command was Captain Abraham Lincoln now his Commander in Chief.... Anderson at this storm center realized his desperate situation, but never considered retreating. A rally at Bryan Hall in Chicago on January 5 had loudly praised the Major's stand as General Swift read: "RESOLVED: That we heartily approve of the decisive and patriotic course of Major Anderson at Charleston and that in him we see the type of hero of New Orleans." But on this fatal date in

---

* Healy's portrait of Beauregard given by Bernard Baruch to the Charleston Museum has in the background portraits of those who fired the first shots. The *Charleston Courier*, April 8, 1861.

April, nothing could save the ill-equipped, ill-armed little band of defenders when they received the message that shelling of the fort would start before daybreak....

It was therefore a terrific shock to Healy walking under a clear sky to hear suddenly the boom of cannon. He halted, looked up, peered across the bay... spurts of smoke floated from that little fort he had painted a few days ago. In spite of the early hour people came tumbling out of houses, rushing to the water's edge, and all around him he heard the terrifying word: WAR!

Charleston's quiet streets suddenly swarmed with excited people calling to each other as they converged to the water front for a better view of the forts. All day and night the bombardment continued; conflicting rumors spread though no one doubted the ultimate end for that brave handful of men. April 13, the flag was shot, and all at once billows of smoke indicated worse than the discharge of arms. When the Charlestonians realized that fire had broken out among their hard-pressed enemies, they sent Colonel L. T. Wigfall, who, under flag of truce, passed through the blazing gateway to offer assistance and demand surrender.

When Beauregard's terms of surrender were finally accepted and the white flag raised, the United States flag was lowered by order of the commanding officer after he had obtained a salute for his flag. As Major Anderson handed over his sword, General Beauregard's aides refused to deprive him of it and the noble company evacuated the fort with dignity. Romantic days, but romance would soon give way to the horrors of war....

Back at the Willington house, Healy found great agitation. The master of the house had been told that if that "Yankee painter" did not leave by sundown he would be tarred and feathered. The artist laughed, but his Southern friend, on the contrary, looked serious. "Mr. Healy," said his host, "a carriage shall be at the door in an hour; you must leave town, otherwise they will prove as good as their word."

And instead of returning to New Orleans, seething with all the terror and distress of war, George Healy traveled straight to Washington to report what he had seen, heard and gathered from the attack on Fort Sumter.

Of the many portraits painted before Ft. Sumter some disappeared in the cataclysm, others remained in homes miraculously spared, while yet others, hidden in old trunks, bales of cotton, or some overlooked cache reappeared later to rejoice the hearts of their returned owners. When the Northern armies reached Louisiana in 1862, Mr. Wallis called on Barrière, the framer, to look after his pictures, and these were safely transported, cased in cotton. And a strange incident saved another portrait—that of Mrs. Hayward painted in 1850. During the war one day a Union officer in Beaufort, South Carolina, noticed a picture lying in the middle of the street. He picked it up, saw the signature, took it with him to Philadelphia where, later, he sent it to Mr. Gabriel Manigault of Charleston who, in turn, sent it to the Taylor family, thinking it might be a portrait of Mrs. Taylor's aunt; it is now in the Taylor collection.

Many a tale of luck or ill luck with his work came to Healy in after years; but when the "Yankee painter" was forced out of Charleston on that fateful Fort Sumter day, he said good-by to his happy Southern winters. Never now would he be asked to paint the hundred and seventy great men of South Carolina who were to adorn the walls of Charleston's new capitol. He might see and paint Southern friends again in Paris, London, Rome, Washington, or New York—but the tie was broken, the project of a long residence South shattered; Thomas and William, whom he continued to help and hold in his thoughts, would seldom be able to reunite and form the patriarchal group George had always hoped for.

At the White House President Lincoln listened intently to Healy's account. How well those two men understood each other! And like Healy's brothers in the South, Mrs. Lincoln also had relatives in the opposing forces ... When Healy asked Mr. Lincoln if he would let him make a quick sketch while they talked, without hesitation the President walked to the armchair the artist was already drawing forward and sat down in listening attitude ...

Even in that rapid sketch, the expression was dramatic, the eyes expressing deep sorrow, the attention tense as if trying to find some way, some solution to an impossible tragedy ...

When Healy explained that he had laughed at his host's hurry to send him out of Charleston, there was no smile in Lincoln's features. The full tragedy of that almost unbelievable situation was all too real—a portent of all the dangers ahead. Like the artist he felt a true American pride over the noble attitude of the combatants after Anderson had been forced to surrender and his victors had refused to deprive the little company of its arms ... Yes, they should have been brothers-in-arms instead of combatants ... When and how would peace with honor come?

Always, in every portrait Healy painted of Lincoln, there would be that depth of feeling that sprang from a great soul, and that the artist had felt from their first close contact. But this quick, vivid sketch could not offer the hopeful effect of Healy's first portrait painted in Springfield four months ago ... both men knew what anguish was still ahead of them, of all Americans ...

Sharing the same thoughts, the same hopes followed by a dread of disunion in this wonderful country of theirs, the two men would remain silent or suddenly bring up some small fact that unexpectedly illumined the horror of this exploding war ... Unwilling to break into the President's thoughts, Healy concentrated on his rapid painting and from the small canvas emerged that amazingly thoughtful face that could retain, even in the dreadful anxiety of the moment an unbreakable faith in the future.

Later, in Washington again, Healy would have a temporary studio for the many portraits ordered by generals, politicians or merely residents who could not afford the time to visit their painter in Chicago, Healy would again paint Lincoln in 1863 and 1864 "a few months before the assassination" as his daughters would later write in affidavits requested of them—portraits the artist would use later for his favorite historical composition: The Peacemakers.

Chapter XXII

THE CIVIL WAR

WAR was raging. Families were disrupted. George Healy heard nothing about his two brothers as communication with the South was well-nigh impossible—save in Maryland which, to his great satisfaction, sided with the North. His sister Agnes had become a widow; she no longer felt the urge to direct a girls' school. She busied herself with war work, but with the war over she would feel lonely, at loose ends. Then memories of the convents she had attended would take on a healing, benevolent aspect. She went to New York, made a retreat at the Convent of the Sacred Heart, visited at Kenwood, Albany, Mother Hardey—a lifelong friend of her brother George—and then entered religious life.

The cleavage was complete. There were now three distinct units among the children of Captain Healy and Mary Hicks: George's family, showing definite New England traits in spite of its wide cosmopolitan experience; Agnes Dyson, now a nun in charge of Thomas's little motherless girl Mary, while Thomas lived in Port Gibson with his sons who would have their roots in Louisiana and Mississippi. One day the father placed little Mary in charge of a train conductor and all the child carried in the way of address was a letter to Sister Agnes, New York! To the credit of the conductor, the convents, and the police, the child aged five arrived safe and sound at Kenwood. There she was to remain until graduation under the austere wing of Mother Dyson, who lived into her eighty-fifth year and was buried on May 25, 1902, in the little cemetery on the hilltop.

But all this was still far in the unknown future when Healy returned to Cottage Hill in June, 1861, facing unexpected and serious financial difficulties. It had seemed so natural when all Chicago flocked to his studio to spend without counting, but the rich harvest expected from his Southern tour had vanished in the smoke of Civil War; he had renounced payments, but his effects and a number of pictures as well as painting material and the lay figures so necessary for his work were still held in New Orleans with things "of great use to me and very little to our Southern brothers who have seized them," as he wrote on June 30. . . .

Chicago was in a turmoil—aflame with war fever. The artist helped in every way he could, sending pictures to raffles, painting the flag presented to Frémont's regiment. . . . Harassed with slow payments and mounting debts, he tried in vain to sell some of his property and to collect the thousand dollars still due him from the congressional appropriation of 1858 for the Buchanan portrait. But the Treasury, burdened with the unexpected war drain, was empty, and defaulted on this and other non-essential agreements. Healy wrote directly to James Buchanan, telling him of his urgent need, and after a long-drawn-out correspondence that led nowhere, finally offered him the painting at half price. In August, 1861, he received from the ex-President an exasperated and discourteous letter refusing to buy at any price or to have anything to do with the matter, since it was not a portrait ordered by him personally! "Oh, very well," said Healy dispiritedly, "let us forget the incident . . ." and left Buchanan hanging on his studio wall.

Overage for military service, he paid for an alternate and then for two, though still deeply in debt; the thought that had troubled him vaguely for a long time crystallized and haunted his sleepless nights: America, founded as a refuge for individuals persecuted in other countries and eager to carry out an ideal of freedom, should never have allowed slavery into this new hard-working paradise—a monstrous error. It denied American Christianity and made a mockery of the dignity of human beings; it scorched the souls of those who profited by it even worse than the souls of their victims.... The present conflict might not be wholly one of principle, Healy admitted; interests and rivalries battled through it—but fundamentally it was inevitable because a great wrong had to be righted.

Louisa quieted his troubled spirit by repeating his own belief in art's mission. Though war devastated the land, education should not be neglected; art was a necessary part of life; he, the bearer of God's special gift, must keep on carrying his message of art and beauty to all parts of the country. Painting was his mission and nothing must interfere.

She, who always felt so keenly every moment of his absence, encouraged his response to any and every call, not allowing her loneliness ever to hamper his movements or his sense of freedom. Happy in the security of a home truly their own and free from the dread of those endless ocean separations, she adjusted herself to the informal, easy atmosphere of a community gathered from roots that were, like her own, far removed from the Middle West, but which had formed here a strikingly American region with large vistas and a great future.

While her husband painted the flag for Frémont's regiment, she reviewed with him the amazing, romantic career of that stormy petrel, son of a French father and a Virginian mother. Frémont was at once appointed Major General in command of the Western Department with headquarters in St. Louis. He was the hero of the West; his explorations on the Pacific Coast, his planting of the American flag on many peaks were legendary; Frémont's hatred of slavery, his loyalty to the Union, and his dislike of Buchanan made him particularly sympathetic to the artist, and it was a spirited portrait Healy painted on the flag.

Healy also painted the young, ardent Irishman, Colonel James A. Mulligan, who had raised the 23rd Illinois Volunteers—the noted "Irish Brigade." His gallantry, his patriotism inspired the artist. Their sympathy was instantaneous. As editor of the *Catholic Weekly,* he was interested in all Healy told him of Mrs. Goddard's translation of Spanish religious books. Healy also told him how he had just missed painting a portrait of the Bishop of Cuba.

In the war Mulligan was to become the subject of stories and songs and his men long repeated his last command at the battle of Kernstown on July 24, 1862: "Lay me down and save the flag...."

That first war summer of 1861, Healy perforce remained with the family at Cottage Hill, painted a few heads, "but not enough to support the family," he wrote.

The death of Mrs. Longfellow on Tuesday, July 9, 1861, saddened the Healys; they could not believe that this gay, vital young woman was gone; but a letter from Mrs. Goodwin gave them all the details:

...Mrs. Longfellow was with us on Saturday previous to her death to say good-by for the summer, intending to go to Nahant on the following Thursday.... We remarked upon her great beauty. She wore the same light muslin dress which afterwards enveloped her in flames. The papers gave you a very correct account of the sad disaster; her two younger girls were with her in the library and while making impressions in wax for them a lighted match or some part of it must have fallen upon her dress for she found herself on fire, rushing to the study where Mr. Longfellow was, who instantly tried to put the hearth rug about her; she escaped from him to the entry. His cries of fire brought the servants with water, but too late to save her life. She was soon placed under the effects of ether and remained through the night conscious at times and, when speaking, perfectly calm, regretting that she was the cause of so much trouble....

The scene at the funeral was one of exquisite beauty....

Mr. Longfellow is still confined to his bed; his hands only were burned, but his physician thinks that he will have the use of them uninjured.... He does not trust himself to see his friends or to speak of his loss.... Mr. Nathan Appleton was very feeble at the time of Mrs. Longfellow's death; he was told of all the circumstances; he said but little and calmly sank to his final rest on the morning after her funeral.

In October, Healy told Mrs. Goddard of the latest transaction to pay off his debts:

"Our Lord has helped me by inducing my neighbor Thomas B. Bryan to offer to take upon himself $18,500 of my $23,000 debts for my interest in Graceland Cemetery. I have no doubt this property will be in five years worth one hundred thousand dollars, and yet I rejoice in his good fortune, and my relief: I mention this to you, because you have always taken so much interest in my affairs; although in a depressed condition, they are not as bad as they have been. I shall try to paint a whole length of Jackson for Congress between now and February; should I succeed in this matter it is my intention to call at Wheeling with Agnes and perhaps take her with me to Washington to see you and Madame de Barros....I look every evening for the dispatches from Washington, which city I now consider safe. I feel encouraged about Missouri and Kentucky to say nothing of Maryland: I hope your father is now satisfied with the efforts of the Government."

Repeatedly, Healy mentioned with regret the critical attitude of Representative Vinton toward Lincoln's administration; he wished the two men knew each other better, for then they would assuredly understand and appreciate one another.

In the midst of inner distress and intense work, Healy's talent ripened. He painted vigorously, enthusiastically, at top speed—and speed with him meant better inspiration. He responded with alacrity to any demand. He would pay for this later with physical weariness, eyestrain, and insomnia, but at the moment there was no stopping him; the fever of activity had reached every fiber of his body while his mind seemed forever on the alert. So keyed up was he that his insomnia increased to the point of danger, which Louisa noticed with alarm.

For Congress he painted a full-length portrait of Andrew Jackson to hang in the Capitol. Mr. Robb, of New Orleans, was at this time in Chicago, posing for his portrait. He eyed the uniform Healy had ordered.

"I did not realize the General was so tall," remarked Mr. Robb.

"Just about your size and figure," Healy replied, and was delighted when, watching his sitter's face, he saw the idea spring up that he had hoped might present itself.

"Would you like me to pose for you in the uniform, Mr. Healy?" So it was arranged, and in a letter to Mrs. Goddard written in November, 1861, Healy mentioned this offer, adding:

"Mr. Robb is truly very kind: he has a fine figure and will work with me to the end."

He also referred to the horse in the background:

"I have made studies from horses to introduce one in the picture; the last study is from the head of the horse I bought from Dr. Huntington when he was in Chicago; when you see the Jackson portrait, you will see a likeness of this creature with a handsome head...."

By January 3, 1862, the portrait was sent to Washington, as Healy started on his winter work in various cities. But before his departure, on December 28, 1861, the Chicago *Tribune* published a flattering notice:

Healy's Jackson

At Mr. Healy's studio on Lake Street will remain on exhibition a few days his full-length picture of the hero of New Orleans. It was painted by the artist on a Government order, and will be taken to Washington on the 3rd of January. While here, it will repay richly a visit from our lovers of art. Mr. Healy's fertile and busy pencil has done much that is excellent in the direction of historical portraiture. A keen and thorough artist, faithful in his details and skillful at fixing prominent traits, his productions will have a permanent national value, and become more valuable with time. His Jackson is beyond all question a noble work of art. It is a full-length portrait, the leader and his war steed. The latter is skillfully introduced, and made subordinate to the chief subject, who stands just ready to mount, but turning for a far-off piercing glance, his whole soul in his countenance, with that characteristic firmness, decision, promptness, and—"I take the responsibility." One can almost imagine that the stern visage is such as the living hero would have worn at learning that the rebel guns had opened upon Fort

Sumter, or, rather, weeks earlier, before the rebellion had taken shape. Turn and compare it with the sad, placid visage of poor Mr. Buchanan, opposite, with the lack-luster eye, and infirm weak old mouth, and the art is true to its trust that tells even on this canvas in the comparison of men. A Jackson would have saved the Government—such a Jackson as Healy has painted—and such he was.... There is no tampering, nor timidity, nor half measure in Mr. Healy's picture, and he is too good and true an artist not to have put them there had he found them in his subject.

Remembering Andrew Jackson's fiery and direct approach, Healy thought sorrowfully of the constant bickerings among leaders from whom the one great hero had not yet risen. Heroic they all were, in combat, but the leader of men, the one who would be followed through defeat or victory, the one who could hold on and save the Union was not recognizable.

When McClellan replaced Winfield Scott in November, 1861, Healy, like many others, hoped and believed that this, the youngest general entrusted with so high a position, would be the man. But here it was January, and what was he doing? Drilling, training, drilling! Until even the long-suffering President was reported to have exclaimed:

"If you don't intend to use the Army, General, won't you lend it to me?"

From the other side of the Atlantic distressing news reached the Healys. Their dear friend Dubourjal, whose presence they missed so much, lay desperately ill. The doctor to whom Healy had written answered that there was no chance of recovery. Healy's instinct was to secure passage across the ocean and hasten to his friend's bedside. But it was impossible—the ports were closed, money was scarce. So George wrote to assure Dubourjal that his little investment of years ago had multiplied so that the income would provide for all his needs. He must not worry. As soon as possible George would join him.

With gold at a premium Healy never failed to send each quarterly remittance, and regularly the Frenchman wrote: "The bankers, Messrs. Munro, inform me that the money is at my disposal ..." and in May, 1863, having received news of Mrs. Phipps's death, Dubourjal added touchingly: "Poor dear Grandmother! God has relieved her of her long suffering.... I hope she is happy and I must confess a feeling of envy—and yet I should wish to prolong my life, so as to prolong my gratitude. Your sincere friend—until the end...."

One day, after the end of war, the dreaded black-bordered *faire-part* came, announcing to the Healys that on December 8, 1865, their beloved Edme Savinien Dubourjal had gone to his rest. He was seventy, eighteen years older than his American friend and companion.

As in life, so in death a comic element often filters into the midst of tragedy. Letters arrived from the miniaturist's relatives who had done nothing to relieve the horror of Dubourjal's four bedridden years. These letters, more and more insistent, claimed the capital from which had come that nice regular income!

Chapter XXIII

WAR PORTRAITS

THE YEAR 1862 opened with a burst of activity that did not slacken. Worry, fatigue, war anxiety, nothing seemed to quell George Healy's ardor. From Washington, where he left his Jackson in the hands of the framer and his daughter in the tender care of Mrs. Goddard, he went on to Wheeling and Baltimore, where work awaited him.

An 1862 exhibit in Chicago lists ten Healy portraits: General Hooker, James Robb, Judge Burnett, Senator Yates, Thomas Sully, Judge Mason of Virginia, Samuel F. Vinton of Ohio, Henry Farnum, George Peabody, and Lord Palmerston—the latter painted years earlier but considered timely because of Palmerston's upholding of the North at this beginning of the war, while the majority of British government officials favored the South more or less openly.

The New York exhibit that same season showed three Healy portraits: Archbishop McCloskey, Bishop Duggan, and Romaine Goddard. He also painted the Archbishop of Baltimore and the Kennedys, General Rosecrans at Wheeling as well as Major and Mrs. Clary, Longfellow, Mary Ely, Mrs. Otis in Boston... Whatever estimate one gathers from letters or papers that later escaped the Chicago fire, it is bound to fall short of the actual number, and the 577 Healy portraits mentioned by Tuckerman as painted during the eleven years of the artist's residence in Chicago no longer seem exaggerated.

As General McClellan sat for his portrait Healy felt a surge of happiness.

"General," Healy told him, "had I painted you first, General Beauregard would undoubtedly have reminded me of you as you now make me think of him."

"How is that?" queried the startled Northerner.

Healy smiled. "You are both the artist's delight. Masculine beauty is met rarely enough in our profession, and accompanied by dignity, dash, and gallantry it is indeed a great treat."

"Enough, enough!" McClellan laughed. "Military training, it makes us all alike...."

Much-traveled and well-read, speaking French, German, Russian, and Spanish, McClellan had made an excellent envoy; he was sent to the Crimea as United States observer and on his way was received at the brilliant Court of Napoleon III. To Healy's intense surprise, this officer did not find the Empress Eugénie as beautiful as reported; in fact, he did not think her beautiful at all!

"An unsurpassed blonde beauty," protested the artist, "perhaps a little cold, perhaps a little hard, but very beautiful! She will probably grow into graceful and fascinating old age...."

In the natural course of conversation they turned from the Empire to the earlier regime of Louis Philippe and to the American artist's relations with the French King. At this present moment two of the late King's grandsons, the Comte de Paris and the Duc de Chartres, were acting as McClellan's aides-de-camp, having been permitted to serve without taking the oath of allegiance and without pay.

Healy remembered the little fellows whose father Ferdinand, Louis Philippe's eldest son and heir to the throne, had died in a carriage accident in 1842. There would be no more Orléans on the French throne nor would the Bourbons occupy it long.

In American politics McClellan was astounded to find Healy an ardent admirer of Abraham Lincoln. How could an artist accept as the leader of a great and picturesque nation that uncouth,

lanky lawyer? The General did not hide his contempt for the man
he resented as Commander in Chief. While believing in the young
enthusiast's military acumen, Lincoln patiently suffered the officer's rudeness while McClellan continued his thorough preparations for a smashing victory which did not come.

And Healy, under the spell of his agreeable model, wrote to
Mrs. Goddard:

"I am glad to see the country beginning to understand McClellan. I expect great things from him."

Everyone was fighting the war in those days—armchair strate-
gists whose moving pins on maps could not picture the horror and
destruction. Despite his ignorance of military affairs, Healy, too,
wrote to his friend Mrs. Goddard: ". . . it seems to me it would be
better to clear the Mississippi with the balance of our forces, rather
than run against masked batteries in Virginia. But no doubt our
new Commander in Chief will do the right thing at the right
time. . . ."

However, they were not all military models who came marching
into Healy's studio. That year 1862, richly varied, took the artist
to many cities painting poets, speakers, prelates, and a goodly
number of ladies, young, old, or middle-aged. He made a portrait
of Mrs. Goddard's niece on the verge of marriage with M. de
Barros, which he sent to the New York exhibit. Painting constantly on his way home, Healy stopped at the Sullys' and made
another portrait of Sully, later shown in Chicago. In Washington
he delivered his Jackson at the Capitol and received two new
orders for portraits of Presidents Harrison and Tyler—the latter
having died in Virginia in January.

Agnes left Mrs. Goddard to visit her father. Journeying eastward
to Boston, they stopped in Wheeling, Baltimore, Philadelphia, and
New York. In Boston, George Healy and Agnes decided that
Boston should be their next home; they had so many friends there,
the atmosphere of New England suited them so well! They
wanted to come East.

Abraham Lincoln
SIXTEENTH PRESIDENT OF THE UNITED STATES
1809–1865

Ulysses Simpson Grant
EIGHTEENTH PRESIDENT OF THE UNITED STATES
1822–1885

William T. Sherman
AMERICAN SOLDIER
1820–1891

Robert E. Lee
AMERICAN SOLDIER
1807–1870

"The Peacemakers"
SHERMAN, GRANT, LINCOLN AND PORTER

Pierre Gustave Toutant Beauregard
AMERICAN SOLDIER
1818–1893

John Q. Adams
SIXTH PRESIDENT OF THE
UNITED STATES
1767–1848

Andrew Jackson
SEVENTH PRESIDENT OF THE
UNITED STATES
1767–1845

John Tyler
TENTH PRESIDENT OF THE
UNITED STATES
1790–1862

Martin Van Buren
EIGHTH PRESIDENT OF THE
UNITED STATES
1782–1862

James Buchanan
FIFTEENTH PRESIDENT OF THE UNITED STATES
1791–1868

James K. Polk
ELEVENTH PRESIDENT OF THE
UNITED STATES
1795–1849

Millard Fillmore
THIRTEENTH PRESIDENT OF THE
UNITED STATES
1800–1874

Franklin Pierce
FOURTEENTH PRESIDENT OF THE
UNITED STATES
1804–1869

Chester A. Arthur
TWENTY-FIRST PRESIDENT OF THE
UNITED STATES
1830–1886

25

George P. A. Healy
SELF PORTRAIT
1813–1894

Mrs. G. P. A. Healy
LOUISA PHIPPS HEALY
1819–1905

Agnes de Mare and Her Son
ELDEST DAUGHTER OF HEALY

Tiburce de Mare
HUSBAND OF AGNES HEALY

Jeanne de Mare
YOUNGER DAUGHTER OF AGNES
HEALY DE MARE

Marie de Mare
OLDER DAUGHTER OF AGNES
HEALY DE MARE

27

The Healy Garden in Paris
MRS. HEALY AND DAUGHTER EDITH

"The Boating Party on the Thames"
EXCURSION OF THE HEALY AND WHITEHOUSE FAMILIES

Jennie Bryan
LATER MRS. JOHN BARTON PAYNE

Emma Thursby
AMERICAN SINGER
1845–1931

31

Charles Goodyear, Sr.
AMERICAN INVENTOR AND INDUSTRIALIST
1800–1860

Meanwhile the fortunes of war rose and ebbed, the list of casualties mounted, the tales of horror grew louder and more bitter. That essential Union of the States Daniel Webster had so eloquently proclaimed and fought for seemed broken beyond repair.

In this exalted atmosphere, civilian portraits might seem tame, yet one model inspired Healy: Orestes Brownson, lecturer, writer, editor, a man to conjure with—big in body and intellect—fearless, ardent, in his denunciation of slavery and his Christian preachings. A convert to Catholicism, he had belonged to the Transcendentalists at one time, but even Brook Farm could not follow his progressive pace and many bishops caviled at his interpretation of Catholicism, although Bishop Duggan, Healy's friend, fully approved of Orestes Brownson.

Healy asked the latter to give him a few sittings. They became so animated in conversation that Healy had time to make two three-quarter length portraits, one of which he gave to Miss Brownson. Later, in Paris, he again painted this man he so admired.

Brownson's patriotic views so forcefully presented in his magazine and his spiritual eloquence did much, Healy felt, to awaken interest and diminish prejudice among his anti-Catholic Chicago friends. Bishop Duggan filled Bryan Hall "with most of our nicest people who were highly interested when he spoke of his journey to Rome," says one of Healy's letters. "Mrs. Douglas * was present and took tea with us to meet the Bishop the next evening. Saturday morning she left for home; she was much depressed the two or three days she was here, going daily to the grave of her late husband...."

A letter from Eliza Starr to a friend allows us a glimpse of the enthusiasm aroused by Healy's portraits:

"You heard that Dr. Brownson was here this winter.... Mr. Healy's portrait I consider little less than a miracle, which was

* Mrs. Stephen Douglas, widow of the "Little Giant."

replied to by Mr. Healy in this wise: 'Then it is a likeness, for Mr. Brownson is only less than a miracle.' You must see the portrait. It has been sent, together with those of the dear Archbishop and Mr. Longfellow,* to the New York exhibit. . ."

It was during the winter of 1862 that Healy was able to sell his Cottage Hill home; receiving only $4,000 when he had paid $13,000 for it; but especially with the desperate illness of the aged Mrs. Phipps, his wife found living in the country intolerable. Her mother, whose mind wandered, resisted her daughter's care and fought every measure intended for her comfort until the family found a person who devoted her entire time to her and satisfied Mrs. Phipps until the end. This occurred shortly after they moved to Chicago, and that delightful lay nun, Eliza Starr, gives another echo of Healy life in her diary of that winter. She mentions a visit from Mrs. Healy:

"After Mrs. Healy left, Mother said: 'She is very entertaining, and why must I fall asleep?' 'Oh,' I said, 'you are tired. . . .' It was no matter either with Mrs. Healy; she knows all about old ladies; her mother lived to be over ninety and she was most faithful in her attentions to her. . . ."

In the Healy letters dated from their new home at 247 Illinois Street one can almost hear the sighs of relief and content at being in the city.

Chicago, it was said, had never been more prosperous. The movement of troops from this center, the mounting army needs, the influx of people fleeing battlegrounds, all contributed to make Chicago with its Great Lakes port and ships and its railroads a strategically important and industrially active center.

---

* William Dean Howells wrote: "It shows Longfellow at the most characteristic period of his life, in the freshness of his powers in the time of his greatest enterprises, when he had already won a world-wide fame as a poet and had begun his greatest scholarly achievement as the translator of Dante. It is interesting to see him while his face is still that of youth and strength.

"I had the company of the picture many years in the old reading room of Ticknor and Fields, and I never wearied of its color and dignity and ideal fidelity to Longfellow's fineness."

On Christmas morning, 1862, Healy wrote from Chicago to Mrs. Goddard:

"...I am happy to say we all enjoy the city after having been so long in the country: and this has been a delightful day since early this morning; between five and six Georgie and Kathleen were up and delighted with what they found—he with his sled and skates, etc., while she with her great doll and its variety of dresses formed a subject for a charming picture. In the fullness of her joy Kathleen exclaimed, 'I do believe I must go up the chimney and kiss Santa Claus!' "

When George Healy informed his friends that he and his family intended to move East, commissions poured in and sitters flocked to his studio. For once he felt obliged to cancel his proposed visit to Louisville, Kentucky, where he had spent part of every winter for several years. Healy counted many friends in that Border State and had been following with bated breath the rivalries in the Kentuckian Congress which was now definitely siding with the North. Grant had emerged from obscurity with brilliant victories at Fort Henry and Fort Donelson in Kentucky and now the two generals who would symbolize for the artist Northern success, Grant and Sherman, were carrying out the Mississippi plan Sherman had long ago declared essential for victory.

Chapter XXIV

THE CAPTAIN FALLS

IN 1863 two names began to emerge high above the usual horizon of military fame—Grant and Sherman. Grant's victory at Vicksburg turned the tide, which up to that time had seemed controlled by General Lee—that officer to whom the President had offered command of the Union armies. When the great Virginian, not without an inner struggle, decided to remain with the South, it was a blow. How often since that first shot at Fort Sumter, Lincoln wished he could have retained Lee's allegiance!

But now a man in absolute contrast with the Southern leader, a short, silent, serious officer, was showing the qualities needed to wear down that Southern courage and tenacity. "The Hammerer" they called Ulysses S. Grant—for the South felt the impact of his blows; before the country sensed his genius, Grant spelt danger to Lee. Both Grant and Sherman had seen their stars rise after Shiloh, but it took the siege of Vicksburg to arouse national recognition.

When the armies under Grant marched along the Mississippi into the Southwest, George Healy studied every bulletin.... How familiar all that country was to him—that Mississippi the artist had followed so many times in picturesque river boats or riding a horse along the tall green levies on his portrait journeys to New Orleans, and then again on his way up through Tennessee and Kentucky, usually switching over to the Ohio River route.... Once only had he stopped in Mississippi to visit his brothers after their move from Natchez to Port Gibson. And now, even as he exulted over the Grant and Sherman advance, his heart constricted while he read of an attack on Port Gibson May 1, 1863, where Grant's armies had lost 853 men. Where were Thomas and William? What were they doing, what were they feeling? Now that his house could hold them all, he could not reach them.

So vivid was every stage of the war that in later years, when George Healy, then intimate with the Shermans and the Grants, would speak of them, his sitters as well as his children and grandchildren could visualize each incident, each personage, and live over with him what had now become history.

That Grant never doubted final victory, Healy knew. There would be indecisive battles, some defeats, but on the whole Grant's assurance that they "had" Lee was justified. Modest he remained, but not hesitant. Easygoing, much of the time careless about his appearance, not too exacting over detail, Grant could on occasion become a strict disciplinarian and as a ranking officer would not brook what he considered a lack of respect. He showed this when at Chattanooga Hooker sent an officer of his guard to meet him at the station instead of going himself. "If General Hooker wishes to see me," Grant coldly informed the officer, "he will find me on this train," and when Hooker promptly appeared, his tardy offers of hospitality were declined.

But he could accept seeming rudeness in a good cause. An officer not recognizing the rider urging his horse on a wooden bridge shouted:

"Turn back, you darned fool! That bridge is slippery as glass!"

Some hours later Grant recognized him:

"You are the man who prevented me from venturing onto the bridge, Colonel?"

"Yes, sir!" replied the worried Colonel.

"I wish to thank you. You saved me from a silly, foolhardy action."

And the following year, when Secretary of War Stanton complained of Grant's drawing upon some of the Washington defenses for his Army, the General—for whom Congress had revived Washington's title of Lieutenant General—replied:

"I think I rank you in this matter, Mr. Secretary."

"We shall have to see Mr. Lincoln about that," said the Secretary.

"All right," agreed Grant, "Mr. Lincoln ranks us both," and they went to the White House.

Stanton asked Grant to state his case, but the latter said he had no case, was satisfied; the cabinet member then stated his objections. The President, who had rejoiced at Congress's recognition of Grant, exclaiming, "Thank God! At last I have a General!" now gave the Secretary of War a typical answer:

"You and I, Mr. Stanton, have been trying to boss this job, and we have not succeeded very well with it. We have sent across the mountains for *Mr.* Grant, as Mrs. Grant calls him, to relieve us, and I think we had better leave him alone to do as he pleases." *

In Washington, Healy knew General Sherman's younger brother, John, who, when Salmon P. Chase was named Secretary of the Treasury, had succeeded him in the Senate, a post he would occupy until also named Secretary of the Treasury in 1877. John Sherman and his family ordered their portraits; during the sittings, the artist heard much talk and praise of Generals Sherman and Grant, and followed with keen personal interest the progress of these Union leaders.

When John Sherman had urged his brother to take up again his military profession abandoned at the time of his marriage, Sherman hesitated. He hated war; his famous "War is hell!" came from a deep-seated conviction. But at Baton Rouge, where he headed the Military Seminary, the sudden seizure by Governor Moore of the United States Arsenal infuriated him. He called this "the worst act so far of the revolution!" and impulsively William Tecumseh Sherman returned North to offer his services, an important turning point in history, indeed!

Appointed Colonel in the 13th Infantry, he was assigned to

* Quoted in William Connant Church, *Ulysses S. Grant.*

command a brigade in General McDowell's army. His determination to keep the press away from his troops, however, for fear of careless unveiling of plans to the enemy, made him extremely unpopular with these powerful makers or destroyers of reputation and started his long calvary of slander.... Sherman's critics circulated a rumor that the officer was losing his mind. Nervous, quick, active, always working under high tension, sensing the mistakes made by his superiors, pleading in vain for re-inforcements, taking sudden decisions, the General seemed at times erratic enough to justify the suspicion.... Later, when Sherman's reports were finally published, these same accusers ate humble pie, admitting that his predictions had been correct, his sudden movement wise. All, except Secretary of War Stanton, who never defended the General even though he knew him to be right, and who at the last resented viciously Sherman's generous terms to Joe Johnston —an incident quickly closed by Grant's immediate and friendly intervention.

Healy went frequently to Washington, painting portraits of every member of the President's Cabinet, of many generals, of wives devoted to war work, and listening to comments about the two leading Northern generals.

Grant and Sherman worked in perfect harmony. The supposedly erratic officer showed a keen understanding of Grant's quick mind and slow speech. How silently and brilliantly Grant and Sherman carried out the strategy they had outlined after Vicksburg! Perhaps Sherman felt then that his silence to the press had borne fruit. Before his superior officer's words were out of his mouth, Sherman would express comprehension, agreement, and expound his own appreciation of all the possibilities involved.

Neither had it taken Sherman's men long to understand and appreciate him. His courage and warmheartedness endeared him to them; familiarly, they called him "Old Tycoon" or "Uncle Billy," and any one of them would have given his life to protect him, had Sherman ever allowed it. At Shiloh the General had received shots in the shoulder, through his hat, and in his hand, and had fought on while four horses were killed under him! They all believed he bore a charmed life. No other leader, unless perhaps Lee with his Confederate followers, could obtain such devotion and confidence as Sherman's men showed during those heroic marches.

A great soldier, Sherman suffered the lasting hatred of the South because of his famous "March through Georgia" which carried out the terrible and effective "scorched-earth" policy of modern warfare. Yet, in that same march during which his tired but enthusiastic troops ate their fill, the war-hating General had saved young lives on both sides, shedding the blood of animals to feed his soldiers, and carrying destruction to the earth rather than to the men.

News trickled slowly. Of all the journalists who followed the armies and telegraphed stories to the North, Charles Anderson Dana was one of the closest to Lincoln and Lincoln's Cabinet. Healy knew him and snatched at every report from his pen. When word came of Sherman's March to the Sea, Healy's interest reached a new peak, because in Savannah, the Admiral whose fleet was to support Sherman happened to be the man of whom his friend Mrs. Goddard spoke so often—in fact, the man he knew she was going to marry, Admiral John Adolph Dahlgren....

Of all the officers at the Washington Navy Yard when war broke out, only two had not joined the seceding states—Dahlgren was one of them. In February, 1863, he received the "Thanks of Congress and a ten-year extension to his term of active service." The Dahlgren name still stands high in the annals of the United States Navy.

In his fertile mind, the artist pictured that joining in the South of Sherman and Dahlgren: the punctilious naval officer greeting on his temporary flagship, the *Harvest Moon,* his military confrere, thin, nervous, quick Sherman. That night, the General wrote to Mr. Lincoln to offer Savannah as a Christmas gift.... And while the enemy was still looking for him between Atlanta and Savannah, Sherman and his men were on the march again, northward this time—a harder feat than the first three-hundred-mile trek in twenty-four days, for this was winter turning to spring with its rains and freshets, and they had five hundred miles to cover before they could rejoin Grant's army.

In Washington, Healy heard that Lincoln, eager to witness the final developments, had boarded the *River Queen* in March, 1864, to visit Grant's headquarters at City Point. Mrs. Lincoln accompanied him. At the same time, Sherman, leaving Schofield in charge, had also started for City Point, to consult once more with Grant. On March 28 Grant, with Sherman and Admiral David D. Porter, called upon the President on the *River Queen*. Their conference lasted an hour or so, repeated the next morning—the last time they saw one another before Lincoln received Grant's dispatch: "Lee has surrendered!"

The interview at Appomattox was dignified, simple, pathetic, and friendly. With infinite tact, Grant allowed the officers to retain their side arms and let the men who owned horses keep them for the plowing.... When the worn-out gray-coated men had stacked their arms, they sat around, exhausted, tears running down their weather-beaten cheeks. Grant ordered his troops to cease at once their victorious demonstrations; instead, the Union men in their proud blue uniforms joined their ex-enemies, bringing them rations that were sorely needed.

How different were these two heroes—Grant and Lee—the one, a polished Southern gentleman, refined, handsome, educated; the other, gruff, squat, solid, reticent; both perfect officers and magnificent riders; both endowed with the same human understanding, the same love of country and men, the same great heart—like Lincoln, ready to bind the country's wounds "with malice toward none, with charity for all." But their fineness could not always prevail against the hatred bred in many hearts during the fight.... When, a little later, Sherman, animated with the same sentiments,

gave Joe Johnston assurances of peace and good will, Lincoln was
no longer there and Stanton ordered the agreement canceled.
Swiftly, Grant hurried to Sherman's camp and remained with
him until Johnston signed surrender terms copied exactly on those
of Lee and then sent word to the Secretary of State: "General
Johnston has surrendered to General Sherman." No word of his
part in this.... The painful incident was closed, but its portents
worried—and not without cause—those who dreamed of reconciliation.

With all the North, Healy thrilled at the burst of enthusiasm
that greeted Grant on his arrival in Washington after Appomattox.
That evening the Lincolns were going to the theater and wanted
the Grants to be their guests, but General and Mrs. Grant took an
evening train for Burlington, New Jersey, because they had
promised their boys to visit them at school as soon as they arrived
North.

Every detail of that terrible night remained etched in the minds
of all who had fought with Lincoln to preserve the Union and
constantly reminded Healy how often Fate dealt her cruelest blows
at the least prepared moment, plunging men's hearts from the
highest elation to the deepest sorrow.... Lincoln enjoyed the play
Our American Cousin; it was more than half over and no one
showed the least restlessness in this moment of pure relaxation.... Then a shot. A man jumped from the President's box onto
the stage, shouting and brandishing a weapon. Pandemonium
broke loose as the shocked whisper grew to a roar: "The President
is shot!"

Wilkes Booth, the assassin, had opened the box door, put a
pistol to the President's head, fired, then had seized a knife he
carried in the other hand to strike at Major Rathbone who tried
to grab him. Booth leaped to the stage and vanished before anyone
realized what had happened.... In his chair the President still
sat, head drooping forward, eyes closed. Rathbone, bleeding profusely, rushed to the door and opened it to a young officer and

two surgeons. A hasty examination of the President's wound showed it to be fatal. The President was carried to a house across the street.

The long vigil was interrupted by constant messengers. Lincoln's son Robert came with Major Hay; Dr. Stone, the family physician, was there, and all the members of the Cabinet save Mr. Seward who, attacked by another member of the murderous gang, lay at home between life and death. Grant, called back when his train reached Philadelphia, hastened to throw a cordon of troops through the city. All night Washington was in an uproar—but in the house of mourning the silence grew more and more oppressive save for the automatic moaning from the unconscious President's lips. In the morning this stopped: peace settled over the gaunt face.

At twenty-two minutes past seven in the morning of April 15 he was gone. Stanton quietly remarked: "Now he belongs to the ages."

Only those who, eighty years later, lived through the stunning news that their President also, after seeing them through four terrible years of war more modern and even more savage, had suddenly died, can realize the choking sorrow that spread in the land. Incredulity, horror, grief—silent processions through the streets of every city, tears, blessed tears of loyalty and love....

George Healy mourned as Lincoln's funeral train slowly went on its way to Springfield followed by prayers of a grief-stricken nation. Chicago's very life seemed to stop as the funeral cortege passed through the city. There Lincoln had scored his greatest triumph, and the hundreds of thousands who lined the streets or crowded the windows wept not merely for the leader, the great man, but for their friend—to so many there the personal friend whose place no one could ever take.

Healy looked one last time upon that still face he had seen in laughter and in sorrow. The artist could not contain his grief. The crime that had cut short the hour of triumph—a triumph so dearly bought and so richly deserved—made one doubt Providence... but no, one must pray, and Healy, like thousands of others, turned to his church. All churches were open, the services everywhere were crowded.

Chapter XXV

RECONSTRUCTION

No ONE could fill the place of Lincoln, least of all the man who must succeed him—Vice-President Andrew Johnson, willing but unlettered, tactless, quick-tempered, and totally unfit for statesmanship. He meant, insofar as he perceived them, to carry out Lincoln's intentions—but the understanding, the brotherhood, the deep humanity were missing, and there followed black years, for Johnson, who did not lack personal courage, committed blunder after blunder, while Congress opposed him more and more violently. The culmination came in an unheard-of crisis, unique in United States annals—a demand for impeachment. During March and April, 1868, the decision hung in the balance, and in the end one vote only prevented the trial from being continued. The bitterest enemy of the South, a tempestuous, narrow, but clever and eloquent magnetic leader in Congress, Thaddeus Stevens, was responsible for most of this unrest and injustice. Many deplored the restrictive measures against the South and the vulture-like swoop of carpetbaggers upon that once-happy, sunny land.

The men who had fought hardest—the great generals on both sides—were the outstanding and generous ones, striving nobly, but alas often hopelessly, to close the breach and bring back the early unity of American states. Lee, refusing all the various honors offered him by the dissolving Confederacy, accepted the presidency of Washington College, because it was with the youth of the country, he felt, that he could work best toward the ultimate reconciliation.

All this George Healy followed with passionate interest. He had at last got in touch again with his brothers; they were safe, thank God! And if still too close to the past events for visits, they could again tie the broken thread.

Between 1863 and 1867 Healy had spent as much time in Washington as in Chicago. In 1864, he had shared the nation's ardent faith and hope as victory grew closer and closer. With the overwhelming majority of his fellow citizens, he had acclaimed Lincoln's re-election, and had painted another Lincoln portrait which remained in his possession, and later Robert Lincoln ordered a full-length seated picture for which Healy used the same pose but with an armchair more suitable to Lincoln in the White House.

The Healys had not moved East in 1864, as they expected. Instead, they bought a big frame house at 259 Wabash Avenue; it was surrounded by fine trees, a good-sized lawn and flower beds, and situated among the homes of friends so that Mrs. Healy and her two eldest daughters, Agnes and Mary, could easily join in Chicago's social life. It was rather exciting for the girls to think of their father in Washington, Philadelphia, New York, Boston, St. Louis, painting portraits of the men who were making history.

Edith, Maria, and Emily were at Wheeling and Healy had promised the nuns a portrait of General Sherman for their big fair to take place in March and April, 1866, for the benefit of the wounded. There were so many still to care for, and the Government relied mostly on patriotic individuals to assume the heavy burden of social welfare.

In the Wabash Avenue house, Mrs. Healy, as usual, took charge of financial matters and relieved her husband as much as possible of all material cares. He was as busy as he had been during his first two years in Chicago, but the worries of depression years, the anguish of war, the emotional strain of this terrible civil strife had taken a heavy toll. Louisa noticed a fatigue he seldom admitted. Their debts at last cleared, they tried now to prove themselves more provident, and with the help of their dear friend, Ezra B. McCagg, to make a few wise investments and to have a secure income. This did not prevent the artist from accepting poor land deals occasionally instead of cash payments for his work. Louisa did not chide; she laughed a little ruefully one day when her husband told her of his experience that afternoon:

"The recorder looked at me queerly, dearest, when I handed him the deed and asked if I really wanted it recorded. I said, 'Of course!' 'But, Mr. Healy, it will cost you five dollars.' 'I know; that is the usual amount, isn't it?' 'Yes, but, you see, Mr. Healy, this land is under the lake!' "

However, some lots grew in value, especially the made land beyond the Water Works on the North Side. For years this land caused him and the other owners—Potter Palmer, McClurg, et al.—long and costly litigation that in the end had to be carried to the Supreme Court in Washington, because of the mad Irish squatter named Streeter who claimed rights to that whole shore and threatened with a vicious-looking gun anyone coming too near "his land"! Streeterville became a legend in the city....

Constant travel and ceaseless work finally undermined Healy's iron constitution. His eyes troubled him, and this could not pass unnoticed; he cut down on reading and writing, but not on his painting. Headaches recurred more and more frequently, insomnia plagued him. Louisa became thoroughly alarmed. A trip abroad might rest him. She suggested his going over to see Dubourjal, but before Healy could dispose of the work on hand and make arrangements for the voyage, word came of Dubourjal's death. No—he would not go abroad now. The demand for portraits might never be so brisk: returning veterans pleased their families by posing in uniform—especially the officers. The most in demand then was that of General Sherman, and the sittings established between artist and model a firm, delightful, and lasting friendship.

The lean, tall, erect figure, the deeply lined face with sharp dark eyes, reddish hair and beard, seemed at first a little forbidding; but the eyes would light up, the mouth smile and words tumble out so full of life that immediately the artist saw in him a fellow Irishman full of spirit, quick at repartee, and ready for the enjoyment of life after tragic years.

Vivid in his descriptions, Sherman would suggest pictures that immediately took shape in the artist's mind. When the General told of the messenger's arrival, shouting, "Lee has surrendered!" Healy could see the men throwing their caps in the air, slapping each other on the back, yelling to the bearer of such wonderful news: "You're the man we've waited for all these years!"

Healy asked about Admiral Dahlgren for whom Sherman expressed great respect; it interested the General to know that the charming and fashionable Mrs. Dahlgren who had married the Admiral the preceding August was a friend of long standing with the Healy family.

"Mrs. Sherman, I believe, knew her as Mrs. Goddard," Healy said.

"Oh!" exclaimed the General. "Now I place her. Yes, my wife admires her; they belong to the same church, you know."

"So do I," continued Healy.

"Really!" Sherman sounded surprised but added that though he didn't hold much on those things, he felt that the Catholic Church must be very fine since it satisfied a soul as beautiful as his wife's.

As usual, during these sittings the talk invariably turned to Lincoln's wit, magnanimity, greatness, and understanding. How different things would be now, could he have lived to carry out his plans for peace!

Having finished the portrait for Mrs. Sherman, Healy asked the General to give him a few more sittings for the picture he had promised his daughters. The convent at Wheeling was organizing a fair and the painting was to be raffled. Sherman laughed:

"A raffle—a fair—a convent! Man, that doesn't sound right!"

"But it's for the wounded!"

"All right! All right! But I don't see what pretty girls want with an old codger like me!"

Healy protested: "Everybody wants your portrait, General."

And when that second portrait was done, Healy wanted a third to send to the Paris Exposition opening at the Palais de l'Industrie in the spring of 1867.

"Aren't you getting tired of my face?" asked Sherman, but he rather enjoyed his new popularity after the hard years of criticism.

When Sherman's portrait for the fair arrived at Mount de Chantal, Edith wrote in her diary, "Wednesday, March 14, 1866. The picture arrived at half-past three o'clock. As I was in French class, I did not know it until four. I went after Sister Eulalia and we got Thomas and another man to open the box; it is splendid and has a beautiful frame...."

Nuns and girls worked like beavers, and when at last the fair opened, though tired, excited, and happy, they sold a great number of tickets for the raffle of Sherman's portrait, one of the heavy buyers being General Hancock. Mrs. Healy and Mary came on from Chicago for the occasion, which became a great social event and brought in considerable sums for the wounded. It had been a long business, very exhausting, but something of which all could well be proud. Its closing date, April 9, 1866, marked the end of Edith's schooling, for the Healys had taken a great decision and Edith was coming home to pack all her things and help the family close the Chicago house.

"Leaving? Oh, no! Mr. Healy! You can't leave us now! We need you. That academy of design, that art gallery you planned—surely you have not given up the idea...."

But even as they spoke, Healy's friends noticed the fatigue which had so worried his wife and made her propose this great change —undoubtedly he was on the verge of a nervous breakdown; he must stop. Even his work showed it; a new stiffness, a loss of the buoyancy that gave life to his painting.... So again Louisa suggested his going abroad—to have his eyes treated—to renew contacts in London, in Paris; but he pleaded too much work on hand...in six months he would do it. Louisa Healy knew then that she must act, or this would go on indefinitely until he collapsed.

"Very well," she told him, "we shall go ahead, the children and I, and you can join us as soon as you have finished the orders. Now, George, don't accept new ones, and I shall find an apartment wherever you like...."

"You'd leave me all alone here?" George asked, dismayed.

She smiled, satisfied. He would not remain too long, she knew.

"Well, Agnes might stay with you through the winter. Mrs. Dahlgren has invited her and Silvia de Pau. It might do Agnes good to have a Washington winter—she's so dreadfully shy and unworldly."

So it was arranged. In June, Mrs. Healy would sail for France with five of her six girls and young George.

In Chicago, the artist saw with satisfaction one of his cherished projects take shape. With his friend, the sculptor Volk, he had wished to organize a Chicago art school and gallery, but financial support lagged. Now that prosperity had returned and peace seemed established, H. H. Crosby, owner of the Crosby Opera House where Healy had his studio, formed an art association widely advertised.

The Chicago *Tribune* published in June, 1866, a congratulatory letter to Crosby signed by forty-six prominent citizens including G. P. A. Healy.* It was a practical beginning, a hope for the future.

* H. H. Crosby, Esq.

Dear Sir: We have been pleased to learn that you have decided to adopt the "Art Union" principle in the disposition of your Opera House.

While we should be glad to know of your success in such an enterprise under any circumstances, it would add greatly to our gratification to reflect that, in accomplishing your own wishes, you had given additional impetus to the development of aesthetic taste amongst us; that this would be only the natural result of the distribution, as proposed, of a large number of first-class paintings and engravings, we have no doubt, and we

Healy and Agnes saw the family off on the *Ville de Paris* sailing from New York June 16 on "the most lovely day imaginable," says Edith's diary. No mention of tears, which undoubtedly marked their good-bys. And on board, while most of the family succumbed to seasickness, Edith experienced her first romance—a shipboard encounter with a handsome Spaniard that was to pass with the swiftness of summer clouds. Alas! in Paris, at every concert, every play, at the riding hour, at the driving hour in the Bois de Boulogne, her eyes strained in vain to catch a glimpse of the gallant dark-eyed, dark-haired fellow passenger! Christmas passed; he had promised he would see them before Christmas. . . . And then one day at the Cirque Napoléon, listening to a symphony concert, she saw him!

"I could not listen. . . . I seemed alone and to see no one but him who would not see me. I watched him but he was wrapped in the music and his thoughts were far from me. The piece finished, and still I had my eyes fixed on him. Then it struck me that the people were leaving, and that I must do the same. I asked Mama to wait and let the crowd go first, but she said 'better not,' so I lost him from view—perhaps never to see him again."

Meanwhile, in Washington, George Healy was being lionized as he never had been before, and retiring, self-effacing Agnes suffered tortures throughout that extremely social winter. Mrs. Dahlgren entertained constantly for her daughter Romaine, for Agnes Healy, and Silvia de Pau. When Mr. Little of Boston became attentive to her, Agnes did not know what to do . . . and how they teased her!

In the spring of 1867, with her father, she returned to Chicago to close the house they had all learned to love. George Healy painted a few more portraits. He gave to the embryo Art Institute those

congratulate the public upon this fact, as well as upon the no less important one that they possess in your own well-established integrity satisfactory guarantee that the enterprise will be fairly and honorably conducted. With every wish that you may succeed, we are, dear Sir,

Yours very truly . . .

paintings which a few artistically minded citizens had spoken of buying for that purpose but never had bought. Now with a nucleus in their hands, he hoped it would grow and that Chicago would soon actually possess an art institute.

A tribute of appreciation signed by a group of Chicago's leading men, many of whom were patrons of Healy, was presented to the artist on June 15, 1867, shortly before his departure for France.

Mr. Healy
Dear Sir:

The undersigned, your friends, are unwilling that you should leave without expressing to you our regret at your departure and our high appreciation of you as an Artist, and our friendship and regard as a man. For years with your refined and genial family you have brightened our social circles.

As an artist, you came among us when Art was little known and appreciated. By your taste and varied culture; by the many examples of highest excellence for which we are indebted to your pencil; by your generous liberality towards your profession; and by your ever kind encouragement towards young artists, you have created a School of Art in the North West, the influence of which in refining and elevating the people will be permanent.

Wherever you go, you and your family will ever be objects of affectionate interest to us. With earnest prayers for your continued happiness, we look forward with the hope that at an early day we may welcome you home, as an honored and permanent fellow-citizen.

Chicago, June 15th '67

W. B. Ogden	W. L. Newberry
Mahlon D. Ogden	Mark Skinner
Chas V. Dyer	I. N. Arnold
Edwin H. Sheldon	C. Beckwith
Geo. F. Rumsey	Thomas Drummond
John B. Stevens	W. Hoyne
Wm. Bross	Edw. I. Tinkham
E. W. Blatchford	Grant Goodrich
	E. G. Larned

At 259 Wabash Avenue, father and daughter made a last inspection tour. As they stopped in each ghostly room with its shrouded windows, covered furniture, stacked pictures and cases, the artist thought it was well they had not sold the house, after all. It contained so many paintings, such a quantity of letters that were part of American history and European life. How could he have carried along this accumulation of priceless souvenirs? There were volumes of history in this house, records of conversations with his noted models, a gallery full of his work, his progress, his failures, covering now nearly forty years. Agnes, too, felt sentimental about their home, and as they walked out with a final locking of the front door she turned to her father:

"It will be nice, won't it, to always have this home to come back to?"

In New York, they stopped for Louisa's niece, Emily Hanley, of whom Agnes was very fond; all the cousins got on well together, and Healy had invited Emily to spend a few months with them in Paris. They sailed June 28. The Chicago *Tribune* of July 3, 1867, carried this note:

"G. P. A. Healy, the well-known artist, Miss Healy, Miss Hanley ... sailed in the French steamer *Pereire* for Havre on Friday last."

Chapter XXVI

A FRENCH WEDDING

ON JULY 9, 1867, Healy with his daughter Agnes and Emily Hanley took the family by surprise, arriving in Paris a day earlier than expected, for it had been an easy crossing. How the tongues wagged! There was so much to tell on both sides that letters, even daily letters, could not explain ...

The Paris apartment was too small for such a crowd and immediately George and Louisa Healy started house hunting; Louisa insisted on getting out of the city as she felt that her husband needed the rest as much as the children needed the country air. Healy suggested Versailles but Louisa protested: it would be almost as bad as Paris; he would get no rest. Finally they decided on Saint-Cloud, just outside the city but charming with its hillside garden villas and the view of that towering Palace surrounded by an immense park.

Meanwhile, the girls took their cousin sight-seeing. Of course, all of them first went to the great Exposition at the Palais de l'Industrie. In the Fine Arts Section, Healy's portrait of Sherman attracted much attention. The next day, it was Versailles and its Palace, and by evening the iridescent waters of the celebrated terraced fountain—the *Grandes Eaux*—playing that day. During the afternoon they had taken Emily through many green and flowered corners of the great park where they used to play as children. Emily was entranced with the long rows of Lombardy poplars, stately sentinels of so many French parks and French roads. Instinctively Agnes and Mary looked around for the friends of their childhood who, like them, must now be grown up; they recalled Grandmother Phipps talking by signs with Madame de Mare, who refused to learn English, while Tiburce and Albert ran races with them.

"Remember, Agnes," said Mary, "how Tiburce used to call you *'ma petite femme'?*"

Agnes laughed. "I wonder what's become of him?"

She would soon know, for a few days later her father brought Monsieur de Mare and Tiburce to the house; he had met them at the Louvre where Tiburce was secretary to the Comte de Nieuwe-kerke, now Director of the Louvre and formerly Napoleon III's favorite Minister of Fine Arts. They were amazed to learn that Johannes de Mare had been in America with Tiburce, doing some engraving for the United States Treasury.

"But why didn't you let me know?" Healy asked.

It was Tiburce who answered:

"Oh, Father didn't want to see anybody! His idea was to sail right back to France, and our cousins de Milhau used to lock his studio door to prevent his getting out...."

"Mais, cher Monsieur," said M. de Mare, " it was *really* too much like commercial work.... Still, I did some scenes of early American history that were interesting; you may see them someday; they are signed John de Mare."

The Healys thought it dreadful that Tiburce had not been any-where save in New York and Washington, but he had brought back a certain ease of expression in English which pleased them. After a few visits, Tiburce asked the American father's permission to court Agnes. He really *did* mean to make her "his little wife"! Louisa felt rather dubious—she always distrusted the French, especially in regard to marriage; the novels they had read were not encouraging, and the fact that the would-be son-in-law was an artist did not insure financial security. But Agnes's heart made the decision.

And so it was that the quietest and least worldly of the Healy girls became the center of attraction on September 9, 1867, when, at Saint-Cloud, in "the prettiest, sweetest little home in the world," as Edith said, wedding preparations went on.

Early in the morning, clouds had threatened but the sun won out; the air was balmy, and lining the road bordered on both sides by those long, straight green poplars Emily so admired, crowds of villagers waited in their best Sunday clothes to see the wedding cortege.

In the house, excitement reigned, the girls flitting from room to room with baskets of flowers, aligning presents on the tables, calling to one another, receiving the Paris guests as they entered. . . . In all this confusion Louisa's quiet voice called up:

"Agnes, are you ready?"

"Yes, Mama," came in a rather faint voice, and down the stairs came the Madonna-faced bride in her heavy white silk dress veiled in a cloud of light tulle held by orange blossoms. George Healy met his daughter at the foot of the stairs to head the procession; then came Tiburce with his mother on his arm; M. de Mare and Mrs. Healy in her soft gray silk; Mary in her white silk dress and bonnet with M. Langlé, while immediately behind came another of Tiburce's cousins, the Comte de Vernon, escorting Edith who also wore a white silk dress and bonnet. Other guests followed as the procession left the house, and the villagers shouted their good wishes, while little girls threw flowers all the way up to the church.

There, Archbishop Kenrick in his purple robes and handsome lace waited beside the excited parish priest. The Healys' American friend had promised to perform the ceremony and had been their guest at Saint-Cloud for several days. After the ceremony, the procession re-formed, many friends following. At the house, they found the doors wide open and the first thing that met their eyes was a lovely portrait of Agnes which her father had finished just in time and which the girls framed entirely with bridal flowers. Just below the picture a table held the wedding cake, while on the sideboards more substantial refreshments awaited the guests. It was gay and charming, up to the sad moment when Agnes said good-by to her parents.

Less than six weeks later George Healy and Emily Hanley were on board the steamer *Ville de Paris,* this time bound for New York. Louisa had found it quite useless to expect her husband to rest in the country or anywhere else. They talked it over and finally decided they would move to Rome for a year, since Agnes and Tiburce had gone there and so many of their friends lived in Italy.

"I'd better go back and paint a few of those portraits for which I had no time last spring," said the artist. "We shall need more money than I thought," and seeing her distress, added: "Dearest, I shall not stay long this time ... you can leave Maria and Emily at the Sacred Heart in Blumenthal since that is their choice, and George at school in Paris. By the time you, Mary, Edith, and Kathleen are settled in Rome, I shall be back."

Louisa sighed. These constant separations were hard on her, but she knew that the sight-seeing her children wanted would soon pall on the artist; George grew restless every time he was kept from his paints and studio. Besides, she agreed with him that their calculations had not included a wedding, a long journey, and an installation such as might give Mary and Edith the social life they needed. She could always count on her husband for "bringing home the bacon," as Americans quaintly put it.

For a few misguided weeks, Mary had spoken of becoming a nun, but her mother shrewdly suspected this sudden vocation of being the result of some girlish heart distress; she insisted on a reasonable delay before taking such a drastic step. Had not Agnes, too, in the midst of Washington's social whirl, told her father she wanted to enter a convent? ... And here she was, happily married —a far more normal life. Mary protested; parents never did understand the tormenting soul needs of their children ... but she promised to wait and spend a year in Italy. Emily Hanley, on the other hand, could not remain a whole winter away from her lonely father, now a widower, so she sailed with her uncle on October 16.

Mrs. Healy took Maria and Emily to the Sacred Heart Convent in Blumenthal where the nuns received them with open arms; she saw George comfortably settled in his Paris school, and, rather reluctantly, she gave up the pretty house at Saint-Cloud. They had a last dinner there for a number of American friends who had been present at the wedding; among these were the McCaggs. They discussed the coming journey and Mr. McCagg, convinced that women knew nothing of practical matters, insisted on lending his courier to Mrs. Healy. Under this expert guidance, their luggage was safely sent ahead and a carriage secured for them on the train so that the four of them, Louisa with Mary, Edith and little Kathleen, enjoyed comparative comfort until they reached the mountain pass at the frontier between France and Italy. From there on, traveling became harder. They were transferred to a coach that terrified Edith. "Look where I would," she confided to her faithful diary, "I saw nothing but danger.... I thought the horses would fall on that slippery snow, that the diligence would follow the horses and we follow the diligence so that all, together, we would roll down one of those awful precipices...." After thirteen hours of the shivery ordeal they reached Turin and again took the cars, their former privacy invaded this time by an enormous and talkative Italian whom Edith dubbed "the giant."

Forty-eight hours later they were in Florence—and there learned of fighting in Rome. Impossible to continue their journey.... Garibaldi had entered the papal territory.

Garibaldi—a name to stir the blood of liberals, particularly American liberals who had known him during his years of exile in New York, but to Edith who had heard of him only from the sisters at Mount de Chantal he was a devil, intent on attacking the Pope! Yet she was too eager about Italy to let politics worry her.... For a month the travelers remained in the Tuscan capital, more entranced with it each day. They thoroughly enjoyed their enforced stop along the Arno—all but little Kathleen, who ran across from the Uffizi to the Pitti Palace with her hands over her eyes not to see "all those pictures any more."

It had been disappointing not to find their friends, the Marshes, at the American Legation. Mr. Marsh had been very ill, they were told, but was better and might return in a week. On the other hand, most unexpectedly, they met Bishop Duggan who could give them no news from the outside, and advised them to stay quietly at the hotel.

As soon as their presence became known to the American colony, several of Healy's friends called on his wife. William Hart, the extremely tall painter who greatly admired Healy, delighted Edith with his stories and vitality; "a jolly old bachelor" she said of him, and after a while added "such a good, kind old man," though Hart was ten years younger than her father. From studio to studio they went with him, meeting artists, answering questions about America which many of them had not seen for years, admiring works of art, or silently criticizing them. They saw a number of sculptors who naturally gravitated to Michelangelo's native Tuscany; Hiram Powers, Thomas Ball, Meade, and the popular Italian Santarelli. In the evening, at the "table d'hôte," they would review their day, the drives, the visits, and sometimes exchange conversation with tourists whom Edith described in her diary:

"We have a queer set of Americans here; happily some of them are gone; one party found nothing to admire in Florence; one lady had been to Mr. Powers' studio. 'But,' said she, 'I am not accustomed to see ladies and gentlemen naked, so I can't tell whether they are good likenesses or not,' at which her husband turned to Mama and informed her that he knew for a fact that *them* artists *paid* men and women to sit for them! "

The Marshes arrived and gave a party for them, so charming that Edith wished she could remain a month at the Legation! And even Kathleen became reconciled to this city too full of pictures and churches when she discovered a little girl of her age at the Balls'. Mrs. Ball was equally pleased to find a young friend for her Lizzie—such a relief from adult company!

News came at last from Agnes, who assured her mother that she and Tiburce were quite safe in Rome and awaited their arrival with great impatience. Mrs. Healy also heard from the children at school, all in good spirits; most important of all, the _Ville de Paris_ had reached New York safely; she ought to hear from her husband soon. Now they could enjoy their sight-seeing without any overhanging cloud of anxiety. Mary and Edith took long walks in the country, visited churches, palaces, galleries, while Mama wrote to each member of the scattered family.

It was almost with regret that by the middle of November they decided to continue their journey; nowhere could the sky be quite so blue as in Florence nor give such an impression of depth and lightness. . . .

Rome at last! Agnes and Tiburce met them, took them to the apartment they had secured for them at 41 Via di Porta Pinciana, not far from their own little studio. Garibaldi, defeated by French and papal troops, had been forced back to his island of Caprera— the refuge he had bought in 1854 with money earned in New York. There he bided his time.

The Healys saw Pope Pius IX, heard the Christmas services at St. Peter's, met many American friends, went to parties, joined moonlight excursions to the Coliseum, and rides in the morning sunshine, followed a hunt with Mr. John Bigelow and, best of all, formed warm friendships with the talented laureates of the Villa Medici, the "Prix de Rome" * whom Tiburce de Mare had introduced to his sisters-in-law.

---

* "The Prix de Rome" was founded under Louis XIV to encourage Fine Arts in France. In 1803, the French Government bought the beautiful Villa de Medici where the "Roman" laureates lived. The prize is given each year to one painter, one sculptor, one architect, and one musician; every other year to one engraver; every three years to a metal and stone engraver, and it gives each one four or five years in Rome at the Government's expense, a year of travel included. Each year a work is sent to Paris. A "Prix d'Athènes" also exists for Frenchmen—archæologists and Greek scholars.

Edith expressed intense surprise one day when she found her sister Mary in tears at the thought of giving up all this if she became a nun. "I believe she is very fond of society," Edith confided to her diary, "and begins not to be so desirous of going to the convent." Mrs. Healy wisely made no comment. It was not impossible that Charles Bigot, a laureate of France in Athens on a visit to his comrades of Rome, had something to do with Mary's change of heart. Nor was the tall blond Charles Bigot her only admirer; the Director of the Villa Medici, Ernest Hébert, a painter of note, also showed himself quite attentive to Miss Healy; and his charming old mother, who kept house for the "Prix de Rome," invited and visited the ladies often.

Chapter XXVII

"THE PEACEMAKERS"

Whilst his family traveled through Europe prior to settling in Italy, George Healy was working in America, spending the winter of 1867-68 in Chicago and Washington. It was not merely to paint portraits this time. Once more the dream of a large historical picture held him.

Sherman, in his vivid manner, had told the artist of a last interview with Lincoln toward the end of the war. General Grant, Sherman, and Admiral Porter had visited the President on board the *River Queen,* and there had outlined the last moves of the conflict. Immediately Healy's active imagination pictured the scene: these four men—Lincoln the central figure—preparing for peace. He would call the picture "The Peacemakers." The idea haunted him, and there followed an exchange of letters with General Sherman and General Grant. Quite characteristic were the missives between the two Generals:

Sherman to Grant:

Washington, Jan. 17th 1 P.M.

General,

Healy of Chicago wants to paint your portrait to make a picture of yourself, Mr. Lincoln and myself as we sat in the steamer at City Point. Are you willing? What shall I answer Healy?

Yours,
Sherman

On the back of the same note came Grant's reply:

I have sat so often for portraits that I had determined not to sit again. The object Mr. Healy has is such, however, that I may change my mind in this case, but before giving a positive answer I will see when it will be convenient for him and me both. Answer that I will reply to his dispatch soon.   U. S. G.

Then Sherman wrote to Healy:

Washington, January 21, 1868

Dear Healy:

On getting your telegraph message I sent it to Grant and he returned it as you will see, and I answered you accordingly.

Grant is now at Richmond. I want to get off next week and I don't know when the General can give you a sitting.

I was at Annapolis on Sunday. Admiral Porter reminded me that he too was with us on the occasion of our visit to Mr. Lincoln on the *River Queen,* and says he kept a Journal and made notes of our general conversation. He says he will give me a copy of that part, also a full diagram of the cabin of the *River Queen,* dimensions and description, etc. When it comes I will send it to you.

In haste
Sherman

Before this Healy had received a long, detailed letter from the General recounting as he remembered it the whole scene at City Point. It offers an intimate and personal view of those concerned, and of the last stages of the Civil War:

Washington, D. C., Jan. 13, 1868

Geo. P. A. Healy, Artist
45 Opera House, Chicago

My dear friend:

I feel much flattered at your proposed picture and I will be most happy to aid you all I can. I will see General Grant in a day or so and collect more material as I progress.

Now I have only time before the meeting of a Board that will assemble within half an hour to describe:

After my army had reached Goldsboro, and made junction with Schofield, I knew there was but one more move on the arena of war to close it out. United with Schofield, I was not afraid to meet Lee and Johnston united in an open field. I proposed to march straight for Rushville; that would have shut off all supplies to Richmond—compelling Lee to leave—force him to attack me, avoiding Grant.

This was in March 1865—Grant still investing Richmond and Petersburg—gradually enveloping him around by the South and West. Knowing it would take me some days to collect enough food in my wagons and make arrangements to get some on the *Roanoke,* I concluded to go in person to City Point, Va., to see General Grant. I telegraphed down to my Q. M. General Easton at Morehead City to hold for me a suitable steamer and went down myself by rail. I found the captured Blockade Runner *Asia* all ready and proceeded in her to Old Point Comfort and City Point.—General Grant was living close to the wharf in a row of huts. He knew I was coming, met me and took me to his cabin. This was about 3 P.M. An hour or so later the General said we must go and see Mr. Lincoln who was visiting City Point in the steamer *River Queen* then at the dock. We walked down, went on board her, sent our names to him and followed to the "After Cabin" where he alone received us, with marked empressment. I had not seen him since 1861 when I was with the Army of the Potomac, when I had seen him several times. At first he looked haggard and careworn. I understand he had come down to the Bay to escape the cares and harassments of political life. As we engaged in conversation he warmed up and looked more like himself. We did not sit to a table nor do I recall having any maps or papers. We merely sat at ease, in such chairs as happened to be there. I think I can get a diagram of that cabin or it may be a sketch, if so will do it. Now my memory is thus:

General Grant gave a general statement of the actual state of affairs and only expressed an uneasiness lest Lee should attempt to escape before we were all ready. He stated that at that moment Sheridan was crossing from the North to the South side of the James to move around the line of investment, to get on the extreme left of General Meade's army, ready to make the final movement on to the south side railroad, the only remaining channel of supply to Richmond, and that would force Lee to come out of his intrenchments to fight or to run. Else surrender.

Mr. Lincoln seemed very much pleased and at the same time anxious.

He repeated several times that he was perfectly satisfied to leave the whole thing to us.

Once or twice he addressed his conversation to me, in a pleasant jocular strain, laughing heartily at the stories he had heard of the Runners, of turkeys, etc. and our high state of living. He laughed at my former troubles with the Sanitary Commission and the Christian Commission and told an apt illustration of the confusion this super Philanthropy had sometimes occasioned. We sat less than an hour and excused ourselves. We then went up to Grant's Quarters where Mrs. Grant was. After some conversation Mrs. Grant said to her husband: "Mr. Grant, did you see Mrs. Lincoln?" "No," said Grant, "I did not ask for her." "Well," said Mrs. Grant, "you are a pretty pair. Now you have put your foot in it." The next day, having arranged to start back for Goldsboro, the General and I called again, partly to correct the blunder of the day before. This time the *River Queen* was anchored off in the stream and we went off in a tug.—We found Mr. Lincoln as before, and our conversation was resumed—after of course inquiring for Mrs. Lincoln, who was unwell and did not see us. Mr. Lincoln was anxious about the safety of things in North Carolina in my absence, but I vouched strongly for General Schofield whom I had left in command. Still, I told him I would depart that day, which I did.

I will try and find out if the *River Queen* is still in existence and if so the shape, dimensions, etc. of the After Cabin where we conversed. No plan was then hatched. It had already been resolved upon, and he was merely told of its character.

Whether this group will warrant an historical picture is for you to say. I want you to paint Mrs. Sherman at your best leisure, a picture to match mine, to be transmitted to our children.

Board has come. My best regards to friends and your family.

Your friend,
W. T. Sherman

The exchange of letters was followed by separate sittings from Grant, Sherman, and Porter which the artist was able to work up into a 68 x 48 sketch. Begun in America, the large historical picture was to be completed in his studio in Rome.

Chapter XXVIII

ROMAN INTERLUDE

IN Edith's diary we find:

"Rome, Thursday April 23, 1868. Today we received two charming letters from Papa. He was in such good spirits about his picture of Grant, Sherman, Lincoln, and Porter. Mr. McCagg bought the first small one and it is supposed the Government will buy the large one which Papa will paint here in Rome."

To Healy, this third historical picture would mark another great, perhaps the greatest, moment of American history. He had shown Franklin pleading the cause of freedom and Union at the Court of France; then Webster in Washington eloquently defending that Union. Now he would express the greatness of simple men who had victoriously tested the willingness of Americans to kill and die in order to save this same Union. . . .

The tangles left by Johnson's administration made Grant's sittings necessarily few and short, nevertheless most interesting. The taciturn General talked easily on military matters and when the painter expressed surprise that so many West Pointers who had sat to him seemed to have left the service several times before war broke out, the President explained:

"In peacetime, Mr. Healy, there isn't much of interest for an officer outside of exploring, surveying, bridge building, or civil engineering—that is what McClellan and Beauregard chose. . . ."

The artist hesitated about questioning the President as to his own choice, but the latter forestalled him:

"Yes, I know: you've heard that I was a farmer and then a

merchant—money, that's all: we needed money—and I'm a cavalry man, not an engineer...."

When Healy praised the generous restraint Grant had shown in victory: "Lee would have done the same for me, had he won...." And when Grant spoke of the women in war, the President chuckled: "I was thinking of a story my wife repeated to me. Someone asked Mrs. Lee why she gave hospitals so many of the General's perfectly good socks. 'Because,' she answered, 'when they put on the General's socks they want to start marching again!'"

It was surprising and refreshing to find his quiet sitter animated and talkative. They mentioned horses: Julia Dent seemed as fond of horses as her father and her husband; this gave George Healy an opportunity which he never neglected: he spoke of his own wife and children! And Grant spoke of his son Frederick, then at West Point: throughout the first weeks of war young Frederick would wait for his father's return from the day's work, challenging him every evening with the same words:

"Want to fight, Mister?"

"I'm a man of peace—but I'm blessed if I let a man of your size get away with this!" and the two would mix, and the boy would win....

What fine, simple people these are! thought Healy. The growing intimacy with the Grants and the Shermans increased still more his feeling of devotion and admiration for his countrymen. Lincoln, the central figure of "The Peacemakers," he represented seated in a simple armchair such as he probably had used for his earlier portrait of 1864, leaning forward, chin on hand, face intent.... Sherman on the edge of a chair faces him, arm extended, emphasizing a point with his hand. Thoughtful, quiet, at ease, his piercing eyes turned to Sherman, Grant watches. They are speaking of the last move—success within their grasp. At the right, Admiral Porter, face framed in heavy whiskers, imposing with all his gold braid, listens to the unfolding plans. Through the cabin window the curved end of a rainbow adds light and color....

"I shall call this 'The Peacemakers,'" Healy had told his sitters —and all agreed.

The various sittings over, Healy had packed his material and once more was on his way to Europe. Mrs. Healy breathed easier: at last George was coming back! He would know whether to encourage or discourage Mary and Edith's active participation in the Villa Medici's activities. The girls received much attention from some of these young men and Louisa still retained some of her English prejudices against what she labeled Latin Europeans. . . . Emile Pessard dedicated some of his new compositions for the harp to "Miss Edith"; Charles Bigot, a visiting laureate of the French Academy of Athens, was assiduously attentive to "Miss Mary," and even the Director, the well-known and much-run-after artist Ernest Hébert, seemed to have singled her out. Henri Régnault, the genius of that group of painters, joined in their improvised concerts. At Easter, the young people gave Gounod's "Ave Maria."

Summer was upon them when Mrs. Healy and her daughters left Rome. Just before the family's departure for Bagni di Lucca, Mary and Edith were invited to hear Liszt—a very great treat—and on the day they left, all the remaining young men of the Villa accompanied them to the station: no wonder beautiful and fashionable Lucca seemed tame without their little court of artists and musicians!

Then one night, at three in the morning, the bell rang—and there stood "Papa" with Maria, young cousin Emily, and George whom his father had picked up at school on their way to Italy! Home life took on an accelerated tempo. Tiburce and Agnes felt surrounded by their exciting, ever-moving family, though they were planning then to move to Rome where Tiburce had some interesting commissions for engravings in the Eternal City.

In the midst of these happy family reunions rumors of war between France and Germany grew louder and more threatening. They all moved back to the city, although Rome did not seem too secure, and yet it seemed incredible that war should again ravage these sunny climes....

While Mrs. Healy took the school children back to France and England, George Healy arranged his new studio and started on his plan for the larger picture of "The Peacemakers." Fortunately for him General Sherman came over to Europe with young Frederick Grant. They were all enthusiasm about the historical painting. Indeed, by this time George Healy had become the interpreter of American history and its great men. The Civil War had had its repercussions—and exaggerations—in European countries. To these the painter brought vivid interpretations of a new world seeking progress in democracy and unity.

At the studio in Rome the father painted all their portraits as well as one of Mr. Freeman and also that of Dr. Georgi who was attending Agnes and who, on August 29, delivered her of the expected boy—though contrary to all the others Edith had prepared a baby girl's outfit.

It was a pleasant, uneventful summer. Healy painted several views, including the celebrated Devil's Bridge. The artist's diary of the Roman period is missing, so Edith's more biased comments must serve as guide.

How exciting Rome became to the two young girls with their lionized father home! Friends flocked to the studio almost before it was made habitable; news from home was avidly received; Italians seemed eager to meet the much-talked-of artist who had painted all the heroes of America's Civil War; the French, on the other hand, came to renew contact with an old friend, or, as in the case of the young Prix de Rome, to discover if this father from across the ocean were friend or foe....

As in his early days in England, when Healy, a young man, had moved among the great, here in Rome the artist, much older and now famous, moved also among a select yet very different society. Mary and Edith played hostess together or in turn for their father, and tried to fill the tasks their mother always seemed to carry out so easily and capably—but they could not please as she did. Edith complained: "I go every morning and read about an hour and a half to Papa, but of course that is not what Mama's reading is, so he looks rather glum...." Then two weeks later: "Mama's with us again! what a blessing! Papa looks brighter and we all get along much better now that she is with us to keep all our tempers within bounds."

In spite of new orders for portraits, of sketches in Rome or in the country, the all-absorbing work for Healy that winter was "The Peacemakers." The large canvas was in progress, the smaller one used as reference. The girls had suggested his introducing a table in the cabin of the *River Queen* to break what seemed to them too hard a line, "but he will not," Edith said of her father, "for nothing of the kind was there in reality and he wishes this to be a true historical picture."

The artist also worked on other portraits, a very fine one of Liszt at the piano. These sittings fascinated the painter as he watched the magic fingers and listened to the waves of melody or thunder cascading from the piano. He achieved a superb black-and-white contrast: the Abbé's cassock, the white marble-like chiseled features, the deep, dark eyes looking way beyond the earth, the long, almost white hair—and the hands, those sensitive, nervous, powerful hands... What a model! Spiritual, inspired, religious—a composer whose innovations startled, but whose pianistic fireworks made him the greatest virtuoso of his time, probably of all times.

Liszt was already a legend. Even as they talked religion, Healy's thoughts unconsciously raced back to the Paris days when his model had scandalized the city by eloping with Countess d'Agoult! Cosima, born at Lake Como, the youngest of three children from this illicit union, was also to have her own wild romance with Wagner....

Women pursued Liszt wherever his concerts took him. After the glory of Weimar and the new all-absorbing romance with

Princess Sayn-Wittgenstein, he thought of marriage; at last, in 1863, the musician and his Princess were to consecrate their union in Rome, the Pope having finally given his consent—the church was already decorated with bridal flowers, the ceremony to take place in the early morning. At the very last minute the Wittgensteins persuaded His Holiness that her annulment had been obtained by fraud. Roman gossip persisted in whispering that the great Liszt became an Abbé to avoid marriage with the Princess... in truth, both renounced earthly love in a mood of religious fervor that night, when Pius IX's messenger arrived suddenly to blast their happy preparations. That was six years ago. The Princess still received only in the evening when Liszt appeared; sometimes he would hold the guests under his spell, playing to them; more often she, dynamic, intelligent, half hidden in the smoke of her big cigar, would lead the conversation letting Liszt interrupt with his music.

Healy, fascinated by the pianist's hands, asked permission to have casts made by his friend Barbedienne, the bronze-artist who happened to be in Rome. This was done, the mold destroyed, and the bronze hands, a unique treasure, remained in Healy's studio until the painter's death—later passing into possession of his musically gifted granddaughter, Jeanne de Mare.

Most available records mention that Roman winter of 1868–69 as a particularly social one. George Healy, always popular, took his wife and daughters to innumerable parties, balls, plays, receptions, or whatever entertainment attracted them. More and more, however, Mary had to drop out as cold after cold kept her confined to the house. But Edith reveled in the gay doings, unwilling to see how hard this perpetual parade under candle, lamp, or gas light was on her father: his eyes "cooked," he said, and he suffered acutely. "But it is the only way to see people," complained Edith with small compunction as she let him escort her to the Hookers, Wards, Goulds, Rogerses and Armstrongs, the Crawfords and Cushmans.... The Healys also entertained. Arthur

Shee, President of the Royal Academy, and his wife came that winter, exchanging many civilities with them; but the highlight was Longfellow's arrival with his daughters for a New Year's Day dinner given for them, bringing together both Liszt and Longfellow.

In answer to Liszt's invitation one day, Healy and Longfellow went to Santa Francesca on the outskirts of town; dusk had settled over the landscape. As they pulled the bell, the door of the monastery opened, and they looked into the dark recesses of a corridor. At the top of the steps Liszt appeared holding a lighted candle, his face illumined by its rays. It was like an apparition; the poet leaned over to his companion, whispering: "Oh, Mr. Healy, you must paint that for me!" This request was gratified later when Liszt returned from Weimar.

On concert tours the composer did not wear his religious robe, but at each return to Rome a new fervor accompanied his donning again the Abbé's cassock. In such mood Healy painted him, and the charming little portrait, showing a long, thin, ascetic figure and inspired face, now hangs on the wall at Craigie House.

The Longfellows remained in Rome long enough for Healy to paint the poet and his daughter Edith walking under the Arch of Titus. In the foreground a group of artists includes Healy himself and the sculptor Launt Thompson standing, while, seated at work, is the landscape painter Sanford Gifford.

As the months passed, Mary Healy seemed to grow more feverish, coughing a great deal and often forced to abstain from the happy reunions of the Villa Medici. One of the early laureates, Charles Gounod, now reaping great fame in Paris with his opera *Faust,* visited his friend Hébert at the Villa Medici. He heard the latter speak of Mary Healy and gave a whole afternoon to the young American girl, casting over her the spell of his charm, beauty, and genius. Edith in her diary wrote, "Mary was delighted and I really think it did her good."

Liszt, Longfellow, Gounod—what a trio for the girls! No

wonder Bagni de Luca seemed tame after they left their little court of artists and musicians.

As usual new plans were in the making. Healy had meant to join Gounod, Hébert, and some others on an Eastern tour; he would meet them in Constantinople at the end of summer.... Meanwhile, they all went to Naples, saw the Appletons again. Emily wrote from England about Kathleen's first communion in May and George made his in Paris.

They spent June in Venice where Maria was courted by the artist Vanutelli, but the sprightly Maria decided in favor of the convent. They all visited the Armenian convent where Healy painted his well-known "Armenian Bishops."

Healy left his family for England to paint John Walter of the London *Times*. To follow George Healy as he hastened through countries and continents makes one dizzy! Art with him was not merely a discovery in beauty, it was an exploration of the globe.... Brush in hand, ready to sketch landscape or figure, the artist went from Venice to France, to England, to America, and back again to join his wife and daughters at Ostend for a couple of summer months. The Uffizi Palace requested a self-portrait for the special Hall of Artists, the first American artist to receive this honor.

The Franco-Prussian War came as a clap of thunder; Healy's sympathies naturally were with France, and his daughters felt keenly the impact of such a war on their friends of the Villa Medici. Several had already gone: Regnault, the young genius, the adored of everyone, hastened home from an artistic journey in Morocco and from Paris wrote back to the Academy: *"On bat Maman! J'accours!"* *

Trapped in Switzerland that summer, the Healys found it hard to get news of their friends in France, England, or Italy. Communication depended upon the movement of troops. The only way George Healy could get money was to go himself to Paris or London and carry back what they needed.

* "They are beating Mother France! I come running!"

In June, 1870, at Lucerne, Agnes, Tiburce, and baby George came to spend a week with them before leaving Italy forever; in Brussels that following September little Louise de Mare would be born, almost within sound of German cannon.

In her diary from Frankfort, Edith Healy wrote with a pang of jealousy: "Papa monopolizes Mama, but it's for so short a time that we must not complain," and during a rainy spell at Lucerne she added: "Papa found it hard not to be at work, but he was with Mama, wrote all his letters, yet complained of the cold and calls our beautiful place a 'howling wilderness'—how dreadful!"

One of Mary's admirers, the French writer Charles Bigot, was with them when news came of his brother having been drafted—and he rushed back to France.

At the end of summer, the father, taking Maria and Kathleen to school in England, let Mary accompany him. The trains were filled with troops, the railroad stations impossible of access; and Mary's hope of seeing Charles Bigot in Paris was doomed. But they reached England and somehow got back to Italy.

At the Villa Medici, almost empty these days, came the shattering news of Regnault's death at Buzenval.

With Clairin he was at the murderous battle of Buzenval on January 19, 1871. With evening, came the order to retreat! Regnault did not answer the roll call. Clairin, terrified, called:

"Henri! Henri!" No answer.

The Roman comrades who with him had hastened to defend *"la patrie"* found him among the dead at Père-Lachaise.

Would the sound of cannon forever pursue the Healys? Must they lose more friends yet, after the carnage of an American Civil War? The Commune in Paris made victims while at Versailles the Prussians strutted and goose-stepped, and furious rebels sacked and burned! The Hôtel de Ville, the Tuileries went up in flame.

It seemed strange to Healy that so many Americans sided with Germany in this sudden war. To them Bismarck seemed a clever big giant and Prussia an interesting kingdom.

Louisa May Alcott was in Vevey, Switzerland, when war broke out, and she wrote home: "Hooray for old Pruss!" The proclamation of a French Republic, however, was to change this view and perhaps her sittings to G. P. A. Healy in Rome evoked in her a sympathy for French life and French character which the American artist understood so well.

They were pleasant sittings. The Healys and the Alcotts' acquaintance dated back to the 1840's in New England, and these sittings often turned into family visits. Mary Healy became happily excited when Louisa Alcott expressed interest in her writing and promised to speak to her American publisher about it. So it happened that one of Mary Healy's first American novels, *Storm Driven,* was published under the patronage of her favorite author.

One day the artist laughingly quoted his youngest child's expressed wish: "I must have a million babies and one little boy!" "What will you do with them in winter when it gets cold?" asked her mother. "Oh, I'll wrap them in newspaper and put them on a shelf to go to seed. . . ." Louisa Alcott immediately exclaimed: "Oh, Mr. Healy, may I use that in a book?"

"Of course, my dear." And in *Little Men* the chapter "Round the Fire" contains a charming picture of little Rob on his mother's knee telling a tragic tale with great earnestness, "Once a lady had a million children and one nice little boy. . . ."

Louisa Alcott's great idol, Ralph Waldo Emerson, the Sage of Concord, came to Rome at this time. Healy thought of painting his portrait as an offering but felt deterred somewhat by an artist friend's experience. This man had sent Emerson, in token of his deep admiration, a small painting which he considered one of his best and had it beautifully framed; the great philosopher thanked him charmingly, but returned the frame, saying he could not accept anything of such value.

That winter Pope Pius IX sat to Healy, who always recalled these sittings with reverent joy. The Pope had charm, wit, and culture, and possessed an inexhaustible fund of information and apt stories. One day the conversation turned on the Carmelite Father Loyson, Père Hyacinthe, whom Healy had heard preach at Notre-Dame. The priest, refusing to accept the infallibility of the Pope, separated from the Church, and afterward married an American. With a twinkle in his sparkling eyes, His Holiness remarked:

"He has taken his punishment in his own hands."

The artist also liked to quote the Holy Father's gentle rebuke to a visiting American who rebelled against bending under the Pope's benediction:

"My son, an old man's blessing never did harm to anyone."

It was Pope Pius IX also who, when an old woman blocked a long procession of pilgrims while she fumbled in her pocket for the rosary, hurried her along saying:

"It's all right, my good woman, the blessing reaches into the pocket."

Like the Pope, the artist could at times be impatient. On one occasion the Pope arose from his seat to look over the artist's shoulder, and Healy, earnestly at work, exclaimed rather abruptly: "I beg Your Holiness to sit down!" The Pope laughed, saying: "I am accustomed to giving orders, not receiving them; but you see, Mr. Healy, that I also know how to obey," and submissively went back to his chair. What Healy did not mention in his *Reminiscences of a Portrait Painter* was that the Pope, greatly pleased with the artist's work as well as with the character and personality of the American, made him a Knight of Saint Gregory.

In Rome, as in Paris and Chicago, the painter showed himself a friend to struggling confreres. While enriching his interesting collection, he made sure that his purchases happened at a most opportune time for the artist whose work he bought. Healy's reputation as a kind and wise critic also brought many youths to seek his advice. John Sargent's father brought his son to Healy's studio and, as Sully had told George as a boy, so Healy advised John Sargent to make painting his career.

Rome, a Papal State which should have been closely bound to

Napoleon III, strangely enough remained aloof from the fight with Germany. And after the war was lost, France scarred, the Emperor exiled, and a new republic proclaimed, Rome, instead of Paris, became the Mecca of artists and a resort for royalty.

In 1871, a young and charming girl, the Princess of Oldenberg, sat to Healy for a portrait destined to her fiancé, the Duke of Weimar. She confided to her painter that she loathed the very sight of her future husband! The American was profoundly shocked that in this nineteenth century there should still be such tyranny about marriage and joined her cousin, the fascinating Elizabeth, Princess of Rumania, in urging the girl to tell her father her fears and horror of this fiancé. The breaking of her engagement on the eve of marriage caused great scandal.

Enchanted with her cousin's portrait, Elizabeth ordered one of herself, full length, in the Rumanian costume, as a surprise to her beloved husband Prince Carol of Rumania. Princess Elizabeth seldom lost an opportunity of wearing the national dress. Its vivid colors were becoming. The artist described it as "a sort of embroidered blouse with long, loose sleeves, open jacket, a red skirt embroidered in gold, red Morocco boots, and a thin veil covering the whole, also embroidered in red and gold." *

These sittings began a charming friendship between an oldish man and a beautiful young girl—a friendship which extended to the whole Healy family.

Emboldened by the young woman's sincere interest in his talk about wife and daughters, Healy one day asked his sitter if she would enjoy a very simple home gathering at dinner with Mrs. Healy and the girls.

"But I shall delight to dine with you, Mr. Healy. It will be such fun," the fun being partly her attending duenna's and chamberlain's annoyance at their princess's plebeian tastes.

That evening remained for all of them one of the most charming, intimate memories of Rome. They talked at length while en-

* *Reminiscences of a Portrait Painter.*

joying the good dinner, and afterward the gifted composer of the Villa Medici, Charles Lefebvre, charmed them with the delicacy of his playing. Putting out the lights, the young women sat on the floor by the fire listening with emotion to the "Moonlight Sonata," Elizabeth holding Mary's hand and punctuating every shade of melody with a pressure of her fingers.

Later Edith was asked to play the harp. She gave Pessard's composition dedicated to her. The Princess enjoyed it all the more because she herself was quite proficient with the harp. A poet also, the Queen soon made quite a name for herself under the pseudonym of Carmen Sylva. She asked the subject of Mary's novel and hoped to see the book in print.

In the course of his painting the artist learned that Princess Elizabeth was in Rome to recuperate from the effects of childbirth, and he encouraged the young mother to speak of that adorable baby girl, for every time she mentioned little Marie her face would light up with infinite love—a sensitive nature, too sensitive for the trials and intrigues that surround a throne.

The portrait of Princess Elizabeth completed, George Healy was once more on the wing. Capri's balmy atmosphere delighted him; the brilliance of sea and sky made him bring out canvas, palette, and easel, while his daughter Mary breathed the vivifying air and dutifully drank goat's milk. But when he had done several views and a few portraits—a priest, a shepherd boy, a peasant girl balancing a basket on her head—Healy went to England, saw the Salon in Paris, then traveled south, planning an orgy of painting in Spain. He was free at last to study Velasquez, El Greco, Goya....

Chapter XXIX

HOLOCAUST IN CHICAGO

OCTOBER, 1871. In Chicago, the Healy house stood closed. A keeper attended to lawn and trees; the grounds extended from Congress to Van Buren Street facing Wabash Avenue; throughout the summer trees and bushes had yielded their fruit; now autumn yellowed the leaves. In the house, treasures awaited the return of their owners and the ruthless activity of packers and shippers.

On Sunday morning, October 8, an unseasonably warm and sultry day, hot winds blew the dust in one's eyes. Churchgoers wore their lightest summer clothes and longed for clear, crisp autumn air. As they passed the Healy house, friends wondered how much longer the blinds must remain drawn; they asked themselves whether indeed the artist's family, now living in Rome, would ever come back.... Healy had been over the preceding winter, bringing his completed "Peacemakers," but he had now returned to Rome where American friends visited them and brought back tales of a delightful life, full of art, social gatherings, and travel. Recent letters spoke of the father's projected visit to Spain and the daughters mentioned their summer wanderings, the troublous times in France, their consequent change of plans, but said nothing of reopening the Chicago home.

The wind blew higher and higher; people hastened to their Sunday dinner, their visits, their weekly relaxation from toil. Along the Lake's blue waters strollers tried to find a cool breeze. Chicago was a happy city, rich, proud, and successful. The population, well over 25,000, was divided into three distinct groups—

each one almost a city in itself: the South, North, and West sides, this latter the only one without lake shore.

Rumors of a fire on the West Side reached the center of town; but this was no rare occurrence and would soon be under control. ... A southwest wind gave small hope of rain to wash the atmosphere; the lawns and wilting autumn flowers needed sprinkling; fortunately Lake Michigan and Chicago's great Water Works supplied all the water needed.

A little after midnight alarm bells were tolling. Citizens awoke from their restless slumber, looked out of their windows, and were startled by leaping flames in the distance; in the darkened streets, people were moving; streams of water played over large buildings. Wind carried the flames far and wide—the lumberyards in the west seemed like a giant lighted torch....

Was it Mrs. O'Leary's cow that with a flick of her tail upset the lamp and set fire to a dry barn? or, as others have it, Mrs. Scully who went to attend a sick cow and setting down her lamp saw it turn over while the dry hay all around became a sheet of flame? Every self-respecting Chicagoan had a barn and a cow, nothing simpler than an accident of this sort—Chicago always had the name of "Windy City."

For a time it seemed that this sudden devastation of the lumberyards might confine the fire to the West Side; then a sudden violent summer wind carried sparks way across burned areas, literally flying over to Michigan Avenue, to Wabash Avenue, and from the South finally leaped to the North—a gas tank exploding, the river not wide enough with its flimsy narrow wooden bridges to stop the blazing inferno.

That night of October 8–9, hope still remained and people tried to save their homes. The Wabash Avenue Methodist Episcopal Church was saved by trojan work by the minister and his boys who covered all exposed parts with sand and dirt, but from home to home alarm spread, and soon it was *sauve qui peut* in the crowded streets when news spread that the Water Works were gone....

Panic seized many, while heroic individuals continued to save, help, reassure an infinite number who, otherwise, might have perished. A burning hell with streets so crowded that even the mildest and kindest pushed, shoved, carrying what they could, hiring or stealing any available conveyance. . . . Screaming Negroes, Chinese, ghostly figures from the underworld rubbed elbows on Michigan Avenue with the fashionables—a well-dressed woman was seen dragging a trunk by a cord that cut her fingers . . . all trying to shield their eyes and hair from burning dust, bitter fumes, and blinding smoke. More fantastic still were frightening firebrands: roofs, pieces of sidewalk, porches flying through the air like avenging demons. Dantesque images of barefoot prisoners set free from a burning jail ran madly, seizing clothes to hide their telltale stripes, thieving, grabbing, dying perhaps, or killing. . . . Crazed animals herded toward the Lake ran amuck in every direction.

What nightmares must have haunted the survivors, and how terrible the sound of fire engines forever stamped in their memory!* Later, everyone had some particular incident to recount.

Mrs. Frederick Greeley, daughter of the Congressman Isaac Newton Arnold, told of her children running into the garden, unafraid but excited, to stamp out new spots of fire, then a voice calling from the street: "Mr. Arnold! the Water Works are burning!" and quickly they let out the animals from the barn, gathered some favorite treasures, and headed fast for the "Sands," the Lake Shore, hoping and praying that no lives would be lost and that part at least of their home might stand—a futile hope. But Isaac Arnold proved himself one of those undaunted Chicago giants who rebuilt vigorously and would allow no mourning over the disaster.

Mrs. Frederick T. West's own picture of her father battling with the flames made every Chicagoan relive those unforgettable hours.

---

* In his book, *Great Fires in Chicago,* Mr. Goodspeed gives an unforgettable picture of the frenzied hours: "Dust, smoke, flame, heat, thunder of falling walls, crackle of fire, hissing water, shouts, braying trumpets, roaring wind, confusion . . ."

He realized the impossibility of checking that raging, sweeping fire and suddenly recalling his friend McCagg's aged mother, he called out: "Does anyone know anything about Grandma McCagg?"

Receiving no answer, he plunged through the flames toward the McCagg home. Mrs. West felt terrified: surely her father would never return alive....

But he found the old lady and her daughter Carrie sitting quietly in their parlor, unaware of their danger. There were dreadful moments when the feeble "Grandma" could walk no farther and her rescuer had not strength enough to carry her! Then Providence sent the painter Sullivan dashing by in an express wagon; in a jiffy they lifted Mrs. McCagg and Carrie into the vehicle and all escaped safely.... *

By some freakish phase of that fantastic fire, though the McCagg house had vanished, the glass conservatory was found still standing when ashes grew cold enough for the owners to take stock of their loss.

Nothing in the history of pioneering in the United States is more stirring than this sudden cataclysmic destruction of a city which had grown magically within a space of less than forty years. The same spirit that had built it, the same men who had believed in it and made it a reality, brought forth again a miracle of faith, energy, and success. At once, in one accord, and almost overnight, Chicagoans began to rebuild. Following their Mayor Roswell Mason's exciting and heart-warming example as he stood at his post in the threatened courthouse, issuing orders, telegraphing other cities for more fire engines, they all joined in organizing immediate relief. By Monday evening, while the fire was still burning, food, clothing, supplies of all kinds started to pour in from neighboring towns by wagon or rail. Soon cities from the Atlantic to the Pacific, from Great Britain and France, from Germany, the Netherlands, Austria, and other European or South

* Caroline Kirkland, *Chicago Yesterdays.*

American countries sent their quota of relief, reaching into the millions....

Yet there were a few comic notes. Dr. Moody used to tell of one article Mrs. Moody's heart was set on saving:

...This was a portrait in oil of Mr. Moody by the artist Healy, which hung on the wall of their parlor after their return from the first trip to Europe in 1867...this portrait Mrs. Moody prized above anything the house contained....She urged Mr. Moody to save it for her. The ludicrous side of the situation at once appealed to him notwithstanding the terror of that awful night.

"Take my own picture!" he said. "Hell, that would be amusing! Suppose I am met on the street by friends in the same plight as ourselves and they say: 'Hello, Moody, glad you have escaped; what's that you have saved and cling to so affectionately?' Wouldn't it sound well to reply: 'O, I've got my own portrait!' "

No entreaty could prevail on Mr. Moody, but the canvas was hastily knocked out of the heavy frame and carried off by Mrs. Moody herself —the one relic rescued from their home.*

Robert Lincoln, in like manner, took time enough to snatch from their burning home the Healy portrait of Mrs. George Lincoln Dunlap....

But only much later did these incidents come to light; memories at first seemed blocked by the nightmare of fire, the tolling of bells, and the horror of powerless fire engines.

"Never shall I forget," wrote Mrs. McCormick-Goodhart, "the sea of flames we saw on crossing an arm of the river, nor the awful grandeur of the scene...as far as eye could reach in every direction, houses, trees, pavements, and roads were burnt to cinders, iron railings twisted, dead animals found in the streets, desolation...."

The lovely Healy home on Wabash Avenue, this safe refuge they had clung to in the city that sheltered them eleven years, was now but a pile of ashes.

* *Life of D. L. Moody* by his son.

And all unconscious of disaster to come, George Healy was in Madrid, happily copying Spanish masterpieces at the Palace Gallery, and writing enthusiastic letters to his wife in Rome. In September, 1871, he told her of seeing the unfortunate Empress Eugénie whose fairy castle had suddenly collapsed with the defeat of Sedan—for which the French held her responsible.... In her native city, while the Emperor sickened in the prison of Wilhelmshöhe, she was trying in vain to rally partisans to their cause. In a letter to his wife on September 19, 1871, Healy writes:

I had just resumed my work in the Palace Gallery when I was informed that Her Majesty was coming. I continued painting until I saw the Director showing her the different masterpieces. Then I approached her, and bowing I said: "Your Majesty remembers Mr. Healy?" She smiled and inclined her head very kindly, saying: "You are settled here, Mr. Healy?" I answered that I was settled in Rome, where I hoped to end my days. She exclaimed: "It is difficult in these troubled times to say where one will end one's days!" I expressed my deep sympathy for her and for France. She thanked me, bowed, and passed on. It was very interesting to see this lady whom I had received at my studio in Paris before she had any idea that she was destined to occupy a throne. I also met her at the Maberlys'. Then we were presented at the Tuileries when she was a young and radiant Empress. Now I met her in the city of her childhood, dethroned, a sad, middle-aged woman dressed all in black. Her eyes are still beautiful. After she had left I thought of all I might have said to her... but it is just as well that I said just what I did, because it was simple and natural without being at all gushing.

Less than a month after reading this letter in Rome Mrs. Healy and her daughters, Mary, Edith, Maria, and Emily, heard the terrible news of the all-consuming fire that had destroyed Chicago.

"Mama, we must send for Papa at once!" exclaimed Mary.

Pale, but always quiet and sensible, Mrs. Healy said:

"Why? What could he do from here? Wait until we know

what damage there is." The idea that thousands of homes could be destroyed in two days and an unnumbered host of people killed never entered their heads. Newspaper reports, more lurid with every issue, seemed utterly unbelievable. Yet the repeated accounts, the telegrams that came to all Chicagoans in Rome—and there were many—forced the truth on them. Reassured as to the safety of their closest friends, they began to realize their own loss. . . . Still, Mrs. Healy's great concern was to soften the shock to her husband as much as possible. She wrote to urge him to finish the work he meant to do in Spain and return only when that was done, since there was nothing he or they could do about their loss at that time and at that distance.

Nevertheless, it was a frightened group that sat in the cozy Roman apartment, reading accounts repeated from many American papers. From the New York *World* they read the reprint of Alexander Freer's story which suddenly brought the whole picture vividly before them. He was at the Sherman House that Sunday night when the fire suddenly spread to the South Side. . . . "The wind was blowing fiercely from Clark Street to the River, the flames lighting the houses on the East side of Clark Street. . . ." He went to his sister, to take charge of her children. "While we were talking Mr. Wood burst into the room and said the fire had reached Wabash Avenue and was sweeping all above it. . . . We drove as rapidly as we could into Wabash Avenue, the wind sweeping the embers after us in furious waves. The storm of falling fire seemed to increase every second and it was as much as we could do to protect ourselves from the burning rain and guide the horse through the flying vehicles. Wabash Avenue was burning as far down as Adams Street. . . ."

"Wabash Avenue!"

The Healy girls turned horror-stricken faces to their mother who, like them, remained speechless over the thought of their beloved home burning, burning. . . .

George Healy returned from Spain as quickly as he could,

bringing with his own work several canvases of Spanish friends: a self-portrait by Rosales, two small pictures of Madrazzo... these might help form the nucleus of a new Art Institute in Chicago if the one for which he had left so many pictures before his departure had also vanished in the flames....

Before leaving Madrid, he had received a warmly sympathetic letter from his good friend General Fox and his wife Lady Mary. Englishmen are great believers in insurance, and the General hoped Healy's property was well protected in that manner—a vain hope. He also said that he had written to the British Minister in Rome and to his mother, Lady Holland, then in Italy, to arrange new contacts for the American artist. This brought a new influx of sitters, most welcome to the indefatigable Healy.

There were still many Americans in Rome; to Healy's studio came several members of the Samuel Ward family, of the Carter family from Chicago; he painted a charming portrait of lovely young Helen Carter who had made her social debut in Rome with Maria Healy. A picture of young Margaret Armstrong dates from that period, and as the Shermans remained in Europe longer than the General expected, it gave Healy the opportunity to paint him once more for some new exhibit, while he also made a portrait of Sherman's aide, young Frederick Dent Grant, lately out of West Point and very good-looking in his uniform.

In his *Day before Yesterday* Maitland Armstrong gives a list of American artists in Italy at the time; it is an impressive list, and few of his confreres escaped Healy's brush: Hart, the sculptor; Ward, the painter; Simmons, who made two marble busts of George and Louisa Healy. Miss Crawford, daughter of Healy's late friend, the sculptor Thomas Crawford and sister of the budding young novelist Marion Crawford, sat for a gracious portrait, a duplicate of which remained in the artist's studio.

Still war-scarred, Paris again attracted visitors. While many Chicagoans hastened across the ocean to their stricken city, others insisted on leaving the women of the family abroad until part at least of the promised reconstruction offered shelter and a renewal of normal life. Called to the French capital by sitters from various parts of the world, too busy now to dwell on his losses, Healy found his old studio at 15 rue de la Paix vacant. So he wrote to his wife to give up the Roman apartment and send the contents to their new Paris address. He also wrote to Princess Elizabeth Hohenzollern in Bucharest to ask if she had received her portrait and giving his Paris address.

It was in this studio that the artist received in July, 1872, the telegram from Princess Elizabeth announcing the arrival of her portrait at Sinaïa, and soon after a detailed letter telling him of the success of the surprise they had planned together. Sinaïa, July 2nd 1872—Arrived in perfect health. Much admired—great success. Complete surprise. Letter follows—Elizabeth

Sinaïa, July 12th 1872.

My dear Mr. Healy: Why have you not been gifted with the second sight? Or would the blessing be too great to be allowed to create beautiful things and then watch the effect of them on those for whom they are intended?

The Prince was at Bucharest for several days when I got a telegram with the news of *my* arrival! My excitement no words can describe; no sort of work could be thought of till I espied a big box moving slowly up the hill on which this Monastery lies. The whole house was assembled for the unpacking, working away at the screws. Several hours later, the Prince arrived; the door was shut, he had to open it himself, and then he stood quite still: "Who has done that?" Never surprise was more complete; people said they never saw him look so excited before. But he did not make many words; he lighted it up with dozens of candles, and from seven until nearly midnight he never ceased looking at me. He says the more he looks at it, the better he likes it.

...Since I began my letter, I also had a talk with Philippescu about your coming, and he suggested that you might like better to come to our quiet Monastery instead of Bucharest. Only you must know that we live in cells and have deal tables and no sort of comfort except a

most magnificent nature and the luxury of good air. Perhaps it would
be much nicer to be here together than in the turmoil of town life....
And last, but not least, you'll find a little person who calls herself a
"good maid," "pretty maid," "Papa's own daughter," "Marie," "mon-
key," and of whom I should very much like to have a picture! She is
growing a greater darling every day, our little sunbeam. I wish you
could see her get out of bed with cherryed cheeks and golden curls all
over her head, lying down on the floor to kiss the sunbeam, and the
sun rewarding her by throwing a halo round her innocent head! But I
won't do the very thing I blame: praise my own child! I should only
wish you to take an interest in her.

And now, dear Mr. Healy, I hope I may say: *Au revoir!* My kind
love to all your dear ones.

Yours most affectionately
Elizabeth

This was followed in August by Prince Carol I's urgent invitation
to come to Rumania and paint portraits of himself, his wife, and
little girl, and to remain as long as possible. Once more the artist
was on his way to new horizons.

Chapter XXX

RUMANIA

LEAVING Paris for Rumania, as soon as he reached Bucharest, Healy took a train to Sinaïa and there was met by the Princess herself. Always talkative, she gave him at once the delightful story of her engagement and marriage.

Carol, ruling Prince Hohenzollern, had managed to steer his way through the crisis of the Franco-Prussian War although Rumanian sympathy remained with the French. Then came the question of marriage—an important diplomatic affair. It turned out to be more romantic than political. On a visit to Germany, Charles had met young Elizabeth, Princess of Wied, a particularly charming girl.

Healy received this firsthand account of their hasty courtship from the lips of the Princess herself and described it in a letter to his wife:

September 5, 1872—When she was very young they met in Berlin and of all her partners she thought him the most intelligent...She and her mother (went) to a concert given by Clara Schumann where they again met him. The next day he called on the Princess of Wied.... They all drove to the zoological garden and he walked by her side on the plea of going to look for the monkeys; they were two hours seeking these interesting animals which, somehow, they never found. On their return she noticed that the gentlemen in waiting were laughing over this very long search, but, she added: "I assure you that we did look for them." That evening the Prince paid her mother a long visit. The maid said: "I have never heard Your Highness speak so favorably of

265

any young man." She protested that she had several admirers quite as nice. "But you would not marry one of them." "Nor that one, either!" she exclaimed with a toss of her head. Then she said timidly: "Was not that just like a girl?" As she went to look for her mother, she was quite angry because she thought they would be late for the concert. Then she noticed that her mother seemed much agitated. The Princess of Wied said: "My darling, the Prince has asked for your hand." All she said was: "What, so soon?" This reminded me of your sweet "Very well, dear." A few weeks later they were married.

In another of Healy's letters to his wife he wrote:

Dearest: I slept well last night ... the air here is so pure. I commenced a study of the head of the Princess. She sat from two until half-past five: then she had to go and dress for dinner. After dinner the President of the Chamber was announced and I took some of my new friends to see the portrait of the Princess with which they seemed well pleased. It is too bad that Mary's book sent to Her Highness should not have reached her. She wishes them to be sent under the Government seals.

It was arranged that Healy would paint two portraits of the Prince, but he had to wait until a new uniform was made. In the meanwhile he worked on the portrait of the Princess and her child. On August 22 the artist wrote:

On the whole I had a good night's rest. I awoke very early but did not rise until past five (five in the morning of course). The Mayor of Bucharest came to luncheon and I have promised to paint his portrait.

I had to dance in the evening. Two or three of the ladies asked me to waltz, but I declined. However, when came the gallop the Princess invited me, and off we went! She exclaimed: "Why! You dance very well, Mr. Healy," and the Prince called out: "Bravo, Monsieur Healy."

During the sittings the Prince mentioned Healy's losses in the Chicago fire. The Prince asked Healy how much he received for the sale of his land and when he was told $50,000, Carol indignantly exclaimed: "But, Mr. Healy, that land will be worth enormous sums before long. You should have held on," and when the artist showed indecision about his new residence, the Prince said: "Oh, you must settle in Paris, Mr. Healy, it will soon again be the meeting ground of the world."

Daily, George Healy penned his impressions.

"August 26th—I find the Prince as charming as his wife. They were both with me a great part of the day and asked me to join them in a walk but I stretched a canvas instead."

Golden-haired little Marie liked the artist, and willingly climbed on his knee; she did not even resent the sittings and proved a gay model. Among the rocks and trees on her mother's lap the child looks straight at you. As in her other portrait Princess Elizabeth is wearing the Rumanian costume.

"September 6th— . . . Before twelve this morning, as the weather was fine, I made a study of the valley, and I had a visit from Their Highnesses. She told me that the Minister of War wishes me to paint his little boy, a child about six with a head such as the old masters loved to paint. I began the portrait at one o'clock and before dark it was well advanced."

After another full day's work on the picture he wrote:

"At one time the little fellow sat across the chair, and his attitude was so graceful that I immediately sketched it in. It does much better than the first pose.

"When the picture was done I thanked the father for all the pleasure I had had in my work. He answered: 'Your pleasure can be but of short duration, but mine will last as long as I live.'"

On the occasion of the little Princess's second birthday, according to an old local custom the oldest person present was to break the cake over the child's head. In his letter of that day the artist described the guests' dismay:

"Princess Ghika exclaimed: 'Oh, Your Highness! who will acknowledge being the oldest person present?' The Minister of War said he was born in 1816; the next avowed 1818; but I had to perform, as I was born in 1813!"

Through September and October and well into November the artist remained at Sinaïa. There he worked on the background for the little Princess's portrait.

"October 1st—I made one of my best sketches yesterday. It was painted under difficulties; the wind was high and blew everything about, almost including myself! I ran the blade of my knife through the canvas and then in the bark of a tree. Then I ordered one of the soldiers to hold the canvas while I worked. When he grew tired, his comrade took his place. I stood thus for nearly two hours, and then was glad to sit down. Happily the storm capped the mountains with glorious clouds and I was able to catch the effect.

"The Minister of War and also the Minister of Foreign Affairs asked me to remain long enough to paint their portraits. I answered that it would be impossible this time, but that His Highness had asked me to return next summer, when I should be happy to comply with their request."

On November 27, he could not refuse the Prince's invitation to hear his speech for the opening of the Chambers.

"It was delivered with much dignity. As he had read it to me in French, I was able to follow the Rumanian, which sounded very well. You should have seen me in full dress in one of the Court carriages, bowing with the others as we went along! The Marshal was resplendent in gold lace. The Prince was much more simple. As to the servants, they were so gorgeous that I scarcely recognized them."

George Healy had stretched his visit as long as he dared. His wife wrote of people clamoring for their promised portraits at the Paris studio. So, regretfully, he bade his charming hosts good-by, and, as they accompanied him to his train, it was with renewed promises of a prompt return—though nine years were to elapse before he returned to picture the elevation of Rumania from a principality to a kingdom.

Chapter XXXI

A PARIS GARDEN

EVENTFUL years were to bridge the gap between the first and the second visits to Rumania. George Healy on his return from Bucharest at the end of 1872 gave up his momentary dream of spending the rest of his days in Rome. Paris was the only logical solution. Chicago's marvelous reconstruction was unlikely to yield time for portraits. To Paris the Healys came once more, seeking a suitable studio and apartment.

Healy climbed to the top of a hill known for centuries as Montmartre. In the seventeenth and eighteenth centuries, this hill was covered with famous homes and gardens; now, few of the residences retained their aristocratic greatness and the great parks had been cut into smaller gardens; thickly populated, the neighborhood was haunted mostly by artists, poets, writers. What a wealth of studios to choose from! George Healy decided upon the one occupied during the Second Empire by the Winterhalter brothers, a studio quite familiar to the galaxy of beauties that surrounded Empress Eugénie. From the courtyard of 64 rue de la Rochefoucauld the American glimpsed fine old trees towering over the wall that separated No. 64 from No. 66. He learned that this "hotel" was empty and immediately visited it. He then brought his wife, and they signed the lease at once.

Healy's enthusiasm communicated itself to his family, who exclaimed over the white-and-gold woodwork, the large mirrors, the small conservatory, and the garden with its rococo grotto and bordered lawns—there were even large turtles parading with proprietary air through the sun-flecked alleys. Thick ivy more than a hundred years old gave a feeling of age and privacy, covering as it did the high back wall; on the other side, the lower masonry accorded a view of equally fine trees in the next garden.

"We can give garden parties here!" exulted Kathleen.

"And how easy to dance on these beautiful floors!" added Edith, who had made similar remarks at the Vatican, regretting that the Pope did not give balls!

They found interesting neighbors. Victor Hugo had lived for some time in the rue Pigalle; the sculptor Aimé Millet had his studio Place Pigalle, and a few doors away, in the rue de la Rochefoucauld, Gustave Moreau composed his symbolic pictures. Next door to the Healys, their gardens separated by a wall, lived General Picot, the artist. Of him, Healy made a fine portrait while Picot returned the compliment.

Honors still came to the American artist. In 1873, he received a gold medal from the Emperor of Austria for his Vienna exhibit of the portraits of Pope Pius IX and of Carol of Rumania.

The year after their installation, Mary, the second daughter, married Charles Bigot, writer, professor, polemist—an active "redacteur" of the anti-clerical newspaper *Le XIXème SIÈCLE.* A simple but pretty wedding, many friends attended, and Charles Bigot had to accept the Church wedding—which delighted his own sister, a nun and a very accomplished woman. On February 14, 1874, the day of the wedding, came a telegram from the Princess of Rumania: "Bucharest, February 14, 1874—I send a thousand blessings and the most tender wishes for this solemn day. May God give your dear daughter the happiness she deserves. I could not write sooner because of sickness.—Elizabeth."

At the top of the house which in so short a time had already become known as the Healy home the new couple rented a roomy low-ceilinged apartment. At five every afternoon, Mary Bigot sometimes alone, sometimes accompanied by her learned, handsome husband, would come down for tea with her mother and sisters. In summer they set the tea table in the garden. Agnes and Tiburce de Mare lived on the other side of the Seine, but they and their children soon learned the way to "Mama Healy" and "Nonno" as the young ones called their grandparents. Luxury downstairs, frugal living with feasts of reason upstairs, and across the city the ups and downs of an artist's life with many children —such was the varied existence of the Healys with their two unmarried and their two married daughters.

The other two daughters, Maria and Emily, the prettiest ones, had become nuns. Even George Healy, ardent Catholic that he was, could not bear the thought of their shutting themselves off from life.

Emily at eighteen had declared her intention of entering a convent; her mother opposed this with such feeling that, obediently, Emily desisted—and immediately fell ill. Her vocation was real; the thwarted desire ate into her, and the doctor assured her parents that she would fall into a decline if they did not let her go. Typically, Emily with her keen mind, her active assurance, her gift for organization chose the Sacred Heart. Its great house at Conflans on the Seine, not far from Paris, received her for her postulate and novitiate—later, in the house rue de Varennes in Paris, she took her final vows. The Healy son, George, preferred studying architecture in the French capital to entering college in the United States; so, in reality, the family found itself in closer contact than it had been through the years of schooling and travel. At this time, at least, they could all call Paris their home. And from Cambridge, Longfellow wrote: "I have heard of your beautiful hotel in the rue de la Rochefoucauld. If I could find one like it, I should be tempted to embark at once and go 'where the good Bostonians go when they die'..." *

As in every other capital where he had lived or worked, Healy found himself in contact with opposing parties and opposing views; even his sons-in-law brought two different elements into

* Letter dated October 19, 1874.

their homes. Tiburce, who claimed the freedom of art, still had ties with the old regime through his royalist mother; Charles was a fighting republican, with progressive ideas in education, politics, and art.

The great man of the day now was the first President of this Third Republic, Louis Adolphe Thiers, Monsieur Thiers as he was always called and still remains in history. Short, plump, quick, active, witty, temperamental, learned, Thiers had shown tremendous courage and resourcefulness in France's defeat by Germany in 1871. He it was, Healy remembered, who when the French wanted to fight on and on to the death persuaded them that peace alone would save France. Undaunted, he visited all the courts of Europe, pleading for intervention, or at least neutral sympathy. Prussia was victorious, Prussia was hard. Thiers discussed the peace with Bismarck himself and fought every item of the brutal demand, finally saving for France the stronghold of Belfort. The outrageous terms were met, but in Paris the statue representing the lost province, Alsace-Lorraine on the Place de la Concorde, was draped in black crepe—so to remain until the victory of 1918 returned it to its mother country.

Thiers's portrait was exhibited at the Royal Academy in London early in 1874 and was greatly praised. It also had much success at the French Salon. That same year Guizot died in Paris. When Guizot sat to Healy in 1840 and 1841, he had told the artist:

"Because he is ten years younger than I and our careers have run a somewhat similar course, when I die Thiers will believe that he has ten years more to live. . . ." But Thiers survived his former rival only three years.

Gambetta loomed as the next President of France when McMahon's term of office would expire. Like Guizot and Thiers, Gambetta was of the south, with all its fire and eloquence. A hero he had proved himself, escaping in a balloon to bring succor to Parisians. It was after a long and strenuous hot summer in the United States that Healy began Gambetta's portrait in November,

1876. The sittings were of necessity interrupted when Gambetta fell ill.

Early in 1877 Healy received word that Chancellor Otto von Bismarck would be ready to give sittings on March 5 and expected Mr. Healy at the Chancellery in Berlin at that date. That meant that by the time Healy returned to Paris it would be too late to send Gambetta's portrait to the Salon. Gambetta, sick as he was, meant to be at the Salon; he made an extra effort and managed to give the artist a few last sittings.

At that time an American newspaper reporter called on Mrs. Healy for details of the Bismarck sittings. She wrote them down for him as follows:

On Feb. 25, 1877, Healy received from Mr. Hitt (Am. Minister in Paris) the following letter:

My dear Mr. Healy:

Prince Bismarck sends word through a note from Prince Hohenlohe that he is ready to have his portrait taken, commencing the sittings on the 5th of March and he awaits your arrival on that day.

I am very respectfully your obedient servant

R. R. Hitt

Mr. Healy waited on Prince Bismarck according to appointment; he then learned that it is the custom of the Prince to work every night until 6 o'clock in the morning when he retires to sleep until noon; he then takes a cup of tea, dresses and reads dispatches until 2, when he receives Cabinet Ministers and Ambassadors. At 3, he drives to the Parliament House where he is often obliged to take part in debates. Between 5 and 6, he frequently has to see the Emperor, after which he dines. As the Russian Ambassador from Constantinople had arrived twelve hours before Mr. Healy, the artist had to wait till five before being able to see the Prince to make arrangements for a first sitting. Mr. Healy was not prepared to see so fine a figure of a man, who stands six-feet, three-inches, and is admirably proportioned: his manner is grave but courteous. He was rather alarmed at the idea of 6 sittings of two hours each, but gave the artist two fine rooms and said that in that wing of the Palace of the Foreign Office he, himself, had passed much of his time there when a young man, as the Minister of that day was an intimate friend of his.

After a very good sitting, in which the head was broadly painted in, the Prince said: "This is remarkable, not like the German, French or English schools. Who was your master? Where did you study?"

"First in the United States and then in Europe, but I never had any particular master."

"I can understand that," was the reply. "You evidently study to render the individual character of each sitter; you have more to do with nature than with schools."

After the next sitting, the Princess saw it, and from that time they both took great interest in the work. The Prince came as often as possible, sometimes the sittings were very short; the time he gave most unwillingly was for the hands. He said he never saw an artist so particular about the exact likeness of the hands. "Our painters represent handsome hands and that's all; but, Mr. Healy, I think you are right."

The charming young Baron von Holstein was most kind and took a great interest in the portrait; he speaks English and French as well as a native of each country or as well as Prince Bismarck himself; this is also the case with the Princess and her son and daughter. The Prince entertains rarely at dinner and on account of his health never dines out. Mr. Healy had the honor of dining with the family and meeting a few guests; he handed in the Princess and sat between her and Bismarck; the conversation was most interesting, being principally anecdotes of his (Bismarck's) early life.

On the 23rd of March the portrait was seen by the officers and pronounced to be the man himself; no one seemed more pleased than the Baron von Holstein who said: "I told you it was perfect and an immense success."

Prince Bismarck asked the artist if a copy of the work could be as good as the original, to which he replied: "Never, without renewed sittings. A careful copy could be made, and then with sittings from nature it would be an original." When the price was named, he said: "That is a cobbler's fortune, but my wife says she would prefer it to any jewel I could present her on her birthday, so it must be done."

It was then arranged that Mr. Healy should meet him at Kissingen in June when all the sittings necessary for a second portrait are to be given.

The Princess said: "Mr. Healy, dine with us in your traveling clothes and drive from here to the station," but the artist after thanking her warmly for all the kindnesses he had received at her hands and from the Prince, said he had promised to dine at the minister's, Mr. Davis, which he did and showed his work there before leaving. Mrs. Davis said: "Mr. Healy, I am proud of this as an American. This is the man with all his genius and strength of character, unlike those I have seen of him before."

Mr. Healy on taking leave of the Prince said, "I should like your autograph, but I am told I must not ask for it ..." He replied: "I will write my name on a photograph and send it to you before you leave your Minister's." His leavetaking was as simple as everything else about this great man and his last words were: "I hope I shall meet you again in good health."

Back in Paris curiosity was rampant among all of Bismarck's particular enemies. They were eager to hear Healy's impression and somewhat disappointed that he should return with tales of a familiar, intelligent family life. How could that terrible man show human traits? Thiers felt rather pleased that his archenemy should have spoken of him as a great Frenchman and patriot. Of Gambetta, the Chancellor had said little.

"When France became too burning a subject," explained the artist, "we spoke of America and Americans. He is a great friend of our historian Motley, you know, and I had the pleasure of painting Mr. Motley's portrait in England."

In 1877, when Gambetta heard of the arrival of General and Mrs. Grant on their famed world tour, he asked Healy to present him to the American ex-President. Grant himself told the artist he would very much like to meet the great Frenchman. So it was arranged.

At the Healy table the two men met for dinner before a ball

given in honor of the Grants. Grant spoke no French, Gambetta no English. To Mary Bigot fell the role of interpreter; the translation of so many reciprocal compliments after a while put a strain on her vocabulary and her enjoyment; she was therefore very grateful to Gambetta when the latter, a frank gourmet, turned his attention to the delicacies of the elaborate menu. Meanwhile, the General was confiding to Mrs. Healy that he would gladly forego all those fine messes for a good old-fashioned dish of pork and beans!

The dance that followed brought a galaxy of celebrities to the Healy home and was a great success. It enabled Edith Healy to jot down in her diary that the silent Grant could be a most interesting and talkative person under favorable circumstances. As for Charles and Mary Bigot, they had fallen completely under the charm of Gambetta. The dream all shared at this time of seeing Gambetta at the helm never was fulfilled—suddenly, a short time before those elections that would make him President, Gambetta died—a shot in the hand, gangrene, death. His funeral was the great orator's last triumphal march through the city he had helped to save.

Chapter XXXII

GIANTS ON CANVAS

BEFORE Healy's easel a varied world continued to appear in kaleidoscopic fashion. The elect or the bohemian, millionaire or humble folk, inventors, writers, artists told their story and brought him vistas of foreign worlds or merely a breath of the country; they listened also, for Healy's life was now a long one, an interesting one.

Year after year, the Salon, the Royal Academy, the art exhibits of New York, Philadelphia, Washington, Chicago, listed works of G. P. A. Healy. Critics continued to mention him with praise. It was to him that people still turned for portraits of celebrities. James Gordon Bennett, Jr., of the New York *Herald* sent Henry Morton Stanley to Healy for his portrait.

How thrilling for Healy and his family to hear from Stanley's own lips the details of his sudden call; he was in Spain when Bennett's peremptory telegram brought him back to Paris in 1869. It was generally believed then that Livingstone, the Scottish missionary, had died in Africa. Bennett thought him alive and told Stanley to find him.

With what gusto Stanley recounted that interview with the newspaper magnate!

"But, Mr. Bennett," Stanley had exclaimed, "such an expedition will cost enormously!"

"Very well, draw £1,000: when that is spent, draw another £1,000; when that is gone, draw another £1,000—BUT FIND LIVINGSTON!"

"Shall I go straight to Africa?"

"No. I wish you to be present at the inauguration of the Suez Canal, then proceed up the Nile, then you might go to Jerusalem, visit Constantinople and the Crimea, cross the Caucasus, see Persia, India . . ."

Stanley laughed as he spoke of this multiple assignment which delighted his adventurous soul and explained why he had reached Zanzibar only in January, 1871. His famous "Dr. Livingstone, I presume?" was quoted everywhere. Then during five months in the dark continent the two men had lived a dangerous life in close companionship, and when Stanley left for England, he carried back Livingstone's papers and maps for the Geographical Society in London.

There had been disbelief when, returned from Africa, Stanley told the world of meeting the Scotsman at Ujiji on November 10, 1871, for Livingstone was too ill then to undertake the return journey. It was only when the missionary's body was brought back for interment at Westminster Abbey in 1874 and Stanley acted as chief pallbearer that rumors were quelled; the Queen thanked him and all bowed before the evidence.

"I learned of Livingstone's death only on my return from the Ashantee War," explained Stanley.

Healy remembered hearing that the American accompanied General Wolseley on that expedition. The General's nephew, Sir Charles Wolseley, was courting Nellie Murphy, pretty daughter of Healy's close friends; this seemed to bring them all on familiar ground, favorable to the rapid development of friendly relations.

Stanley's personality was a strange one and the story of his early years somewhat indistinct. English-born, Henry Rowlands led an unhappy youth; he had run away to the United States and, like John Paul Jones of earlier fame, was adopted in the new land, taking the name of his benefactor. The New Orleans merchant, Morton Stanley, intended to leave him a prosperous business; death cheated them both and Henry Morton Stanley, alone again, found himself caught in the Civil War. To Healy, this was both pathetic and familiar: how sharply he remembered the anguish of North and South!

Serving with the South, Stanley suffered the hardships of a Northern prison: turning to the North, he was soon dismissed because of poor health; it was then that he allowed his imagination free rein in the line of journalism, attracting the attention of Gordon Bennett on the watch for new talent. A rover, thought the artist, a turncoat, yet a hero and a great charmer—such was the new model before him, and Healy put into his portrait the vividness of that picturesque wayfarer back from African jungles.

How eagerly they all listened when, either at the studio or taking tea with the family in the garden, Stanley told of his active search for Livingstone among entirely savage and even man-eating tribes! There never was a lull in the conversation. Healy fell under the spell and soon became one of the active promoters of the Stanley Club in Paris—an organization which in later years became the University Club and then the American Club, so familiar to American residents and American visitors in Paris. From his virile portrait of the now famous explorer Healy had his son-in-law Tiburce de Mare make an etching that was very popular. Years later, when Stanley settled in England, Edith Healy after a tea at his house wrote disconsolately that he had grown thin and that his hair, so startlingly distinguished when it had turned white, was now black—which took away much of the character of the head; only the eyes, she admitted, retained their wild look reminiscent of the jungle.

In the studio Stanley asked for details about the great American industrialists: Cyrus McCormick of reaper fame whom Healy had painted some years before after his portraits of Leander McCormick and of Mrs. Leander McCormick, and whom he would paint again as well as beautiful and charming Mrs. Cyrus McCormick; Cyrus Field, George Pullman who always talked of railroads and had to wait so long to see his sleeping cars adopted; Goodyear, N. K. Fairbanks, and so many giants of American progress and power who seemed to look down from the walls upon these men interested in their deeds.

Stanley also liked the recent portrait of Lord Lyons, painted on a commission from E. B. Washburn, whom Healy had known when the diplomat filled a very ungrateful and difficult position as British Minister in the United States in the days of the Civil War. In France, Lord Lyons was well thought of although he never achieved in Paris the popularity of his successor Lord Lytton.

Living in Paris did not mean, as Mrs. Healy had hoped, a slowing up of activities for the artist. And again he suffered spells of eyestrain, headaches, and insomnia. He who had been always so optimistic grew sad when, from both sides of the ocean, news of deaths among his companions of the past reached him—like leaves falling one by one, faster and faster, from the sturdy tree of his friendships. In 1874, Guizot had died in Paris; in 1875 Boston was saddened by the loss of Mrs. Harrison Gray Otis of whom Healy made that year a full-length portrait in the dress she had worn for the Prince of Wales's ball.

Back in the United States in 1875 and 1876 Healy had worked so constantly that instead of visiting in the summer his dear friend Mrs. Dahlgren, a widow now for the second time, he had remained at Rye Beach, ill but still at work, until time for him to sail back to France in September, 1876. And in Paris the following April he learned of the death of Mrs. Dahlgren's son Vinton Goddard. The young as well as the old were being snatched from their circle. In 1877, Thiers died, then in March, 1879, his dear friend Couture passed on to what he hoped was a painter's paradise.

It distressed Mrs. Healy that her husband should insist on accepting commissions when he so needed a rest; she judged severely some of the portraits that lacked life because his hand had stiffened with fatigue, and though his own vital interest in human beings remained as keen as ever, the brain could not always carry its message with the buoyancy of earlier years. With their friend McCagg, Louisa plotted occasionally some journey that would force a temporary stop in his work. Thus it was that Healy with a group of Chicago friends undertook the trip to Alaska. To say that he enjoyed it as much as his companions would be stretching the truth, but he did admire the strange new landscape and thoroughly appreciated his return to civilization. Another time he joined a cruise to Norwegian waters, going as far as Russia. In a little notebook he kept for Louisa there are charming bits of drawing—not all views of the picturesque shores by any means, but a hand holding a fan, a face—his attention held first and last by human movements, human beings.

In spite of the everlasting postponements of his visit to Rumania, the artist remained in touch with his princely patrons. Once at Neuwied, in 1880, he had visited the Princess who was staying with her mother and had invited Healy to join them there. In answer to his acceptance came this wire:

"Neuwied, August 19th 1880
Welcome here on the twenty-first. We shall be so happy to see you. You will celebrate with us on the twenty-second my brother's birthday. Au-revoir.

Elizabeth."

The artist's diary tells of his arrival:

"Yesterday I left Wiesbaden at about eight. The carriage awaited us at the station at Neuweid. . . . We stopped at the Palace of the Dowager Princess with whom I talked at length. After dinner there was excellent music. A young tenor with a beautiful voice sang verses written by the Princess (Carmen Sylva). During the evening twenty singers carrying torches stopped opposite the entrance of the palace and sang. It was in honor of the Prince's birthday. He invited them in and the young tenor sang again. A perfect evening."

The artist wrote with evident pleasure of the next day's events when, in true German fashion, a fete filled with surprises was arranged in the Prince of Wied's honor. With the Marshal of the Palace, Healy started out in the morning, followed by a flower-decked carriage in which the Prince of Wied's children and the driver himself were disguised as birds and angels! The party stopped at an improvised temple on the highest point of their mountain, the Rhine valley spreading at their feet. There the tenor sang, and the Princess of Rumania gave her brother a book written and illumined by herself:

"It is a biography of their deceased brother; it took the Princess several years to do it. When His Highness received the volume, he cried—as did his mother and sister. I was moved by the scene. . . .

"From there we went into the forest. They spread robes and cushions, and an excellent lunch was served. They carried a piano up the mountain; we had more songs, in which everybody joined, and Princess Bibesco played some of Chopin's Preludes. . . . The ladies wore picturesque Rumanian costumes. It made a fine picture subject."

And the following year, in 1881, the painter was at last in Rumania again, for the momentous occasion of Carol's elevation to the throne. To his wife he wrote:

"Palace of Bucharest
Wednesday, Feb. 16th 1881

On Saturday I had my last sitting from de Lesseps. Tiburce considers it my best portrait and thinks it will look well at the Salon. At eight o'clock I took the train to Vienna where I arrived Monday morning. After lunch I visited the Art Gallery, two exhibits of modern paintings, and the Panorama of the Commune. At three in the afternoon I left for Bucharest, and last night at nine the Baroness Witzleben and her son met me at the station here. My old servant Vincent knew me at once in the crowd.

Friday . . . I lunched with my royal model; after the sitting she went to her apartments to receive the guests and to hear good music. Her pianist played parts of Judith by our friend Charles Lefebvre. The Prince came in late from the hunt...I met Philippescu who asked after all the family...

Sunday . . . While I was painting the Princess had the kindness to read me some of her own works."

Another day he wrote that the Princess—soon to be a Queen— held the plate while he mixed the paints for his palette; at which, turning to her husband, he said that he felt as honored "as Titian when Francis the First picked up his brush!"

These daily accounts teem with pleasant little incidents. One evening as he was dining quietly with the Baroness and her son in came the Princess, starved she said waiting for the Prince; so she partook of their soup and relished it.

After a strenuous afternoon at his easel the artist called on the ladies; they wore fancy dress, Turkish costumes.

Healy wrote:

"It would have made a splendid picture if only there had been time—Princess Elizabeth looked like a girl, her dress beautiful, like herself."

In spite of constant work, Healy managed to see many friends. He encouraged young artists; bought some charming sketches by Grigoresco. But when at work, he disliked interruptions however kindly meant:

"A rather funny but most agreeable gentleman came in. He told me he had long admired my portrait of Mrs. Cruger. I was impatient to get back to work."

To send the King of Rumania's portrait to the Paris Salon was his desire, but the time seemed too short. Artist and sitter vied with each other in their eagerness to accomplish this deed; the King posed long hours, the artist worked overtime! At last the portrait was done, packed and shipped. The Postmaster promised that it would reach Vienna on Monday evening, March seventh, and from there a railroad employee would carry it to Paris.

One day, while the Prince was posing for the portrait destined for the Emperor of Austria, Queen Elizabeth rushed in brandishing a telegram! The picture was safe in Paris and would be at the Salon!

Healy was requested to be present at a gala ball given at this time: for once he would have to forsake his work—the sight promised to be worth seeing. Dutifully the painter went to admire the dancers, but he slipped away as soon as he dared and the next morning wrote in his diary:

"I was in bed at half-past twelve. I have just asked my man if it is six o'clock, but he tells me it is only four. He is making a fire."

Absorbed in his work, the artist missed much of the feverish preparations for the Coronation. As King and Queen, the Sovereigns would have a more formal Court, and questions of etiquette turned into affairs of State! Unexpected and amusing details cropped up: the future Queen said that she would reject divorcées among her Court Ladies, at which the dismayed Chamberlain exclaimed:

"But, Your Majesty, there would not be enough ladies to form a Court!"

So they compromised, and admitted the elegibility of those who had not been divorced more than once. . . .

In the midst of all the gay festivities, the startling news of Czar Alexander of Russia's assassination threw a pall over everything. The Court went into mourning: funeral services were held.

"The Prince tells me his wife was greatly affected and overcome. It is the first funeral service at which she has assisted since her little girl's death . . . Nevertheless she wrote a poem this morning, and seeing the progress made on the Prince's portrait, she brought her sewing and stayed with us until ten o'clock. She claims this visit did her good, and that our conversation furnished her with material for writing . . ."

There is a gap here in the diary. The days of official celebration became too crowded with engagements of all sorts, even for the super-energetic artist. On March thirty-first he again wrote:

"5.30 A.M.—Yesterday I worked all day on the Queen's portrait. There is much to do, if I wish to be ready to leave tomorrow."

But he evidently managed to finish it, for on April first he bid Their Majesties adieu, again with a promise to return "next year" —a promise that could not be fulfilled, to their mutual regret.

In that silent interval of the diary, they had become officially "Majesties," this Prince and Princess whom he had known in the prime of their youth and success. A photograph of the Coronation shows G. P. A. Healy among the Court dignitaries during the imposing ceremonies.

"While I was at work the Chamberlain came to request my presence in the throne room. The Prince was evidently much moved and so was his wife. All the members of the Chambers were introduced. . . . . The King's hand, which held his written address, trembled visibly."

Healy left Rumania promptly as his many obligations called him elsewhere. And before long his friends in New York were to welcome him on still another "visit" home. Louisa, tired of not seeing her husband for long intervals, decided to sail with him, taking Edith and Kathleen.

Chapter XXXIII

"WE SAIL NEXT MONTH" . . . 1892

TEN years had gone by since his hasty return from Rumania all the way to New York with, as Edith put it in her diary, a stop in Paris to "drag Mama to several exhibits," adding, "both Papa and M. de Lesseps are amazing men. They never tire. . . ."

But Healy was tired. How crowded those ten years had been. His thirst for work had driven him in spite of himself beyond his strength; also unconsciously—for he always remained supremely modest—he suffered from a partial slump in his undeniable fame. He did not understand the forward and sometimes supercilious attitude of a new generation. But in spite of that the American never ceased to help young artists.

If financial success could have satisfied him, Healy should have been at his happiest. That year of 1881 in America after his second visit to Rumania, he had marked on the inside cover of his notebook the checks received—which did not cover all the payments, many still owing. On that page, his wife and daughters counted more than forty thousand dollars, eliciting a remark from Edith:

"It seems fabulous that one pair of hands, and at Papa's age, could have worked so much."

At almost any page of that agenda early or late one reads such facts:

"At nine yesterday morning I had a sitting from Colonel MacKaye; at noon, one from Mr. Tiffany; and at half-past three one from Governor Morgan. In the evening I had the pleasure of seeing the Agnews; then I called on the Hamiltons—a delightful visit. He is the grandson of Alexander Hamilton and is ninety years old."

His remarks about artists are friendly; one day he mentions Coleman, Blodgett, Beckwith, Blashfield; of the latter, saying:

"I saw fine things in his studio. . . . Mrs. Blashfield is more beautiful than ever."

How he missed William Morris Hunt! And now another friend had died.

"Welsh informs me of the death of my friend Staigg in Newport. The shock is a cruel one."

He traveled on:

"Yesterday morning I reached Louisville to retouch the portrait of Mrs. John Bell which I painted twenty years ago. I stayed until seven in the evening. I arrived here [St. Louis] this morning about nine. Mr. Chapman wanted some slight alteration on the mouth. He took me to lunch at the Club then accompanied me to Dr. Elliot's where I saw the portrait I painted of him in Rome twelve years ago. From there, I went to see Archbishop Kenrick. . . . I leave for Chicago at eight this evening."

Another day:

"I had a long talk with Mrs. Ole Bull about a full-length portrait of her husband. As I cannot find time to do it here she thinks they will come to Paris on purpose and give me all the time I need."

So it had gone for a year. Then Healy joined his family:

"June 1882—Papa is with us. . . . He will probably go to the Château d'Eu to make studies of the head of the Comte de Paris. . . . After he returns we shall go to Wiesbaden, and from there Papa may go to Bucharest. . . . The poor Queen has been so ill all winter that he is doubly anxious to see her."

This third visit to Bucharest did not take place, but he painted the portrait of the Comte de Paris and enjoyed the sittings immensely. At Eu, they welcomed him. The Comte de Paris regretted that Healy's portrait of his grandfather, King Louis

Philippe, had been destroyed in the Chicago fire, for, said he: "We have no good likeness of him."

Edith again, June 28:

"Papa was most kindly received by the Comte and Comtesse de Paris. She is as tall as Papa, and sang in the evening, very well. The Comte sat on Saturday morning and afternoon. Papa painted an entire bust portrait. It is charming in color, firm and well painted, fresh and bold; I dare say much better than the full-length he means to paint from it."

Some time later, in the city, the Comte gave other sittings. He came to the studio and also took tea with the family in their garden. That evening at the theater, Edith noticed with pleased surprise that he and his son, the little Duc d'Orléans, occupied the box next to theirs:

"The Comte sat next to me, so we talked now and then. They were playing 'Le Bossu,' quite romantic."

Not very long after, hostile rumors made the Princes' life in France precarious. Healy alludes to their difficulties with the government after the head of the rival house of Bonaparte issued a manifesto against the Republic:

"January 27th 1883: Colonel MacKaye during his sitting discussed the indecision of the French government. In a few days we shall know how they decide this question of the Princes who are serving in the Army. If they are exiled from the country it is a frightful injustice, and the Republic will suffer. What trouble this manifesto of Prince Napoleon has brought upon everyone!"

The law of exile was passed in 1886, with Boulanger Minister of War. The Comte de Paris and his son the Duc d'Orléans had to leave France. From Eu, several of the most devoted friends and would-be subjects accompanied them to England. There the Comte de Paris gave a farewell luncheon. At Dover, as they watched from the dining-room windows the sea and the ships, one of the guests exclaimed:

"There is the *Victoria* going back to France."

The Comte de Paris rose, walked to the window, looking out long and silently, then he returned to his guests and lifting his glass merely said:

"Gentlemen—to France!"

Thus he bade his final adieu to a throne he would never occupy.

Many Paris events are recorded in the family diaries: the Gambetta funeral, the death of Marie Bashkirtseff, the procession accompanying Victor Hugo's last ride to the Panthéon ... Among the much-talked-of celebrities whom the Healys met was Oscar Wilde, not yet ostracized, and other Englishmen of note: Frederic Harrison, Mr. Wedmore, Sir Charles Wolseley, whom they visited at beautiful Wolseley Hall.

In 1884, his wife and daughters had accompanied Healy to the United States. When the artist went to paint President Arthur in the White House, Edith's diary records:

"We passed from the handsome hall into a fine room where one of Papa's portraits hangs, Adams, I think. It is very good. From that into another, from there through a narrow neck of a room into a large salon where our names were yelled by an attendant; happily Mrs. Logan heard the name, knew it and Papa, and so presented us all to Mrs. McElroy, the President's sister, First Lady of the land. We were passed along as 'Mr. Healy, the celebrated artist, and his family.' There was a: 'Ah! Mr. Healy, the artist!' And with that in our ears we found ourselves out of the reception room and breathing comfortably in a large ballroom."

This American girl, brought up in Europe, criticized the ways of the new world. In Newport, for instance:

"Conversation is of the lightest; indeed the talk is dreadfully commonplace, all chaff and laughing. I overheard some servants yesterday and their talk was a repetition of what goes on in the upper classes. ... People are more divided into sets here than even in Paris. They are all slaves to fashion; you cannot be seen walking at certain hours; you must pay visits only from twelve until two.

On Sundays from five until seven you must walk on the Cliffs; you must go to the Casino on Monday mornings to hear music, but you must sit only on the left of the covered way as the right is 'not the thing.' All the little rules are observed as if life depended upon them."

English society impressed Edith more. She regretted not having been included in the invitation to Lord Lytton's first reception in Paris. The son of Bulwer-Lytton of Pompei fame, Lord Lytton, Viceroy of India and now Ambassador to France, was himself a writer of note under the name of Owen Meredith.

"Parisian society," wrote Healy, "was eager to enter once more the old Palace, so gay in the days of the Empire, so somber since; everyone wanted to see the brilliant successor of Lord Lyons, who has brought back from the Orient a reputation of gracious hospitality. There must have been fifteen hundred guests. . . . Lord Lytton is a man of medium height. His features express intelligence, education, and thought. He has deep-set, light-gray eyes, curly brown hair and dark complexion. He wears many orders and decorations. Lady Lytton, by his side, wore a very simple dress of Louis XV style, much like the dress in the portrait of Marie Leczinska. No music fortunately so that we could hear one another. It was a delightful company. . . . I spoke with Monsieur de Lesseps. Poor man, he seems all broken up."

The great engineer had not only suffered serious checks in Panama because of the insalubrious climate which killed off his men like flies, but also because the money gave out; an unscrupulous financier caused a serious crash which ruined a great many families—even among the poor who had pinned their faith on the name of De Lesseps. The Panama Scandal some years later ended in a very cruel and unjust trial of De Lesseps; it unhinged his mind, and his son Charles offered himself for the prison sentence passed on his father—a tragic ending to a magnificent life.

Healy noticed also at the Lytton reception Count Hoyot whom he had known in Rumania as Ambassador from Austria and whose portrait he was to paint shortly. He saw Clemenceau talk-ing to the German Ambassador. Among the artists he spoke to Munkácsy, the Hungarian painter; to Bartholdi working on his monumental Statue of Liberty.

In Healy's studio, sitters brought echoes of great events with an atmosphere of action and constant change, and around the artist invisible threads were woven to form a slowly growing international spirit. English journalists as well as Ministers ex-pressed their views while he painted: Henry de Blowitz, Paris correspondent of the London *Times,* and John Walter its director. They also discussed French politics and that strange melodrama, the Boulanger interlude, the man on horseback. Even in their sheltered life, the Healys were bitten with this epidemic of en-thusiasm. They watched the handsome General prance by on his black horse, greeted by the joyous shouts of a people starved for glory.

Christmas, 1891, at the rue de la Rochefoucauld was a gay re-union of old friends. A large Christmas tree glitters at one end of the long drawing room. There is music, delicious "gouter," games, and even dancing on the beautiful parquet floor, polished by the feet of many generations. And in the artist's diary this note:

"My grandson, Georges de Mare, came to the studio to say that they were waiting for me. The Christmas tree was all lighted up; about fifty children crowded around it, joy reflected in their faces; the parlors filled with people. Indeed it was the loveliest picture one could see."

Another new year: January 1892. The Healys are back from their extended visit to the United States. George Healy is up. Day will not break for an hour yet: the house, the city, all is quiet.

As he does every morning, as he has done every morning for so many years, the aging artist arises noiselessly, not to disturb the dear ones asleep. He crosses the garden; the penetrating cold makes him draw his overcoat closer around him. Brr! this dampness chills one to the bone! He feels it more this year: is it age coming on? Age ... this thought has obtruded so often of late ... yet he feels strong and his heart is warm as ever: does it not beat like a young lover's at the sound of a key in the studio door, when the wife he has worshipped those fifty-three years of marriage comes to brighten his room with her sweet presence ...

This large, high studio: what a contrast to their first one in Paris in 1839, more than half a century ago. He was twenty-six then, when he painted the King's portrait ... seventy-nine this coming summer ... Incredible! Yes, he is an old man.

Plunged in thought, he walks down to Trinity Church to hear Mass. A daily habit: this communion with God at the break of day lifts the soul and solves problems. Problems? what problem is this that troubles him of late? He is walking back now up the steep, hilly street that leads to the studio and as he looks at the familiar stones, houses, shops—there is no problem anymore. All is clear. He does not belong here.

His love of France and the French never changed him from an out-and-out American, and now he knows: the end of life must be like the beginning—at home. This has been a marvelous temporary home, but to him "home" means America. How strange! So many more years spent abroad than in the United States—so much of his career belongs indissolubly to France and Europe—yet America calls and now the call must be answered without delay.

At breakfast, a punctual meal where the family greet one another with delightful old-time courtesy, George Healy says nothing of his morning thoughts. He must plan and then he will tell his faithful companion who, as usual, will make the plan a reality and inform the daughters of the coming change ...

So, a few days later, George startles his wife with the announcement: "We sail next month."

She looks up in alarm—oh! how she hates and dreads these long journeys...and at once realizes that something vital is at hand.

"Yes, we shall leave Paris. It is changing and we are not. We had better settle in America..."

Is it the restless spirit that seems at times to transform the artist into a rapid, daring traveler?...No. This is something deeper... and final. She has sensed the struggle going on in her husband's mind—but secure in the knowledge that he would come to her with it at the proper moment, she has kept silent, waited...yet she hardly expected such a revolution. And to her America is not "home" any more than France: home is wherever George is.

Her practical sense suggests objections: the lease does not expire for two years...Very well, they may sublet, and if not, pay... "Impossible to pack and ship the accumulation of twenty years within a few months...

"Of course, my dear. You, Kathleen and I will sail first: Edith can attend to everything and join us when we have found a home over there...

"Where? Boston? New York? Washington? Chicago?

"Chicago, I think. We have so many friends there—and the property.

"What about the married daughters and grandchildren?"

"Better not tell them until after the sailing. Let them think this an ordinary journey: it would be a heart-breaking separation..."

"The Manoir in Normandy? We signed the lease for next summer..."

"Let Edith have them there as usual..."

Yes. His mind was made up. They would sail...

The daughters took this announcement with a good deal of excitement. Kathleen, never quite in sympathy with French life and attitude, was beaming. Edith looked at her father with a mixture of pride and horror when he so blithely informed them that she would have all the trouble! After all, had she not always taken it upon herself to more or less rule the roost: now she was given a chance with a vengeance!

And in March 1892 Mr. and Mrs. Healy and Miss Kathleen Healy sailed from Le Havre, leaving Edith in a storm of trunks, furniture, leases, lawyers, landlord . . . She complained, but rather enjoyed the incredible confusion!

Agnes and Mary who had viewed this journey as another of their father's unpredictable moves, realized that this meant indeed more than a visit to America and their indignation covered very deep sadness when word came that their father had bought a house in Chicago at 387 Ontario Street—the street that had been their first address there in 1856 . . .

And Chicago, in a fever of preparation for the great World's Fair of 1893, stopped long enough in its task to accord the returning artist a warm and enthusiastic welcome.

In June, Edith had the rest of the family at Pennedepie in Normandie: Mary and her very sick husband Charles Bigot; Agnes and her children save Eric de Mare then at sea in the French Merchant Marine; some guests also, among them the great harpist, Hasselmans, who could not bear the thought of the Healys' leaving the rue de la Rochefoucauld. Hearts were heavy when, at the end of summer, after having shipped off a terrifying number of enormous cases, Edith herself packed her trunks and sailed.

Busy as it always was, Chicago paused long enough to accord its returning artist a hearty welcome. Edith arrived in the midst of a hectic series of dinners, receptions, teas, and kept asking her new or old friends: "But why do all the women go together and the men go by themselves?" She would see that in the Healy home at least sexes and ages would mingle as they did in Europe.

The Chicago World's Fair of 1893 made of their home a focal point for French exhibitors and visitors. But Edith missed that summer because on April 15 Charles Bigot died and as soon as the cable came she took passage to rejoin her sister Mary.

Ocean crossings now belonged to the younger members of the family, and with the spring of 1894 some of the grandchildren made their first trip to America. Agnes brought over her three daughters, Louise, Marie, and Jeanne—and even the little one proved herself such a poor sailor that the ship's doctor told the whole family never to set foot on a ship again.

The *Mikado,* delightfully given by the d'Oyly Cartes, came from London and George Healy with his houseful of women occupied a row at the theater. He was over eighty and enjoyed the operetta as much as his youngest grandchild.

But he who had been so active, directing personally the placing of every picture as soon as the cases were opened, agile and forgetful of years to the point of climbing stool or ladder, finally was forced to a slowing process. One morning that preceding winter, on his way to early Mass, he had fallen in the snow. A kindly workman passing by helped him up, but Healy forgot the accident and continued his daily trips to the studio a block and a half away. The summer of 1894 began early and was very hot. One day, starting as usual, the painter turned back; the next day he could not rise. Consternation spread through the house; an old friend, Dr. de Lasky Miller, informed the family that nature was closing his active career. The end was near.

Hot June days—dragging out in silence and sorrow. The loving companion by his side night and day; the daughters, and the son back from France, there, ready to answer the least sign; the grandchildren, awed and oppressed, making their first conscious contact with death. Friends surround him; two of them, young men, claim the privilege of watching him in turn.

On June 24, 1894, George Healy sinks into unconsciousness, rallies again, wanders anew. Some vision brings to his face a tranquil radiance. He feels the pressure of a dear little hand, senses the hovering presence of his sorrowing wife: how can he let her know that, in this realm he is now entering, time vanishes? The past crowds in, and it seems only yesterday: France, England,

Rome, Boston, they all blend—space of no more moment than time. Light, a wonderful light.... *Corot, was it not? who hoped they might still paint in heaven*... There it is—color, light, beauty eternal. . .

He lay there, hardly breathing, eyes closed; he was going before her, and in her despair Louisa questioned herself fiercely— had his life given him what he wanted? This tremendous work he had done so faithfully, was it only a substitute for the many great pictures he had dreamed and planned? Had family cares hampered his art? Her eyes, blurred with tears, could not read the answer, but his daughter, bending over him, caught it, in a faint murmur that reached and echoed in Louisa Healy's heart and would echo throughout eleven slow years of her patient waiting to join him.

"Happy—so happy."

In the cathedral to which flocked the people of Chicago, Father Agnew began with deep feeling:

"Well done, thou good and faithful servant . . ."

And all who were there felt the everlasting truth of these words. Throughout his life George Healy had served his God, his country, his family, his friends. He served the art he loved.

INDEX